Economics

FOR THE IB DIPLOMA

Constantine Ziogas

OXFORD
UNIVERSITY PRESS

Great Clarendon Street, Oxford OX2 6DP

Oxford University Press is a department of the University of Oxford.
It furthers the University's objective of excellence in research,
scholarship, and education by publishing worldwide in

Oxford   New York

Auckland   Cape Town   Dar es Salaam   Hong Kong   Karachi
Kuala Lumpur   Madrid   Melbourne   Mexico City   Nairobi
New Delhi   Shanghai   Taipei   Toronto

With offices in

Argentina   Austria   Brazil   Chile   Czech Republic   France   Greece
Guatemala   Hungary   Italy   Japan   Poland   Portugal   Singapore
South Korea   Switzerland   Thailand   Turkey   Ukraine   Vietnam

Oxford is a registered trade mark of Oxford University Press
in the UK and in certain other countries

British Library Cataloguing in Publication Data

Data available

ISBN: 978-0-19-838999-6
10 9

Printed in India by Manipal Technologies Limited

Paper used in the production of this book is a natural, recyclable product made from wood grown in
sustainable forests. The manufacturing process conforms to the environmental regulations of the country
of origin

Acknowledgments

This work would not have been possible without the help of all my past and present IB Economics students.
I also would like to thank Manuel Fernandez and my colleagues on the OCC who assist my work on a daily
basis with their questions and comments. My biggest thanks of course go to my Kris for too many reasons to
include here.

Dedication:

To the best children a father could hope for, Daphne, Myrto and Elias.

Cover photograph: Travel Ink/Getty Images

Contents

Introduction

This book is designed to provide students with a step-by-step approach to practising the skills they need for success in examinations. The most troublesome points of the syllabus are broken down into easily digestible pieces which the student can use in a data response question, producing a commentary or composing an extended essay.

Every topic is included in the order in which it appears in the official IB Economics syllabus guide. Each topic begins with some important points to remember and tips on anything tricky or on how to avoid common errors. These are followed by worked examples and exercises to practise.

There are a wide range of exercises including comprehension, interpretation of diagrams and 'true or false' questions that aim to disperse common myths. Matching economic terms with their definitions and 'fill in the blank' questions provide extra support for non-native English speakers.

Great care has been taken to prepare the quantitative material for higher level candidates. A detailed, analytical approach is adopted that assumes the reader has a limited technical background. The goal is to give confidence to students who are anxious about dealing with algebra or geometry. All higher level material is clearly marked by this symbol **HL** and a dotted line.

Finally, advice is given on writing extended essays, how to produce effective commentaries and how to interpret command terms so students are prepared for every aspect of their course.

The aim of this book is to ensure that all interested candidates are able to answer any 'why' question and therefore develop a deeper understanding of economics. All too often students are aware of the right answer to a question but if asked to dig a little deeper they are unable to provide a meaningful explanation. The same thing happens with diagrams which are seen as 'pictures' and not as logical constructions. This approach leads to mistakes and prevents students from using diagrams effectively in analysis.

Studying economics can be fun and hopefully this book will help students not only to succeed in the final exam but to enjoy their course as well!

Constantine Ziogas, August 2011

Foundations of economics

Remember

The economic concepts presented in this introductory unit will be appearing throughout the syllabus and the course, so you will appreciate their true meaning and significance much later.

Tip

When drawing a production possibility frontier (PPF) curve, make sure that it touches both axes and is not 'floating' in mid-air. Draw it bowed (concave) towards the origin unless you want to show constant opportunity costs.

The concept of opportunity cost applied to a PPF curve refers to the opportunity cost of producing an extra unit of one of the two goods depicted on the axes. You need an increase in the amount of good X produced to determine how much of good Y must be sacrificed.

Example 1

Match each term or concept with the appropriate definition or explanation.

1 Scarcity
2 Efficiency
3 Social scientific method
4 Opportunity cost
5 Rational economic decision making
6 Ceteris paribus
7 Economic growth

a The value of the next best alternative sacrificed
b Everything else remaining constant
c The excess of human wants over what can actually be produced to satisfy these wants
d When consumers aim at maximizing utility (satisfaction) and producers at maximizing profits; in general, when economic agents aim at maximizing some objective function subject to the constraints they face
e Refers to an increase in an economy's total output
f Exists when scarce resources are not wasted, and also when just the right amount of each good or service is produced from society's point of view
g Refers to the collection and analysis of data and the formulation of testable and falsifiable hypotheses about social phenomena

(1, c), (2, f), (3, g), (4, a), (5, d), (6, b), (7, e)

Example 2

Determine whether the following statements are true or false.
Explain your answers. Use a diagram to illustrate if possible.

1 The statement 'official unemployment in Greece has increased in 2011 by more than 2 percentage points compared with the 2010 unemployment rate' is an example of a positive economic statement.

True. It is a statement that can be tested against data. One can check the official unemployment rate in 2010 and in 2011 and then determine whether it has increased by more than two percentage points.

2 The production possibilities curve is a diagrammatic model of an economy.

True. It is a simplified representation of what an economy can produce with limited resources. It assumes that only two goods are produced, but it is still capable of illustrating basic economic concepts (e.g. scarcity, choice, opportunity cost or growth).

3 All resource allocations resulting in a free market economy are efficient.

False. There is no guarantee that the mix of goods and services produced in a market economy is the best from society's point of view. This is one of the reasons a government may choose to intervene.

4 Within the PPF framework, it is increasingly costly to produce increasing amounts of some goods because resources tend to be specialized.

True. Resources are not equally well-suited for the production of all goods. Producing more and more units of good X will only be possible if resources that would be better suited for the production of good Y are used for the production of good X. The number of units of good Y that have to be sacrificed will get larger and larger.

5 A movement along a PPF implies greater efficiency in the operation of the economy.

False. All points on a PPF are efficient as all resources are employed so production involves no waste. This is referred to as productive efficiency. At the same time though, the movement along a PPF may imply that the economy is moving away from one mix of goods (one combination of good X and good Y) to another mix that is the best from society's point of view. In this sense, the statement above can be true as the economy may succeed in achieving allocative efficiency.

Example 3

Explain the meaning of the terms 'allocation of resources' and 'allocative efficiency'.

The easiest way to understand the terms is by picturing an economy endowed with limited resources including 50 trees. These trees are a 'natural resource' and can be used either in the production of books or in the production of tables. The trees available are not enough to produce all the books and all the tables society would like to have. One of the many possible resource allocations is for 20 trees to be 'appointed' (used) in the production of books and 30 trees appointed in the production of tables. Another possible allocation is for 45 trees to be appointed in the production of books and 5 appointed in the production of tables. Each allocation will, given production technology, lead to the production of some specific amount of books and tables for this economy. How many books and how many tables this economy will produce is the answer to the question 'What will be produced and in what quantities?'. Resource allocation determines which goods and services and what amounts will be produced in an economy. To allocate resources means to appoint or assign resources to the production of specific goods or services. If resources are allocated in such a way that just the right amount of each good or service is produced from society's point of view, then we say that 'allocative efficiency' has been achieved.

Example 4

Rewrite the following statements and fill in the blanks by using the terms provided below. Some terms may be used more than once or not at all.

production possibilities	constant
scarcity	production
limited	shift
labour-intensive	'what'
inside	capital-intensive
ceteris paribus	north-east
labour	unlimited

Since resources are (1)_____ while wants are (2)_____, (3)_____ is the fundamental problem all economies face. Societies must choose which goods will be produced and in what quantities. This is the (4)_____ question, the first of the three basic questions all economies must somehow answer. The 'how' question refers to the (5)_____ technology chosen. For example, shirts can be produced employing a more (6)_____ technology, i.e. relying more on machines, or employing a more (7)_____ technology (relying more on labour).

The clause (8)_____ is needed in the statement 'Joey will gain weight if he eats more every day' because if, at the same time he decides to eat more, he also starts training to run the marathon he may end up losing weight. The clause implies that everything else remains (9)_____ and it is necessary in economic statements to be able to isolate the possible effect of a change in one economic variable on another.

A decrease in unemployment in a (10)_____ diagram can be illustrated by a movement from a combination (11)_____ the curve to another point in the (12)_____. There will be no (13)_____ as neither the amount nor the quality of the resource (14)(_____) has increased.

(1) limited   (6) capital-intensive   (11) inside
(2) unlimited   (7) labour-intensive   (12) north-east
(3) scarcity   (8) ceteris paribus   (13) shift
(4) 'what'   (9) constant   (14) labour
(5) production   (10) production possibilities

Example 5

Answer the following questions using the PPF curve in Figure 0.1.

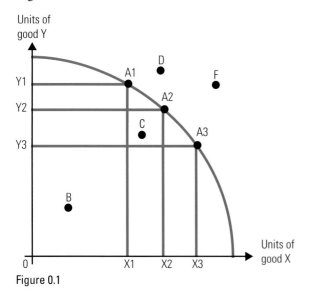

Figure 0.1

1 What do point D and F have in common?

Both points are located outside the PPF. This indicates that the combinations of output each reflect are unattainable given the economy's resource endowments, its technology and its institutional framework.

2 What is the opportunity cost of moving from point A1 to point A2 and producing X1X2 more units of good X?

Within a production possibilities framework, the opportunity cost of producing an extra amount of one good is the amount of the other good that must be sacrificed. If X1X2 more units of good X are produced then Y1Y2 units of good Y must be sacrificed. The opportunity cost of producing X1X2 more units of X is Y1Y2 units of good Y.

3 What is the opportunity cost of producing X2X3 more units of good X?

The opportunity cost of producing X2X3 more units of good X is Y2Y3 units of good Y (Y2Y3 that must be sacrificed).

4 If X1X2 = X2X3, how can you explain that Y2Y3 > Y1Y2?

The opportunity cost of producing more and more of a good increases (the law of increasing costs) as a result of scarce resources not being equally well-suited for the production of both goods. To produce more and more of X, resources less appropriate for X but more appropriate for Y must be used, increasing the opportunity cost of doing this.

5 What do points B and C have in common?

Both points are located inside the PPF and consequently reflect wasted (unemployed) resources, i.e. inefficiency. Given the amount produced of one of the two goods, the economy is able to produce more of the other good by simply utilizing unemployed resources.

6 How would an increase in the size of the labour force of this economy affect the diagram above?

Labour is one of the four factors of production which are assumed constant when constructing the PPF of an economy. An increase in labour will shift the PPF outwards so that combinations of output previously unattainable become attainable.

7 How would a decrease in the unemployment rate of this country be illustrated in the diagram above?

By a movement from a point inside, such as point B, to another point or combination of output to the north-east (such as point C), reflecting at least the same amount of one good and a greater amount of the other good. Note that the labour factor of production is unchanged, so there is no shift.

8 What do points A1, A2 and A3 have in common?

All three combinations of output reflect efficient use of scarce resources because no waste is present (productive efficiency). Given society's preferences (which are not shown in a PPF diagram), only one of the points on a PPF is also efficient in that it is the best mix of goods and services from society's point of view (allocative efficiency).

9 Why is the PPF diagram above a curve and not a straight line?

It is a curve because resources tend to be specialized and not equally well-suited for producing all goods, so the opportunity cost of producing more of either good increases.

10 What would be implied if the PPF diagram was a straight line?

It would imply that the opportunity cost of producing more of either good is constant (which would in turn imply that resources are not specialized).

11 Name factors that could shift the PPF of this economy outwards.

Examples include: an increase in natural, physical or human capital; improved technology; better institutions; etc.

Exercise 1

Rewrite the following statements and fill in the blanks by using the terms provided below. Some terms may be used more than once or not at all.

unattainable	opportunity cost	profits
utility	on	bowed-in
inefficient	rational	
positive	normative	

Consumers choosing the goods they purchase randomly, trying only to satisfy their budget constraint are not considered (1)_____. Typically, rationality requires that consumers aim to maximize (2)_____ while firms try to maximize (3)_____.

The (4)_____ of producing more and more of a good typically increases as resources tend to be specialized. This is reflected in a (5)_____ production possibilities curve. Combinations outside a PPF are (6)_____, while combinations inside a PPF are attainable but (7)_____. The only combinations of output considered efficient are combinations located (8)_____ the frontier.

A (9)_____ economic statement is one that can be tested against data and, in principle, falsified. A statement that includes the word 'should' is most probably a (10)_____ statement.

Exercise 2

Determine whether the following statements are true or false. Explain your answers. Use a diagram to illustrate if possible.

1 The statement 'the government ought to subsidize cotton producers' is a positive economic statement.
2 Assuming the existence of unemployed factors of production, the opportunity cost of producing increased amounts of some goods could be zero.
3 Productive efficiency is not achieved if an economy operates at a point inside its PPF.
4 Scarcity is not a problem in rich countries.
5 If resources were perfectly substitutable then the PPF would be linear.

Exercise 3

Visualize an economy where:

- a government borrows more and more to finance higher and higher government spending
- a country is importing more and more while not being competitive enough to export goods and services
- income distribution becomes more unequal, with the 'rich' enjoying an increasing proportion of national income
- output and incomes are rising by depleting non-renewable resources or at a higher environmental cost.

What is the common thread connecting all of the above?

Can you provide a simple explanation of your answer for each of the above situations?

1.1 Competitive markets: demand and supply markets

Example 1

Match each type of market to the appropriate definition or explanation.

1 Informal market
2 Emerging market
3 Foreign exchange or currency market
4 Bull market

a A market where prices are expected to climb higher and higher
b A market where transactions are not officially recorded and so taxes are not paid
c A market relating to developing nations exhibiting rapid growth
d A market where the buyer is at the same time a seller

(1, b), (2, c), (3, d), (4, a)

Exercise 1

Consider the following markets:

stock market	real estate market
corn market	housing market
commodity market	oil market
capital goods market	street market
fish market	coffee market
bond market	open air market
futures market	the market for teachers
used cars market	telecommunications market

1 What is being exchanged in each? (Check the term using an Internet search engine if you are not sure.)

2 Determine who the participants are in each market and whether they must necessarily be in the same location at the same time.

3 Is the number of buyers roughly equal with the number of sellers in each of these markets?

4 Are the buyers few or many?

5 Are the sellers few or many?

6 Are any of these markets 24/7 markets (i.e. they never shut down)?

7 Are any of them global markets?

8 Are any of them strictly local?

9 Do both sides in these markets share the same information about whatever is being exchanged?

10 What goals do you think each side of each market has?

11 Can you think of ways in which a government could intervene in some of these markets?

Demand

Remember

- Non-price factors affecting demand can be referred to as 'shift factors' because if they change then the demand curve shifts (to the right or to the left). If the price of the good changes then there is no shift of the demand curve, only a movement along it from one point to another.

- Avoid using the expressions 'shifts up' or 'shifts down' when describing changes in market conditions. It may lead you to errors.

- When drawing a shift in a demand curve, many like to draw arrows that show the direction of change. It may be a good idea to draw your arrows 'parallel' to the Q-axis (like this ➡ or like this ⬅) to avoid having them point up or down. This way you will remember that an increase in demand means that **at each price** the quantity demanded has increased.

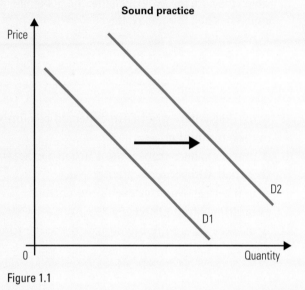

Figure 1.1

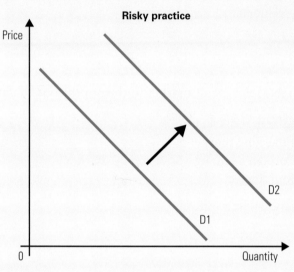

Figure 1.2

Example 2

Explain how the demand for guitar strings could be influenced by an increase in the price of guitars.

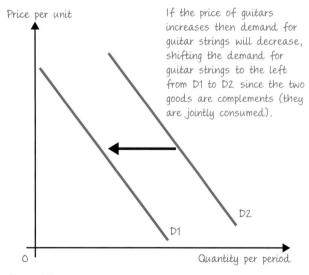

If the price of guitars increases then demand for guitar strings will decrease, shifting the demand for guitar strings to the left from D1 to D2 since the two goods are complements (they are jointly consumed).

Figure 1.3

Example 3

Explain how an ageing population could affect the demand for false teeth.

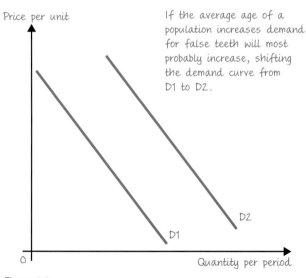

If the average age of a population increases demand for false teeth will most probably increase, shifting the demand curve from D1 to D2.

Figure 1.4

Exercise 2

1 Explain how the demand curve for holidays abroad could be influenced by:
   a higher income levels
   b an increase in the price of airline tickets
   c discounts offered by domestic hotels.

2 Explain how the demand curve for bicycles could be influenced by:
   a an increase in their price (is this a 'shift' factor?)
   b a significant increase in the price of helmets
   c increased levels of pollution.

3 Explain how the demand curve for coffee could be influenced by:
   a medical reports stating that moderate coffee drinking may have certain health benefits
   b a sharp increase in the price of sugar
   c a fall in the price of tea.

Exercise 3

Rewrite the following statements and fill in the blanks by using the terms provided below. Some terms may be used more than once or not at all.

decrease	substitutes	inferior
increase	complements	normal
demand	right	shift
quantity demanded	left	movement along

An increase in the price of watermelons will lead to a decrease in (1) _____. On a diagram this implies that there will be a (2) _____ of the demand curve.

If Coca Cola Co. decides to increase the price of Coca Cola, then the demand for Pepsi will probably (3) _____ and shift to the (4) _____, as the two products are considered (5)_____.

Demand for used cars will (6) _____ when incomes increase if consumers start looking into better substitutes, such as new cars. In this case, used cars are considered (7) _____ goods and their demand curve will shift to the (8) _____. If pizza and hamburgers become more expensive then demand for soft drinks will probably (9) _____, as soft drinks and fast food are (10) _____.

If a government announces that in five months it will increase the tax on heating oil then one may safely assume that the demand for heating oil will now (11) _____ and, thus, the demand curve shifts to the (12) _____. If the price of milk increases then quantity demanded will (13) _____ so, on a diagram, there is no (14) _____ but only a (15) _____ the demand curve.

Simple demand functions

The law of demand requires that the price of a good and the quantity demanded per period, ceteris paribus, are inversely related. In other words, if the price increases then quantity demanded is expected to decrease and vice versa.

Denoting price by P and quantity demanded by Qd, a demand function of the form

$$Qd = a - bP$$

is the simplest form that keeps the requirement that the two variables, price and quantity demanded, are inversely related.

This is guaranteed by the minus sign of the second term, the coefficient of price. In other words, the coefficient of price must be a negative number so that the law of demand holds. This coefficient is referred to as the slope of the demand function.

The functional form $Qd = a - bP$ is an example of a **linear** (a straight line) function, the only form you are required to know. It will always be a straight line, so if you draw it you will be able to plot it using your ruler.

Examples of such linear demand functions include:

$$Qd = 100 - 2P$$
$$Qd = 60 - 4P$$
$$Qd = 5000 - 25P$$

Finding the P and Qd intercepts of a linear demand function

To find the P intercept for a demand function, set Qd = 0 and solve for P.

To find the Qd intercept for a demand function, set P = 0 and solve for Qd.

Example 4

Let the demand curve be of the form Qd = 200 − 2P.

To find the P intercept we set Qd = 0:

$0 = 200 - 2P$

$2P = 200$

$P = \dfrac{200}{2}$

$P = 100$

To find the **Qd** intercept we set **P = 0**:

Qd = 200

Example 5

Let the demand curve be of the form Qd = 700 − 50P.

To find the P intercept we set Qd = 0:

$0 = 700 - 50P$

$50P = 700$

$P = \dfrac{700}{50}$

$P = 14$

To find the Qd intercept we set P = 0:

Qd = 700

Exercise 4

Find the P and the Qd intercepts for the following demand functions.

a Qd = 100 − 2P   **b** Qd = 60 − 4P   **c** Qd = 5000 − 25P

Finding the quantity demanded at different prices

In many exercises you will need to find the quantity demanded at a particular price. For example, you may be asked to calculate a firm's revenues at a particular price. To do that you will need to calculate the quantity demanded at that price. The process is very simple. You just need to substitute the value for price P into the demand function.

In the second column of the table in Exercise 5 you see that if the price (say, in dollars) is $2 then the quantity demanded will be $320 - (8 \times 2) = 320 - 16 = 304$ units (say, loaves of bread).

In the third column you see if the price is $10 then the quantity demanded will be $140 - (7 \times 10) = 70$ units.

In the fourth column you see if the price is $40 then the quantity demanded will be $40 - (2 \times 40) = -40$ units. This makes no sense, so a dash is placed in the cell. Always remember that prices and quantities have to be non-negative numbers.

Exercise 5

Copy the following table and, carefully, fill in the empty cells.

P ($)	Qd = 320 − 8P Qd	Qd = 140 − 7P Qd	Qd = 40 − 2P Qd
0			
1			
2	304		
3			
10		70	
20			
40			−

Plotting a linear demand curve

To plot a linear demand curve follow these steps (taking note of the advice in the tips opposite).

Step 1 Label the axes (include in the label the measurement units to avoid errors).

Step 2 Calculate the **P** intercept (see above).

Step 3 Calculate the **Q** intercept (see above).

Step 4 Locate on the graph paper the **P** and **Q** intercepts (see the tip on this).

Step 5 Connect the two points on the graph.

Step 6 After all this work has been completed go over your graph with a black pen.

Example 6

Plotting the demand function $Qd = 60 - 4P$.

Calculate the price (P) intercept: if $Qd = 0$ then $P = 15$.
Calculate the quantity (Q) intercept: if $P = 0$ then $Q = 60$.
Locate points on the graph paper.
Connect the points.

Plotting the demand function $Qd = 5,000 - 25P$.

Calculate the price (P) intercept: if $Qd = 0$ then $P = 200$.
Calculate the quantity (Q) intercept: if $P = 0$ then $Q = 5,000$.
Locate points on the graph paper.
Connect the points.

Plotting the demand function $Qd = 320 - 8P$.

Calculate the price (P) intercept: if $Qd = 0$ then $P = 40$.
Calculate the quantity (Q) intercept: if $P = 0$ then $Q = 320$.
Locate points on the graph paper.
Connect the points.

Tip

First, always use a pencil and ruler and have an eraser handy. Second, be as precise as possible! To practise, use graph paper and make sure the graph is relatively big, so choose intercepts that are not too close to the origin.

Tip

There is no need to worry too much about choosing convenient spacing for your axes, as on your final exam the axes will include about two values for each variable. This will considerably help you in your work on graphs.

Exercise 6

Use graph paper to plot the following linear demand functions. Make sure you fully label the axes.

1 $Qd = 100 - 2P$ **3** $Qd = 700 - 50P$ **5** $Qd = 40 - 2P$
2 $Qd = 200 - 2P$ **4** $Qd = 140 - 7P$

A note on the slope of a demand function

As mentioned earlier, the slope of a demand function is the coefficient of the price variable. So, if the demand function looks like $Qd = a - bP$, then the slope is $-b$. The slope (as many of you already know from Mathematics and all of you will have learned by the end of Year 2) is given by the ratio $(\Delta Qd/\Delta P)$ or, for small changes in P, by (dQd/dP), the first derivative of the demand function $Qd = f(P)$.

Price in a demand function is the 'independent' variable, and the quantity demanded is the 'dependent' variable. Changes in price lead to changes in quantity demanded. But, even though the independent variable is typically represented on the horizontal axis, in Economics we do the opposite and represent price on the vertical axis.

Why? We do this because Alfred Marshall did this in his book *Principles of Economics* (1890), the first ever textbook on the subject. He did not make a mistake! He was just reading the demand curve vertically, looking at the maximum price a consumer was willing to pay for different quantities.

Does it matter for us? It doesn't matter too much. Just keep in mind that if the absolute value of the coefficient of price increases in value, demand becomes flatter.

For example:
The demand curve $Qd = 100 - 4P$ is flatter than the demand curve $Qd = 100 - 2P$, and the demand curve $Qd = 30 - 2P$ is flatter than $Qd = 30 - \frac{1}{2}P$.

What if the constant term in a demand function changes?

Consider the following demand functions.

$$Qd = 100 - 2P \qquad\qquad Q'd = 300 - 2P$$

For any price, the quantity demanded for the function on the right side will be 200 units greater. Or, equivalently, for any price the quantity demanded for the function on the left will be 200 units fewer.

Check it yourself.

$Qd = 100 - 2P$	$Q'd = 300 - 2P$
Let P = 0	
then Qd = 100	and Q'd = 300
Let P = 10	
then Qd = 80	and Q'd = 280
Let P = 20	
then Qd = 60	and Q'd = 260

If you plot the two functions together in one diagram you see that $Q'd = 300 - 2P$ is to the right of $Qd = 100 - 2P$. The horizontal difference at all prices is 200.

It follows that if you are told that consumers of a product are for some reason willing to buy 200 more units at each price, then to find the new demand function you add 200 to the fixed term:

$$Q'd = 100 - 2P + \mathbf{200}$$
$$Q'd = 300 - 2P$$

Obviously, if demand decreases by 200 then you subtract 200 from the fixed term. Assuming the initial demand was given by $Q'd = 300 - 2P$, then the new demand will be:

$$Qd = 300 - 2P - \mathbf{200}$$
$$Qd = 100 - 2P$$

The new demand curve $Qd = 100 - 2P$ will be on the left of the initial curve $Q'd = 300 - 2P$.

Supply

Remember

- Avoid using the expressions 'shifts up' or 'shifts down' when describing changes in market conditions. It may lead you to errors.

- When drawing a shift in a supply curve, many like to draw arrows that show the direction of change. It may be a good idea to draw your arrows parallel to

the Q-axis (like this ➡ or like this ⬅) to avoid having them pointing up or down. This way you will remember that an increase in supply means that **at each price** the quantity supplied has increased. Notice how the arrow on the right-hand side diagram seems to suggest, misleadingly, that supply has decreased.

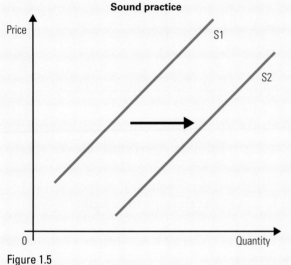

Figure 1.5

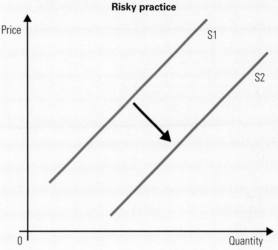

Figure 1.6

Example 7

Explain how the supply of petrol (gasoline) may be affected now if petrol station owners expect to be able to sell at higher prices next week.

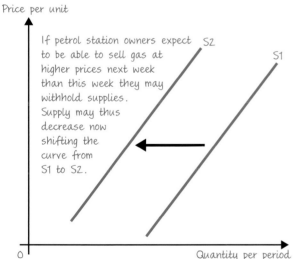

Figure 1.7

Example 8

Explain how the supply of coal may be affected if the coal miners' labour union succeeds in forcing employers to provide full health insurance and life insurance to all workers.

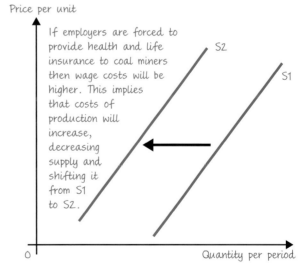

Figure 1.8

Exercise 7

1 Explain and illustrate on well-labelled diagrams how the market supply curve for meat could be influenced by:

   a the higher price of cereals used to feed cattle

   b a subsidy offered to producers by the government

   c a large number of consumers becoming vegetarians (note: be careful here).

2 Explain and illustrate on well-labelled diagrams how the market supply curve for corn could be influenced by:

   a an increase in its price (note: be careful here)

   b an increase in the price of wheat

   c an increase in the price of fertilizers.

3 Explain and illustrate on well-labelled diagrams how the market supply of cod could be influenced:

   a by an indirect tax on cod imposed by the government

   b if the fishing fleet adopts improved fishing technology

   c if the industry has good reason to expect the government to impose severe fishing quotas next year.

HL Simple supply functions

Typically, if the price of a good increases, firms are willing to offer more per period, ceteris paribus. Price per unit and quantity supplied per period are directly related. This is often referred to as the law of supply.

Denoting price by P and quantity supplied by Qs, a supply function of the form

$$Qs = c + dP$$

is the simplest form that keeps the requirement that the two variables, price and quantity supplied, are positively related.

This is guaranteed by the plus sign of the second term, the coefficient of price. In other words, the coefficient of price must be a positive number so that the law of supply holds. This coefficient is referred to as the slope of the supply function.

The functional form $Qs = c + dP$ is an example of a linear (a straight line) supply function, the only form you are required to know. It will always be a straight line so if you draw it you will be able to plot it using your ruler.

Examples of such supply functions include:

$Qs = 10 + 2P$

$Qs = 40 + 8P$

$Qs = -20 + 10P$ (here, you must rule out negative values of Q)

$Qs = 3P$ (here, the constant 'c' is zero, so the supply curve goes through the origin)

Finding the quantity supplied at different prices

In many exercises you will need to find the quantity supplied at some price. Once again, this is straightforward. You need to substitute the value for price P into the supply function.

In the second column of the table in Exercise 8 you see that if the price (say, in dollars) is $2 then the quantity supplied will be $100 + (2 \times 2) = 100 + 4 = 104$ units (say, loaves of bread).

In the third column you see that if the price is $10 then the quantity supplied will be $150 + (6 \times 10) = 150 + 60 = 210$ units.

In the fourth column you see that if the price is $0 then the quantity supplied will be $-20 + (20 \times 0) = -20$ units which makes no sense, so a dash is placed in the cell. Always remember that prices and quantities have to be non-negative numbers.

Exercise 8

Copy the following table and, carefully, fill in the empty cells.

P$	Qs = 100 + 2P Qs	Qs = 150 + 6P Qs	Qs = − 20 + 20P Qs
0			−
1			
2	104		
3			
10		210	
20			
40			

Plotting a linear supply curve

Complete the following steps to plot a linear supply curve. Always use a pencil and ruler and have an eraser handy. Be as precise as possible.

Step 1 Label the axes (include in the label the measurement units to avoid errors).

Step 2 Find the value of Qs if P = 0.

Step 3 Find the value of Qs for some other value of P.

Step 4 Locate the two points on your graph.

Step 5 Carefully connect the two points with a straight line and label the resulting curve 'S'.

Step 6 Since prices and quantities must be non-negative numbers, discard (erase) any segment that reflects negative quantities (i.e. located in quadrant II).

Step 7 After all work has been completed go over your graph with a black pen.

Example 9

Plotting the supply function Qs = 100 + P:

Step 1 Make sure you label the axes: price per unit on the vertical and quantity supplied per period on the horizontal.

Step 2 Find the value of Qs if P = 0:
If P = 0 then Qs = 100 + 0
Qs = 100 units (0, 100)

Step 3 Find the value of Qs for some other value of P:
Let P = 10
Qs = 100 + 10
Qs = 110 units (10, 110)

Step 4 Locate the two points on your graph.

Step 5 Carefully connect the two points with a straight line (and label the curve 'S').

Step 6 All prices and quantities are positive (the graph is in quadrant I).

Example 10

Plotting the supply function Qs = − 40 + 10P:

Step 1 Make sure you label the axes: price per unit on the vertical and quantity supplied per period on the horizontal.

Step 2 Find the value of Qs if P = 0:
If P = 0 then Qs = − 40 + 0
Qs = − 40 units (0, − 40)
Note: You must realize here that a section of the line you will draw after completing Step 4 will be discarded as negative quantities make no sense.

Step 3 Find the value of Qs for some other value of P.
Let P = 10
Qs = −40 + (10 × 10)
Qs = −40 + 100
Qs = 60 units (10, 60)

Step 4 Locate the two points on your graph.

Step 5 Carefully connect the two points with a straight line (and label the curve 'S').

Step 6 Discard the section of the line located in quadrant II, i.e. where negative quantities correspond to some set of prices (all prices below P = 4).
How do you find this vertical axis intercept? By setting Qs = 0 and solving for P:
   0 = − 40 + 10P
   40 = 10P
   P = 4

17

Example 11

Plotting the supply function Qs = 250.

In this case, quantity supplied is 250 units no matter what the price is. The supply curve will be vertical at 250 units. This could be the case for the supply of a farm product, of tickets in a soccer game or a concert, or of rooms offered by a hotel.

For example:
- This year, 1.8 million bushels of wheat were harvested in Country A so the supply of corn will be vertical at 1.8 million.
- The Ocean View tennis court has 4,000 seats so the supply of tickets will be vertical at 4,000.
- The Hilton in New Delhi has 650 rooms so the supply of rooms will be vertical at 650.

Exercise 9

Plot the following linear supply curves. Make sure you fully label the axes and the function.

1	Qs = 10 + 2P	**5**	Qs = 100 + 2P
2	Qs = 40 + 8P	**6**	Qs = 150 + 6P
3	Qs = − 20 + 10P	**7**	Qs = − 20 + 20P
4	Qs = 3P		

A note on the slope of a supply function

The slope of a supply function is the coefficient of the price variable. This is given by the ratio (ΔQs/ΔP).

Price in a supply function is the 'independent' variable, and quantity supplied is the 'dependent' variable. Changes in price lead to changes in quantity supplied.

Supply curves are also plotted in diagrams with price on the vertical axis and quantity supplied on the horizontal, just as in the case of demand curve diagrams.

Of course, it does not really matter as long as you remember that the greater the slope (the coefficient of P), **the flatter** the supply curve you plot. For example, the supply curve Qs = 10 + 4P is flatter than the supply curve Qs = 10 + 2P.

What if the constant term in a supply function changes?

Consider the following supply functions.

Qs = 100 + 20P   Q's = 300 + 20P

For any price, the quantity supplied for the one on the right-hand side will be 200 units greater. Or, equivalently, for any price, the quantity supplied for the one on the left will be 200 units fewer.

Check it yourself.

Qs = 100 − 20P	Q's = 300 − 20P
Let P = 0	
then Qs = 100	and Q's = 300
Let P = 10	
then Qs = 300	and Q's = 500
Let P = 20	
then Qs = 500	and Q's = 700

If you plot the two functions together in one diagram you see that Q's = 300 + 20P is to the right of Qs = 100 + 20P. The horizontal difference at all prices is 200.

It follows that if you are told that the company of a product is willing to offer 200 more units at each price, then to find the new supply function just add 200 to the fixed term:

Q's = 100 + 20P + **200**
Q's = 300 + 20P

Obviously, if supply decreases by 200 then you subtract 200 from the fixed term. Assuming the initial supply was given by Q's = 300 + 20P, then the new supply will be:

Qs = 300 + 20P −**200**
Qs = 100 + 20P

The new supply curve Qs = 100 + 20P will be to the left of the initial one Q's = 300 + 20P.

Market equilibrium

Remember

- Equilibrium in a competitive market exists when quantity demanded is equal to quantity supplied: Qd = Qs. If at some price Qd > Qs, then there is excess demand equal to Qd − Qs and there will be pressure for the price to increase. If at some price Qs > Qd, then there is excess supply equal to Qs − Qd and there will be pressure for the price to decrease. In equilibrium there is neither excess demand nor excess supply. In this situation, the market is said to 'clear'.

- You may need to determine how a market will be affected if a factor affecting demand and/or a factor affecting supply changes. Essentially you may need to determine how equilibrium price and equilibrium quantity is expected to change. These exercises are often referred to as 'comparative statics' as you really are comparing two 'photographs', one showing an initial equilibrium and one showing the new equilibrium after the change.

Example 12

These steps show how to determine the new equilibrium following a change in market conditions.

Step 1 Draw a diagram showing the initial equilibrium, writing at the top which market is illustrated.

Step 2 Determine whether the factor affects demand or supply.

Step 3 Determine whether it increases or decreases demand (or supply).

Step 4 Remember that an increase in demand (or supply) is a shift to the right.
Remember that a decrease in demand (or supply) is a shift to the left.
Note: Avoid using the expressions 'shifts up' or 'shifts down', you may get confused.

Step 5 Draw the new demand (or supply).

Step 6 Determine at the new intersection the new equilibrium price and the new equilibrium quantity.

Example 13

How is the market outcome affected if only demand or only supply conditions change?

If only demand changes (shifts):

If only D↑	P↑ (price will increase)	Q↑ (quantity will increase)
If only D↓	P↓ (price will decrease)	Q↓ (quantity will decrease)

If only supply changes (shifts):

If only S↑	P↓ (price will decrease)	Q↑ (quantity will increase)
If only S↓	P↑ (price will increase)	Q↓ (quantity will decrease)

Example 14

Determine diagrammatically and explain how the market for guitar strings will be affected by an increase in the price of guitars.

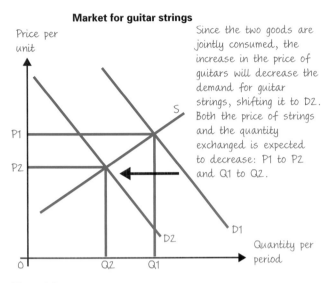

Market for guitar strings

Since the two goods are jointly consumed, the increase in the price of guitars will decrease the demand for guitar strings, shifting it to D2. Both the price of strings and the quantity exchanged is expected to decrease: P1 to P2 and Q1 to Q2.

Figure 1.9

Draw Produce a demand and supply diagram, label the axes and write a title at the top of it so that you remain focused.

Think Consumers buy guitars and guitar strings together, the two goods are considered complements (jointly consumed), so if the price of guitars changes it will be the demand for guitar strings that will be affected.

Think The higher price of guitars will lead to a decrease in the quantity of guitars demanded, so it follows that demand for guitar strings will decrease.

Think A decrease in demand is illustrated as a shift of the curve to the left.

Draw Add this shift to your diagram.

Compare the new with the old equilibrium point: the increase in the price of guitars is expected to lead to a decrease in the price of guitar strings and fewer guitar strings bought and sold per period, ceteris paribus.

Example 15

Using an appropriate diagram, try to find and explain the error in the following.

'In many countries house prices have been rising while more and more people buy their own house. This shows that the law of demand does not hold.'

The conclusion is not true. The law of demand holds. The reason house prices have been increasing is that demand for houses has increased. The shift to the right of the demand for houses has led to an increase in both the (average) price of houses and the number of houses bought and sold. Demand for houses may have increased for many reasons, for example rising incomes, lower interest rates (why?), bigger populations, more divorces or higher rents.

Exercise 10

1   Determine diagrammatically and explain how the market for organically grown eggplants (aubergines) will be affected if the cost of natural fertilizers increases.

2   Determine diagrammatically and explain how the market for air conditioners will be affected by an unusually hot summer.

3   Determine diagrammatically and explain how the market for restaurant dining will be affected if average individual incomes decrease.

4   Determine diagrammatically and explain how the market for eggs will be affected if, as a result of training, egg packaging workers can now pack more eggs in filler trays per hour.

5   Determine diagrammatically and explain how the market for Alaskan king crab will be affected if, at the same time that medical reports confirm the suspected health benefits from consumption of Alaskan king crab meat, wages are increased for trawler men.

6   Determine diagrammatically and explain how the market for DVD rentals will be affected in a city if, following an increase in the number of such stores, the price of renting movies on demand over the Internet is decreased.

Exercise 11

Using an appropriate diagram, explain how at the end of the summer the price at which swimsuits are offered is significantly lower than at other times of the year. This is when swimsuit manufacturers are already designing next year's swimsuits and so offer significantly fewer swimsuits in the market implying a significant decrease in market supply.

Exercise 12

Using an appropriate diagram, try to find and explain the error in the following.

'Improved technology increases supply of a good and leads to a lower price for it. This in turn will increase demand pushing the price back up.'

The equilibrium condition

Since, in a perfectly competitive market, the price at which quantity demanded per period is equal to quantity supplied per period (defined as the equilibrium price), it follows that the **equilibrium condition** is:

(1) $Qd = Qs$

or equivalently:

(2) $Qd - Qs = 0$

Equation (2) states that in equilibrium, neither excess demand nor excess supply exists. In other words, the market 'clears'.

Calculating the equilibrium price and quantity

You may be given a linear demand and a linear supply and asked to calculate the equilibrium price and quantity for this market.

Given that the equilibrium condition is:

$Qd = Qs$

You have three equations and three unknowns:

(1) $Qd = a - bP$

(2) $Qs = c + dP$

(3) $Qd = Qs$

You may use whichever method you find most convenient but it is conceptually convenient to substitute (1) and (2) for Qd and Qs in the equilibrium condition (3) and solve for P. Once you find the equilibrium price you substitute it into either the demand function (1) or the supply function (2) to find the equilibrium quantity.

Step-by-step guide to finding equilibrium price and equilibrium quantity

Let demand be given by $Qd = 100 - 2P$ and supply by $Qs = 2P$.

Step 1 Clearly write the demand function, the supply function and the equilibrium condition one below the other:

(1) $Qd = 100 - 2P$

(2) $Qs = 2P$

(3) $Qd = Qs$

Step 2 Substitute Qd and Qs from (1) and (2) into the equilibrium condition (3):

(4) $100 - 2P = 2P$

Step 3 Solve for P to find the equilibrium price and denote it by P*:

$100 = 4P$

$P = \dfrac{100}{4}$

$P^* = 25$

Step 4 Substitute P* into either the demand function (1) or the supply function (2) to find equilibrium quantity and denote it by Q*.

Substituting the equilibrium price 25 into the supply function (2) gives you:

$Q^* = 2 \times 25$

$Q^* = 50$

Step 5 Double-check your algebra: substitute P* into the other function to make sure you get the same equilibrium quantity.

Substituting the equilibrium price 25 into the demand function (1) gives you:

$Q^* = 100 - (2 \times 25)$

$Q^* = 100 - 50$

$Q^* = 50$

A note on units of measurement

A market demand, as well as a market supply, makes sense only if the time framework is explicitly provided. Both are so-called 'flow concepts' and must be measured over some time period. For example, if you state that your school has 1,000 students and that they demand 300 cheese sandwiches at a price of 1.00 dollar per sandwich, it cannot be inferred whether cheese sandwiches are popular or not as it makes a difference whether the students demand 300 sandwiches per day or per year!

The price must always be expressed on the basis of a 'per unit' of the good in question. It must be, for example, dollars per barrel of oil, or euros per sandwich, or thousands of Turkish lira per ton of cement.

Lastly, quantity (demanded or supplied) is expressed in units per period and these units can be expressed in number of sandwiches or hundreds of bushels of wheat or in millions of barrels of oil, each on some per period basis as explained above.

Example 16

The monthly demand and supply for corn are given by

$$Qd = 500 - 10P \text{ and } Qs = -100 + 50P$$

where price is in dollars per bushel and quantity is in millions of bushels.

Calculate the equilibrium price and quantity in this market.

Step 1 $Qd = 500 - 10P$
$Qs = -100 + 50P$
$Qd = Qs$

Step 2 $500 - 10P = -100 + 50P$

Step 3 $600 = 60P$
$P = \dfrac{600}{60}$
$P^* = 10$
Answer: the equilibrium price of oil is $10 per bushel.

Step 4 $Q^* = 500 - (10 \times 10)$
$Q^* = 500 - 100$
$Q^* = 400$

Step 5 To double-check this answer:
$Q^* = -100 + (50 \times 10)$
$Q^* = -100 + 500$
$Q^* = 400$
Answer: the equilibrium quantity of corn is 400 million bushels per month.

Example 17

The annual demand and supply for coffee are given by

$$Qd = 10,000 - 50P \text{ and } Qs = 20P$$

where price is in dollars per 50-kilogram bag and quantity is in thousands of 50-kilogram bags.

Calculate the equilibrium price and quantity in this market.

Step 1 $Qd = 10,000 - 50P$
$Qs = 20P$
$Qd = Qs$

Step 2 $10,000 - 50P = 20P$

Step 3 $10,000 = 70P$
$\dfrac{10,000}{70} = P$
$P^* = 142.857142$

Note: the direction you will be given is to round off to two decimal places.

Answer: the equilibrium price of coffee is $142.86 per 50-kilogram bag.

Step 4 $Q^* = 20 \times 142.86$
$Q^* = 2,587.20$

Step 5 To double-check this answer:
$Q^* = 10,000 - 50P$
$Q^* = 10,000 - (50 \times 142.86)$
$Q^* = 10,000 - 7143$
$Q^* = 2,857$ (the discrepancy is a result of the rounding off)

Answer: the equilibrium quantity of coffee is 2,587.2 thousands of 50-kilogram bags per year (2,587,200 50-kilogram bags per year or 2.59 million 50-kilogram bags).

Exercise 13

Following steps 1 to 5, calculate for the markets described below the equilibrium price and quantity. Make sure you express these using the appropriate units of measurement.

1 Letting $Qd = 980 - 90P$ and $Qs = 200 + 40P$, describe the market for peaches with price expressed in dollars per kilogram and quantity in thousands of kilograms per month.

2 Letting $Qd = 10 - 2P$ and $Qs = 2P$, describe the market for racing bicycles with price expressed in thousands of dollars per bicycle and quantity in thousands of bicycles per year.

3 Letting $Qd = 2,000 - 40P$ and $Qs = 400$, describe the market for olives with the price expressed in euros per 10-kilogram bag and the quantity in thousands of 100-kilogram bags per year.

4 Letting $Qd = 440 - 10P$ and $Qs = 100 + 7P$, describe the market for T-shirts with price expressed in dollars per T-shirt and quantity in thousands of T-shirts per year.

Exercise 14

Plot on graph paper the five demand and supply functions in the previous exercise, determining on each graph the equilibrium price and the equilibrium quantity. Make sure you label the axes fully.

Calculating excess demand or excess supply in competitive markets

If some price is not an equilibrium price then either excess demand or excess supply will result in a competitive market, and a process that will restore equilibrium will start.

This is what you need to do:

Step 1 Substitute the disequilibrium price into the demand function to find the quantity demanded at that price.

Step 2 Substitute the disequilibrium price into the supply function to find the quantity supplied at that price.

Step 3 Determine which one is bigger:

If Qd > Qs then there is excess demand equal to Qd − Qs.

If Qs > Qd then there is excess supply equal to Qs − Qd.

Step 4 If excess demand exists then there is pressure for the price to rise.

As the price increases, the quantity supplied increases (there is an extension of supply) while the quantity demanded decreases (there is a contraction of demand) until equilibrium is restored.

Example 18

Assume a competitive market where demand is given by $Qd = 980 - 90P$ while supply is given by $Qs = 200 + 40P$. It can be determined that the equilibrium price in this market is 6 while the equilibrium quantity is 440 units.

1 Calculate Qd and Qs at P = 4.

Step 1 At P = 4:
$Qd = 980 - (90 \times 4)$
$Qd = 980 - 360$
$Qd = 620$

Step 2 At P = 4:
$Qs = 200 + (40 \times 4)$
$Qs = 200 + 160$
$Qs = 360$

Step 3 Qd > Qs so there is excess demand equal to:
$Qd - Qs = 620 - 360 = 260$ units

Step 4 Since excess demand exists there is pressure for the price to rise.

As price increases, quantity supplied increases (extension of supply) while quantity demanded will decrease (contraction of demand) until equilibrium is restored at $P = 6$.

2 Calculate Qd and Qs at P = 7.

Step 1   At P = 7:

$Qd = 980 - (90 \times 7)$

$Qd = 980 - 630$

$Qd = 350$

Step 2   At P = 7:

$Qs = 200 + (40 \times 7)$

$Qs = 200 + 280$

$Qs = 480$

Step 3   Qs > Qd so there is excess supply equal to:

$Qs - Qd = 480 - 350 = 130$ units

Step 4   Since excess supply exists there is pressure for the price to decrease. As price decreases, quantity demanded increases (extension of demand) while quantity supplied will decrease (contraction of supply) until equilibrium is restored at P = 6.

Exercise 15

1 Assume a competitive market where demand is given by Qd = 10 − 2P while supply is given by Qs = 2P. It has been determined earlier that the equilibrium price in this market is 2.5 while the equilibrium quantity is 5 units.

Calculate Qd and Qs at P = 1 and at P = 3. Determine in each case whether excess demand or excess supply results.

2 Assume a competitive market where demand is given by Qd = 2,000 − 40P while supply is given by Qs = 400. It has been determined earlier that the equilibrium price in this market is 40 while the equilibrium quantity is 400 units.

Calculate Qd and Qs at P = 38 and at P = 42. Determine in each case whether excess demand or excess supply results.

3 Assume a competitive market where demand is given by Qd = 440 − 10P while supply is given by Qs = 100 + 7P. It has been determined earlier that the equilibrium price in this market is 20 while the equilibrium quantity is 240 units.

Calculate Qd and Qs at P = 18 and at P = 22. Determine in each case whether excess demand or excess supply results.

Calculating new market equilibrium following a shift in demand or supply

You may be asked to determine the outcome in a market where, at all prices, quantity demanded or quantity supplied increases or decreases by some number of units. For example, demand for figs may increase by 20,000 units per year at all prices, or supply of chicken may decrease by 5,000 units per month. Such a development in a market implies a parallel shift to the right (when there is an increase in either demand or supply) or a parallel shift to the left (when there is a decrease in either demand or supply) of the demand or supply curve.

To determine the new demand or supply function you need to add or subtract the number of units so that the constant term increases or decreases by that amount.

Care should be taken to ensure that units are properly accounted for. For example, if demand is in thousands of chicken per month and demand decreases at all prices by 5,000 chickens, you need to subtract 5 from the demand function. Say Qd was 105 − 5P, it would now become 100 − 5P.

Example 19

Let demand for chicken be Qd = 105 − 5P while supply is Qs = 25 + 5P, where P is in dollars per chicken and Q is in thousands of chickens per week. How much will the equilibrium price and quantity **change** if people are now willing to buy 15,000 fewer chickens at each price as a result of lower beef prices?

Step 1   Determine the original equilibrium price and quantity:

$105 - 5P = 25 + 5P$

$105 - 25 = 5P + 5P$

$80 = 10P$

$P = \dfrac{80}{10}$

P = 8, and substituting P = 8 in the supply equation:

$Q = 65$

i.e. the price was $8.00 per chicken and 65,000 chickens were traded weekly.

Step 2   Demand for chicken decreases by 15,000 chickens at each price so:

$Q'd = 105 - 5P - 15$

$Q'd = 90 - 5P$

Step 3   The new equilibrium price will therefore be:

$90 - 5P = 25 + 5P$

$90 - 25 = 5P + 5P$

$65 = 10P$

$P = \dfrac{65}{10}$

$P = 6.5$, and substituting $P = 6.5$ in the supply equation:

$Q = 57.5$

i.e. the price decreased as a result of demand for chicken decreasing to $6.50 per chicken or by $1.50, and quantity demanded and supplied decreased to 57,500 chickens per week or by 7,500 chickens. Note that you are asked for the change in price and output so you need to calculate differences between initial and new levels for both variables.

Example 20

In the above example, even though demand decreased by 15,000 chickens at each price, quantity demanded when equilibrium was restored was only 7,500 fewer chickens. Explain why this is the case.

At the original price ($P = $8.00) quantity demanded was $Qd = 105 - (5 \times 8) = 65,000$ chickens. Since demand fell at all prices by 15,000 chickens, at that $8.00 price only 50,000 chickens were demanded. The problem was that suppliers

were still offering 65,000 chickens at the $8.00 price ($Qs = 25 + (5 \times 8)$). Thus at the $8.00 price there was excess supply of 15,000 chickens and, when excess supply exists in a market, the price begins to decrease.

As price started to decrease not only were suppliers willing to offer fewer chickens in the market (supply contracted) but some households increased their quantity demanded of chicken (extension of demand). Remember: the now lower price provided the incentive to consumers to increase consumption from 50,000 chickens per week to 57,500 chickens per week. We started with a shift of demand (as a result of the availability of cheaper beef) but now there is a movement along (because of the decrease in the price of chicken).

Exercise 16

Let demand for bracelets be given by $Qd = 1000 - 10P$ and supply by $Qs = 200 + 30P$, where price is expressed in cents per bracelet and output is in millions of bracelets per year.

1   How much will the equilibrium price and quantity of bracelets **change** if their popularity decreases so that demand decreases by 200 million units at any price?

2   Explain why at the new market equilibrium quantity has not changed by 200 units.

The role of the price mechanism

Remember

- Changing prices convey information: an increase in price signals to producers that there is excess demand and gives them the incentive to produce more, while it signals to consumers that the good is now more expensive and gives them the incentive to cut back in consumption.

- A decrease in price signals to producers that there is excess supply and gives them the incentive to produce less, while it signals to consumers that the good is now cheaper and gives them the incentive to increase consumption.

- The change in the behaviour of market participants leads to a change in price and thus in more or less produced. A change in the allocation of resources follows.

Tip

To show this process in a diagram do not 'jump' from the initial equilibrium price to the final equilibrium price, but instead choose a price inbetween the two and describe the effect this price change has, first on quantity demanded and then on quantity supplied.

Example 21

Explain why farmers will choose to allocate more land and labour to cranberry production if consumers become aware of the benefits derived from eating cranberries.

Step 1   Start with a diagram illustrating an initial equilibrium in the cranberry market.

Step 2   If consumers become aware of the benefits derived from eating cranberries then demand for cranberries will increase and shift to the right.

Step 3   At the original equilibrium price, excess demand will now exist so the price of cranberries will start to rise. This development is now visible to all market participants and conveys the information (i.e. has signalling power; think of a waving hand) that excess demand in this market exists.

Step 4   The higher price provides the incentive to farmers to increase production, and through this to employ more land and workers in cranberry production, while it leads consumers to cut down on the consumption of cranberries.

Exercise 17

Explain how increased production costs in the fruit juice industry as a result of an indirect tax imposed by the government will decrease fruit juice consumption and production. How could this tax on fruit juice affect in turn the oranges market?

Exercise 18

1   Can you think of why the same increase in price resulting from increased demand for a product may in some cases lead to a large increase in quantity supplied while in other cases to a smaller one?

2   Can you think of reasons why despite increased demand for a good or service and a resulting increase in price, the output of some goods and services may not change? What does your answer imply about factor mobility and factor specialization?

3   A decrease in demand leads to lower prices and provides the incentive to firms to produce less. Resources (factors of production) then are 'freed up' implying that they become available for use (for employment) in other productive activities. Could you think of reasons why becoming available does not necessarily guarantee becoming employed elsewhere?

Tip

- Reading demand and supply curves 'vertically' is useful to understand the meaning of the terms consumer and producer surplus. A demand curve shows for each **extra** unit how much, at the most, the consumer is willing to pay. It follows that the area under a demand curve shows how much a number of units of the good are worth to the consumer.

- Symmetrically, a supply curve shows for each **extra** unit how much, at the very least, the firm needs to earn to be willing to offer that unit (this would be the **extra** cost of producing that unit, referred to as the **marginal** cost). It follows that the area under a supply curve shows what the firm needs to earn, at the very least, to be willing to offer a number of units of the good.

Tip

- Just the right amount of a good from society's point of view will be produced if social surplus is greatest. This occurs at the equilibrium level of output in competitive markets, where demand is equal to supply. This implies that neither too many nor too few resources have been allocated in its production so resource allocation is the best (optimal) from society's point of view.

- Another (equivalent) way of showing that the competitive equilibrium output is the best is by realizing that all units which are worth more to society than what it costs society to produce them are indeed produced up until that unit for which the extra benefits to society are equal to the extra costs society incurs to produce it. At the competitive equilibrium output, the marginal benefit (MB) is equal to its marginal cost (MC) for the last unit produced and consumed.

Market efficiency

Example 22

Consider the diagram below, which illustrates Mr. Green's demand for a particular product.

Assume that the price is determined at P':

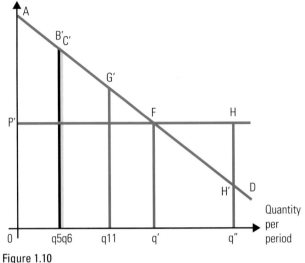

Figure 1.10

Question How much is Mr. Green willing at the most to pay for unit q_5 (say, the fifth unit)?

Answer We draw a line up from unit q_5 all the way to the demand curve: unit q_5 is worth to Mr. Green q_5B' dollars, the black thick line drawn above.

Question How much is Mr. Green willing at the most to pay for unit q_6 (say, the sixth unit)?

Answer We draw a line up from unit q_6 all the way to the demand: unit q_6 is worth to Mr. Green q_6C' dollars, the grey line drawn above.

Question How much are **both** units q_5 and q_6 worth to Mr. Green?

Answer They are worth q_5B' plus q_6C' dollars.

Question Will Mr. Green be willing to purchase unit q_{11} if the price in the market is P'?

Answer Unit q_{11} is worth to him as much as he would be willing and able to pay for that unit, which from the diagram is equal to $q_{11}G'$ dollars. Since the market price is only P' dollars, yes, Mr. Green would be willing to buy it.

Question Given that the price for the good in the market is P', which unit will Mr. Green at the margin be willing to purchase? (In other words, which unit is the very last unit he would be willing to buy?)

Answer He will be willing to purchase all units which are worth more to him (i.e. for which he would be willing to pay more) than the market price. In this case he would be willing to buy up all units up until (at the limit) unit q'.

Question Why wouldn't he be willing to buy unit q''?

Answer Unit q'' is worth to Mr. Green only as much as he would be willing at the most to pay for it which, given his demand, is q''H' dollars. The market price P' is higher (equal to q''H) dollars so of course he won't buy unit q''.

Question What are all units up to unit q' worth to him?

Answer They are worth to him the area below the demand curve up to unit q' or, in other words, area (0q'FA).

Question Since the good is sold at price P' and Mr. Green will buy q' units, how much will he end up spending?

Answer He will spend P' dollars multiplied by q' units, or area (0q'FP').

Question Since Mr. Green would be willing at the most to pay for units (0q') the area (0q'FA) but he actually only spends area (0q'FP'), what is his consumer surplus?

Answer: Since consumer surplus is defined as the difference between how much a consumer is willing at the most to pay for some amount of a good and what he actually ends up paying, Mr. Green enjoys a consumer surplus equal to area (P'FA), the difference between area (0q'FA) and area (0q'FP').

Example 23

Consider the diagram below, which illustrates the supply of Mr. Pink's firm.

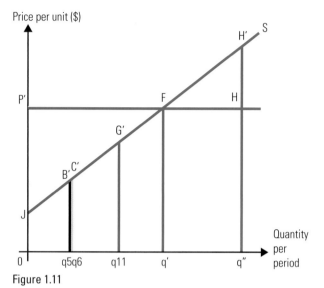

Figure 1.11

Question How much at the very least does Mr. Pink need to be willing to offer unit q_5 (say, the fifth unit)?

Answer *We draw a line up from unit q_5 all the way to the supply curve: at the very least Mr. Pink requires q_5B' dollars, the black thick line drawn above.*

Question How much at the very least does Mr. Pink need to be willing to offer for q_6 (say, the sixth unit)?

Answer *We draw a line up from unit $q6$ all the way to the supply curve: to be willing to offer unit q_6 Mr. Pink requires at least q_6C' dollars, the grey line drawn above.*

Question How much at the very least does he require to be willing to offer **both** units q_5 and q_6?

Answer *At the very least he requires q_5B' **plus** q_6C' dollars.*

Question Will Mr. Pink be willing to offer unit q_{11} if the price in the market is P'?

Answer *Mr. Pink requires at the very least $q_{11}G'$ dollars to be willing to offer unit q_{11}. Since the market price P' is higher, yes, Mr. Pink would be willing to offer that unit to the market.*

Question Given that the price for the good in the market is P', which unit will Mr. Pink at the margin be willing to offer? (In other words, which unit is the very last unit he would be willing to offer?)

Answer *He will be willing to offer all units for which the price in the market is greater than the minimum he needs to earn. In this case he would be willing to offer all units up until (at the limit) unit q'.*

Question Why wouldn't he be willing to offer unit q''?

Answer *Mr. Pink requires to earn at the very least q''H dollars to be willing to offer unit q''. The market price P' is less so he won't be willing to offer unit q''.*

Question What is the least amount that he needs to earn to be willing to offer all units up to unit q'?

Answer *The minimum he requires to earn to be willing to offer all units up to q' is the area below the supply curve or, in other words, area (0q'FJ).*

Question Since the good is sold at price P' and Mr. Pink will sell q' units, how much will he end up earning?

Answer *He will earn P' dollars per unit multiplied by the q' units he sells, or area (0q'FP').*

Question Since Mr. Pink requires to earn at the very least area (0q'FJ) to offer units (0q') but he actually ends up earning area (0q'FP'), what is his producer surplus?

Answer *Since producer surplus is defined as the difference between the minimum required by a firm to be willing to offer some amount of a good and how much it actually earns, Mr. Pink enjoys a producer surplus equal to area (JFP'), the difference between area (0q'FP') and area (0q'FJ).*

Exercise 19

The diagram below illustrates the market for product X. Determine the social surplus enjoyed if the market price is P' and Q' units are produced and consumed. Explain why allocative efficiency is achieved if Q' units are produced and consumed.

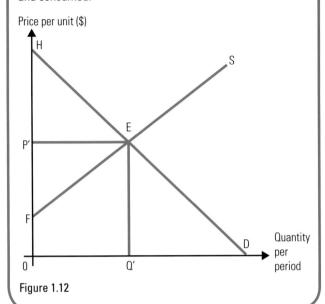

Figure 1.12

Exercise 20

The diagram below illustrates the demand for product X. Determine **the change** in the consumer surplus if the market price increases from P to P'.

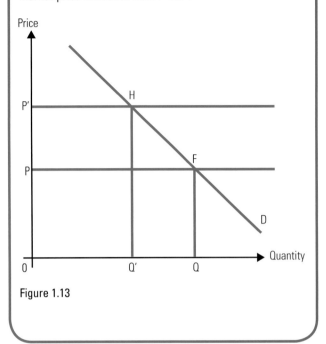

Figure 1.13

Exercise 21

The diagram below illustrates the supply conditions for product X. Determine the change in the producer surplus if the market price increases from P to P'.

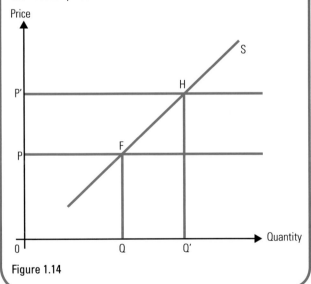

Figure 1.14

Exercise 22

A fall in the price of a good leads to a fall in quantity supplied. But if supply increases then price falls. Use supply and demand analysis to explain why these two statements do not contradict each other. Make sure you clearly explain the difference between a shift of and a movement along a supply curve. Use diagrams and examples to illustrate the points you make.

29

1.2 Elasticity

Price elasticity of demand

Remember

- Make sure you interpret properly the PED of a good. The table below summarizes the range of values for PED and how each should be interpreted (ignoring the minus sign).

If:	Then demand is:	This means that:
PED > 1	price elastic	a change in price leads to a **proportionately greater** change in quantity demanded, or a 10 % increase (decrease) in price leads to a greater than 10 % decrease (increase) in quantity demanded
0 < PED < 1	price inelastic	a change in price leads to a **proportionately smaller** change in quantity demanded, or a 10 % increase (decrease) in price leads to a smaller than 10 % decrease (increase) in quantity demanded
PED = 1	unitary elastic	a change in price leads to a **proportionately equal** change in quantity demanded, or a 10 % increase (decrease) in price leads to a 10 % decrease (increase) in quantity demanded
PED = 0	perfectly inelastic	a change in price leads to no change in quantity demanded
PED → ∞	perfectly elastic	a tiny change in price would lead to an infinite change in quantity demanded

Example 1

The table below presents PED for several products. Interpret each value.

Product	Estimated PED	Interpretation
Apples	− 0.73	Demand is price inelastic; a 10 % price increase will decrease quantity demanded by 7.3 %.
Granny Smith apples	− 1.82	Demand is price elastic; a 10 % price increase will decrease quantity demanded by 18.2 %.
Carbonated beverages	− 0.68	Demand is price inelastic; a 10 % price increase will decrease quantity demanded by 6.8 %.
Schweppes lemonade	− 1.25	Demand is price elastic; a 10 % price increase will decrease quantity demanded by 12.5 %.
Music concert tickets	− 0.45	Demand is price inelastic; a 10 % price increase will decrease quantity demanded by 4.5 %.

Tip

Price elasticity of demand (PED) is always a negative number (as a result of the law of demand), and that is why we usually refer to it **as if it were** positive. In calculations, **never** forget the minus sign.

Tip

Remember that the direction of change in total revenues (TR) is the same as the direction of the change in price (P) only when demand is price inelastic:
If 0<PED<1,
then when P↑, TR also ↑,
If 0<PED<1,
then when P↓, TR also ↓.

Tip

Remember that:
A doubling of quantity demanded implies a 100 % increase (while a halving implies a 50 % decrease).
If price increases by a factor of 4 (i.e. quadruples) then it increases by 300 %.

Tip

The PED equation has three elements, so if you know **any** two, you can always solve for the third.

Example 2

Why do you think demand for apples is price inelastic?

Apples do not have close substitutes. All other fruit, say oranges or melons, may be considered substitutes but they are not as close as, say, Pepsi and Coke or as LG and Sony television sets. An additional explanation may rest on the claim that spending on apples, at least for higher-income households, is typically a rather small proportion of their total expenditures.

Example 3

Why do you think PED for Granny Smith apples is higher than that for other apples?

Granny Smith apples have many more close substitutes than other apples (as it is a much more narrowly defined product). There are perhaps 80 different varieties of apple (Golden Delicious, Red Delicious, McIntosh, etc.) so each variety has many close substitutes. Apples, on the other hand, are a product category and as such have fewer close substitutes. Oranges or pears may be fruit but are not as close substitutes to apples as Red Delicious apples are to the Granny Smith variety.

Example 4

PED varies even along a straight line negatively sloped demand curve. Why?

PED can be calculated as:

$$\left(\frac{\Delta Q}{\Delta P}\right) \times \left(\frac{P_1}{Q_1}\right)$$

This is the product of the slope of the demand curve ($\Delta Q/\Delta P$) multiplied by the original price over quantity ratio (P1/Q1). The slope of a straight line demand curve is constant and equal to the coefficient of the original price but the ratio P_1/Q_1 varies.

Example 5

Why do you think demand is more elastic at higher prices than at lower prices?

Consumers will be more sensitive (i.e. responsive → elastic) to any price change when the price is already high than when it is low. Who cares if something cheap becomes a bit cheaper or a bit pricier? On the other hand, if it is already pricey,

then a relatively greater response will be induced if it becomes pricier or a bit cheaper.

On a more technical level: as a result of the law of demand, as price increases, quantity demanded decreases so the ratio P_1/Q_1 is greater at higher prices.

Example 6

Show why if two straight line demand curves intersect, the flatter one is more price elastic (for small price changes around the intersection price).

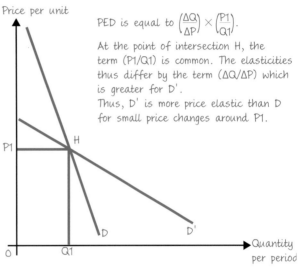

PED is equal to $\left(\frac{\Delta Q}{\Delta P}\right) \times \left(\frac{P1}{Q1}\right)$.

At the point of intersection H, the term (P1/Q1) is common. The elasticities thus differ by the term ($\Delta Q/\Delta P$) which is greater for D'.
Thus, D' is more price elastic than D for small price changes around P1.

Figure 1.15

HL Example 7

Show why if two straight line demand curves are parallel, then the one furthest from the origin is more price inelastic (for small price changes around some price).

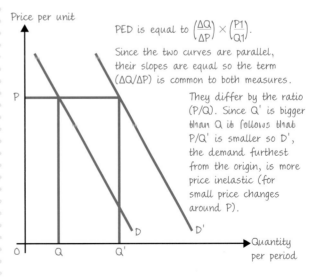

PED is equal to $\left(\frac{\Delta Q}{\Delta P}\right) \times \left(\frac{P1}{Q1}\right)$.

Since the two curves are parallel, their slopes are equal so the term ($\Delta Q/\Delta P$) is common to both measures.

They differ by the ratio (P/Q). Since Q' is bigger than Q it follows that P/Q' is smaller so D', the demand furthest from the origin, is more price inelastic (for small price changes around P).

Figure 1.16

Example 8

Near Mr. Green's office in Athens there is an amazing pastry shop called ALEA which arguably sells the best cheesecake this side of the Adriatic. This cheesecake is very good but very expensive, selling at €30 per kilogram. The owner, Ms. Hical, despite being very much aware of the reputation of her products, is hesitant to raise the price by 10% to €33 per kg.

Explain Ms. Hical's dilemma. Why would she be even more hesitant now that Greece is in an economic crisis?

It all depends on PED for ALEA's cheesecake. Being very good and having a brand name it could very well be the case that demand is price inelastic, in which case revenues for the owner will increase (as quantity demanded would fall, but by less than 10%). On the other hand, since the cheesecake is considered already very pricey, it could be that the current €30 price is in the price elastic region of demand. A 10% price increase would then lower Ms. Hical's revenues as quantity demanded would fall by more than 10%. Lastly, if incomes are shrinking then spending on her product will represent a bigger proportion of typical consumer spending and that too may leave demand for her cheesecake price elastic.

Example 9

Hitome, who is a collector of rare maps, has just bought at an auction two of only three known rare maps of Japan. She proceeds to pick up her two maps on stage and, immediately after the auctioneer hands them over, she lights up a match and conspicuously burns one of the two maps in front of a gasping audience. What must Hitome's estimate of the PED for these rare maps be if we assume her decision was rational?

How could we go about this exercise? Start from what you know: you know the formula for PED and calculating it requires the percentage change in quantity and the percentage change in price. Could these be calculated from the information provided? Let's see.

Burning one of the known three rare maps implies a 33% reduction in quantity. For her action to make any sense, Hitome must expect that it would lead to at least a doubling of the price (value) for each of the two remaining maps. This represents a 100% price increase. Assuming that the price just

doubles, then $PED = -\dfrac{33\%}{100\%} = -0.33$. So she expects PED to be 0.33 or less.

Example 10

Lydia owns a noodle stand on Nathan Road in Hong Kong. She is convinced that by decreasing the price of her noodles by half, her total revenues (TR) will double. Explain to her why this would be the case only if PED for her noodles was -6.0.

Start by what you know: you know the formula for PED and you know that $TR = (P_1 Q_1)$. The new price will be $\frac{1}{2}(P_1)$ so the percentage change in price will be -50%. For the revenues to double if the new price is half the initial price, quantity must increase four times so that:

$$TR_2 = \frac{1}{2} P_1 \times 4Q_1 = \frac{4}{2} \times P_1 Q_1 = 2 \times TR_1$$

But if quantity quadruples, then it increases by 300%. Substituting into the PED function we get:

$$\frac{+300\%}{-50\%} = -6.$$

Example 11

Calculate PED in the following cases.

1   If price increases by 14% while quantity demanded decreases by 10%.

Step 1   Organize what you know. You know the percentage change in price (+14%) and the percentage change in quantity demanded (−10%), so you know two of the three elements of the PED formula.

Step 2   Substitute the values into the PED formula:

$$PED = \frac{-10\%}{+14\%} = -0.71$$

2   If quantity demanded increases by 7% following a 3% decrease in price.

Step 1   Organize what you know. You know the percentage change in price (−3%) and the percentage change in quantity demanded (+7%), so you know two of the three elements of the PED formula.

Step 2   Substitute the values into the PED formula:

$$PED = \frac{+7\%}{-3\%} = -2.33$$

Example 12

Assume that, as a result of a change in price, quantity demanded for a particular product decreased by 20 %. If PED is 1.2, calculate the percentage change in price.

Step 1   Organize what you know.

You know the percentage change in quantity demanded (− 20%) and the PED (− 1.2).

Step 2   Substitute the values provided into the PED formula:

$$- 1.2 = \frac{- 20\%}{\%\Delta P}$$

Solving for %ΔP we get:

$$\%\Delta P = \frac{- 20\%}{- 1.2}$$

$$\%\Delta P = + 16.67\%$$

So, price must have increased by 16.67%. (Remember: two decimals are expected unless otherwise stated in the question.)

Tip

Since quantity demanded decreases, the percentage change will be a negative number.

Tip

If a variable, say price P, increases by some percentage, say x %, then:

$$P2 = P1 + \left(\frac{x}{100}\right) \times P1$$

If a variable, say price Q, increases by some percentage, say x %, then:

$$Q2 = Q1 - \left(\frac{x}{100}\right) \times Q1$$

Examples:

a   If the initial price was £120 and it increased by 5%, what is the new price?

$$P2 = P1 + \frac{5}{100} \times P1$$

$$P2 = 120 + (0.05 \times 120)$$

$$P2 = 120 + 6$$

$$P2 = £126$$

b   If the initial quantity was 2,000 units and it decreased by 45%, what is the new quantity?

$$Q2 = Q1 - 45\% \times Q1$$

$$Q2 = Q1 - 0.45 \times Q1$$

$$Q2 = 2,000 - (0.45 \times 2,000)$$

$$Q2 = 2,000 - 900$$

$$Q2 = 1,100 \text{ units}$$

Exercise 1

Refer to Example 1 on page 30.

1   Why do you think PED for Schweppes lemonade is higher than that for carbonated beverages?

2   How would you explain the very low PED for the latter?

Exercise 2

The table below provides actual price elasticities of demand for oil in Canada.

Price elasticity for:	PED
Oil (short run)	− 0.04
Oil (long run)	− 0.35

1   Interpret these two measures.

2   Explain why PED is (absolutely) larger in the long run than in the short run.

Exercise 3

PED for sushi in Akira's sushi restaurant in Auckland is estimated at − 0.4, and he currently sells 300 servings of unagi (fresh water eel sushi) per week at a price of $9.00 per serving. Calculate the effect on quantity demanded if Akira decides to raise the price to $9.45 per serving. What will happen to his weekly revenues?

Exercise 4

Simply Burgers' most famous hamburger is the 'Atomic' and it is currently priced at €8.45. Hungry Analysts, a market research company, has estimated that customers buy 550 Atomic burgers per day. When the price of the Atomic rises to €9.45, revenues decrease by €935. What was PED for the Atomic?

Exercise 5

Chicken with black bean sauce currently sells at $7.00 and the weekly revenues for China's Fantasy Restaurant are $294.00. If cutting price by 70 cents leads to 63 servings per week, what must PED for chicken with black bean sauce be equal to? What is the percentage change in revenues?

Cross price elasticity of demand

- The larger a positive cross price elasticity of demand (XED) is, the happier the owner of a firm will be if the price of a close substitute rises.

- The larger the absolute value of a negative XED is, the happier the owner of a firm will be if the price of a close complement decreases.

- The closer to zero XED is, the more unrelated the goods are. If the price of kerosene rises, the demand for chocolate chip ice-cream will not be affected. Thus the manager of Kayak Ice-Creams will not be terribly concerned by such a development.

Example 13

The table below presents XED for various products with respect to a change in the price of another. Interpret each of the values.

XED of:	Estimated XED	Interpretation
Gasoline with respect to the price of public transport tickets	− 0.53	The minus sign implies that the two goods are considered complements. A 10% increase in the price of public transport will lead to a 5.3% increase in the demand for gasoline.
Popcorn with respect to the price of cinema tickets	− 0.14	The minus sign implies that the two goods are jointly consumed. A 10% increase in the price of cinema tickets leads to a 1.4% decrease in the demand for popcorn.
Chicken with respect to the price of ground beef	+ 0.23	The plus sign implies that the two goods are considered substitutes. A 10% increase in the price of ground beef will lead to a 2.3% increase in the demand for chicken.
Ground beef with respect to the price of chicken	+ 0.35	The plus sign implies that the two goods are considered substitutes. A 10% increase in the price of chicken will lead to a 3.5% increase in the demand for ground beef. Note that the XED here differs from the value above. It seems that consumers of chicken consider beef a closer substitute than consumers of ground beef consider chicken products.
Breeder's Choice dog food with respect to the price of Natura Pet Product dog food	+ 1.32	The plus sign implies that the two goods are considered substitutes. A 10% increase in the price of Natura Pet Product dog food will lead to a 13.2% increase in the demand for Breeder's Choice dog food. The size of XED suggests that the Breeder's Choice brand is considered a relatively close substitute of Natura Pet.
Coca Cola with respect to the price of Pepsi	+ 0.61	The plus sign implies that the two goods are considered substitutes. A 10% increase in the price of Pepsi will lead to a 6.1% increase in the demand for Coca Cola. Since XED is not as high as the dog food example above it suggests that there is greater brand loyalty for Pepsi than for Natura Pet.

Example 14

When Shaw's, a supermarket in North Dartmouth, Massachusetts, increased the price of whole milk from $0.80 to $1.00, the weekly sales of low-fat milk increased from 25,000 gallons to 30,000 gallons. Calculate the XED for low-fat milk with respect to the price of whole milk.

Step 1   Organize what you know.
You know the old and new prices for whole milk as well as the old and new quantities for low-fat milk. You also know that the two are substitutes so that your answer should be a positive number.

Step 2   Calculate the percentage change in the quantity demanded of low fat milk:

$$\%\Delta Q = \frac{\Delta Q}{Q1}$$
$$= \frac{(Q2 - Q1)}{Q1}$$
$$= \frac{(30,000 - 25,000)}{25,000}$$
$$= \frac{5,000}{25,000}$$
$$= \frac{1}{5}$$
$$= +20\%$$

Step 3   Calculate the percentage change in the price of whole milk:

$$\%\Delta P = \frac{\Delta P}{Q1}$$
$$= \frac{(P2 - P1)}{P1}$$
$$= \frac{(1.00 - 0.80)}{0.80}$$
$$= \frac{0.20}{0.80}$$
$$= \frac{1}{4}$$
$$= 0.25$$
$$= +25\%$$

Step 4   Substitute these values into the XED formula.

$$XED = \frac{\%\Delta Q_{lowfat}}{\%\Delta P_{whole}}$$
$$= \frac{+20\%}{+25\%}$$
$$= +0.8$$

The result is positive, confirming that the two types of milk are considered substitutes.

Example 15

The following table provides data on the price of a brand of shampoo and volume of sales of the same brand of conditioner in June and October 2010 in a chain of supermarkets.

Time	Price of shampoo (£ per unit)	Quantity of conditioner (units)
June 2010	£1.40	68,000
October 2010	£1.60	64,000

Calculate the XED for conditioner to price changes in shampoo and interpret your result.

Step 1   Organize what you know.
This is neatly done in the table provided.

Step 2   Calculate the percentage change in the price of shampoo:

$$\%\Delta P_{shampoo} = \frac{(P2 - P1)}{P1}$$
$$= \frac{(1.6 - 1.4)}{1.4}$$
$$= \frac{0.2}{1.4}$$
$$= +14.29\% \text{ (remember the two decimal places)}$$

Step 3   Calculate the percentage change in the quantity demanded of conditioners:

$$\%\Delta Q_{conditioner} = \frac{(Q2 - Q1)}{Q1}$$
$$= \frac{(64,000 - 68,000)}{68,000}$$
$$= -\frac{4,000}{68,000}$$
$$= -5.88\%$$

Step 4   Substitute these values into the XED formula.
$$XED = \%\Delta Q_{conditioner}/\%\Delta P_{shampoo}$$
$$= \frac{-5.88}{+14.29}$$
$$= -0.41$$

The two goods are considered complements so if there is a 10% increase in the price of this shampoo then we should expect a 4.1% decrease in the sales of conditioner.

Exercise 6

Dunkin Donuts has estimated the cross price elasticities between honey-glazed doughnuts and chocolate frosted doughnuts, between doughnuts and muffins, between doughnuts and lattes and between doughnuts and bagels.

But the manager has mixed up the estimates and he is in trouble. The numbers he has are: + 0.20, + 1.10, − 0.50 and + 1.00.

Help him sort out these estimates, explaining to him why your suggestions are plausible.

Exercise 7

Pick n Pay supermarkets sell both arborio rice and basmati rice. They sell basmati rice at R140 per package and they know that its own price elasticity is less than one. The manager is thinking of increasing the price of basmati rice by 6%, expecting that this would increase revenues from basmati sales. Sales of arborio rice are currently 1,500 packages per week. If XED for arborio rice with respect to changes in the price of basmati rice is + 0.2, and currently about 800 packages of arborio rice are sold per week, what will be the new quantity of arborio rice Pick n Pay will sell?

Exercise 8

The following table provides data on the price of Cape Cod potato chips and volume of sales of Al's Delicious popcorn in June 2010 and October 2010 in the SuperValu supermarkets.

	Price of Cape Cod potato chips ($ per bag)	Quantity of Al's Delicious popcorn (bags)
June 2010	2.40	25,000 bags
October 2010	2.60	28,500 bags

Calculate XED for Al's Delicious popcorn to price changes in Cape Cod potato chips and interpret your result.

Income elasticity of demand

Remember

- Income elasticity of demand (YED) can be positive or negative:

  if YED > 0 then the good is normal,

  if YED < 0 then the good is inferior.

  Focusing only on normal goods:

  if 0 < YED < 1 then demand is income inelastic,

  if YED > 1 then demand is income elastic.

Tip

- The same good or service may be income elastic in one economy or locality and income inelastic or even inferior in another. Why? Because income elasticity of demand depends on the initial level of income and, more generally, on the living standards of the people in the specific market.

- Most, but not all, primary sector products are characterized by a low YED, secondary sector products (i.e. manufactures) are more income elastic while most services (tertiary sector) carry an even higher income elasticity. Assuming that incomes in an economy grow, we should expect that the economy may structurally transform: the relative size of the primary sector will typically shrink while the relative size of the tertiary sector will typically rise.

Example 16

The table below presents YED for three different products. Interpret their values.

YED	Interpretation
1.5	This is a normal good or service as YED is a positive number. Since it is greater than 1 it means that demand is income elastic: a 10% increase (decrease) in income is expected to lead to a 15% increase (decrease) in quantity demanded.
− 0.4	This is an inferior good as YED is a negative number: a 10% increase (decrease) in income is expected to lead to a 4% decrease (increase) in quantity demanded.
0.3	This is a normal good as YED is a positive number. Since it is between 0 and 1 demand for this good is income inelastic: a 10% increase (decrease) in income is expected to lead to a 3% increase (decrease) in quantity demanded.

Tip

A diagram with income on the vertical and quantity demanded on the horizontal illustrates an Engel curve. If it is a straight line that cuts the vertical axis then YED > 1. If it cuts the horizontal then 0 < YED < 1. If it goes through the origin then YED = 1. Note that the slope of the Engel curve alone cannot reveal whether the good is income elastic or inelastic.

Example 17

The table below provides annual per capita income levels in 2005 and 2010 in a neighbourhood of Shanghai and the number of appointments for manicures made in each of these two years.

Year	Per capita income level (000 Rmb)	Number of appointments (thousands)
2005	55	350
2010	61.6	413

Calculate and interpret YED for manicure treatments.

Step 1 Organize what you know.
The table neatly organizes the data; you can easily calculate the percentage change in per capita income as well as the percentage change in the quantity demanded for manicures.

Step 2 Calculate the percentage change in the quantity demanded for manicures:

$$\%\Delta Q = \frac{(Q2 - Q1)}{Q1}$$
$$= \frac{(413 - 350)}{350}$$
$$= \frac{63}{350}$$
$$= 18.00\%$$

Step 3 Calculate the percentage change in per capita income:

$$\%\Delta Y = \frac{(Y2 - Y1)}{Y1}$$
$$= \frac{(61.6 - 55)}{55}$$
$$= \frac{6.6}{55}$$
$$= +12.00\%$$

Step 4 Substitute these values into the YED formula:

$$YED = \frac{\%\Delta Q}{\%\Delta Y}$$
$$= \frac{+18\%}{+12\%}$$
$$= +1.5$$

Demand for this service in Shanghai is income elastic, as expected. A 10% increase in incomes leads to a 15% increase in the demand for manicures.

Example 18

The sectoral structure of an African country in 1987 and in 2007 is illustrated below.

Contribution of different sectors to total output	1987	2007
Primary sector	56.8 %	31.1 %
Secondary sector	5.9 %	8.8 %
Tertiary sector	33.2 %	50.7 %

These changes are the outcome of very many different factors but one may argue that YED has played a role. Discuss the possible role of YED in explaining the sectoral change evident above.

The data above reveal that the significance of agriculture (which dominates the primary sector but is not identical to it) has decreased over a 20-year span from representing over half (56.8%) of this country's economy to being less than a third (31.1%). Part of the explanation can be found in the low YED characterizing agricultural products. If YED is less than 1, say equal to 0.4, then a 10% increase in incomes leads to only a 4% increase in the demand for such products. Demand (and so spending) rises slower than incomes do.

Services, on the other hand, exhibited the reverse path: from being a third of the economy (33.2%), the tertiary sector grew to represent half of the economic activity in 2007. Again, YED could be part of the explanation: services (and note that these include government-provided services) are characterized by a high YED, typically greater than 1. If, say, YED for 'services' is 1.8 then a 10% increase in incomes leads to an 18% increase in the demand (and on spending) in services. Demand for services rises faster than income.

To explain why the contribution of manufacturing was and still is very low (5.9% in 1987 and 8.8% in 2007), more theoretical background is required. Note though that the significance of manufacturing, while still low, increased by almost 50% in 20 years.

Exercise 9

The following table presents actual estimates of YED for various products in the USA.

Income elasticity for:	YED
Goods at Wal-Mart (a large discount store)	− 0.5
Gasoline	0.45
Automobiles	2.56
Public transportation	− 0.36
Furniture	1.48
Electricity	0.20
Restaurant meals	1.40
Water	1.02

1   Which goods or services are inferior?

2   If there was an estimate for luxury dining would you expect it to be higher or lower than the estimate for restaurant meals?

3   What specific evidence is there above that taxi drivers are among those who suffer during bad times?

4   Revenues from the sale of which goods or services rise during bad times? Why?

5   Revenues from the sale of which goods or services suffer the most during bad times? Why?

6   How do you explain the significantly higher YED for water compared with electricity?

7   The term trade or business cycle refers to the ups and down of total economic activity and total income of a country through time. Intuitively, which industry would you label 'acyclical'?

8   If incomes in the USA increased by 4.1%, what would be the percentage change in the quantity demanded of furniture?

9   What evidence is there above that explains why governments tax gasoline? Explain your answer.

Price elasticity of supply

Remember

■   Price elasticity of supply (PES) is a positive number as both price and quantity supplied change in the same direction.

■   Make sure you properly interpret the PES of a good. The table below summarizes the range of values for PES and how each should be interpreted.

If:	Then supply is:	This means that:
PES > 1	price elastic	a change in price leads to a **proportionately greater** change in quantity supplied, or
		a 10 % increase (decrease) in price leads to a greater than 10 % increase (decrease) in quantity supplied
0 < PES < 1	price inelastic	a change in price leads to a **proportionately smaller** change in quantity supplied, or
		a 10 % increase (decrease) in price leads to a smaller than 10 % increase (decrease) in quantity supplied
PES = 1	unitary elastic	a change in price leads to a **proportionately equal** change in quantity supplied, or
		a 10 % increase (decrease) in price leads to a 10 % increase (decrease) in quantity supplied
PES = 0	perfectly inelastic	a change in price leads to no change in quantity supplied
PES > ∞	perfectly elastic	a tiny change in price would lead to an infinite change in quantity supplied

Example 19

The following table presents PES for several products. Interpret each value.

Product	Estimated PES	Interpretation
Oil (short run)	0.04	Supply is price inelastic; a 10% price increase will increase quantity supplied by 0.4%.
Oil (long run)	0.35	Supply is price inelastic; a 10% price increase will increase quantity supplied by 3.5%.
Copper (short run)	0.05	Supply is price inelastic; a 10% price increase will increase quantity supplied by 0.5%.
Copper (long run)	0.15	Supply is price inelastic; a 10% price increase will increase quantity supplied by 1.5%.
Milk (short run)	0.36	Supply is price inelastic; a 10% price increase will increase quantity supplied by 3.6%.
Milk (long run)	0.5	Supply is price inelastic; a 10% price increase will increase quantity supplied by 5.0%.
Housing (very long run; US average)	4.5	Supply is price elastic; a 10% price increase will increase quantity supplied by 45%.

Example 20 (use the table above)

How do you explain that long run price elasticities of supply are all larger in size than short run price elasticities of supply?

In the long run, by definition, more adjustments are possible. In terms of a production process, this implies that firms could acquire more capital goods and could expand their size.
In the long run, the use of all factors of production can change.

Example 21 (use the table above)

Why do you think PES for both copper and oil are so low?

Both the oil and the copper industries are extractive industries. It takes a long time to bring new copper mines into production and it takes a long time to find and bring a new oil field into production. Thus, any increase in demand will have to be satisfied with existing capacity. An increase in price can only bring about a very insignificant output response.

Example 22 (use the table above)

What factors could account for the relatively low long run PES for milk?

To be able to respond in the long run to higher milk prices with increased supply of milk, farmers would not only need more cows but also more grazing land. It is very possible that the constraining factor in this case is the factor of production, land.

Example 23

Calculate the PES for foot massage services in Singapore if the number of appointments offered per week increases from 2,140 to 2,568 when the market price increases from S$50.00 to S$55.00 per appointment.

Step 1   Organize what you know.

You know the old and the new quantity supplied; you know the old and new price for the service. Calculating the percentage changes of both and taking the ratio will provide the answer.

Step 2   Calculate the percentage change in quantity supplied:

$$\%\Delta Qs = \frac{(Q2 - Q1)}{Q}$$
$$= \frac{(2,568 - 2,140)}{2,140}$$
$$= \frac{428}{2,140}$$
$$= 0.20, \text{ i.e. } + 20\%$$

Step 3   Calculate the percentage change in price:

$$\%\Delta P = \frac{(P2 - P1)}{P1}$$
$$= \frac{(55 - 50)}{50}$$
$$= \frac{5}{50}$$
$$= 0.10, \text{ i.e. } + 10\%$$

Step 4   Substitute these values into the PES formula:

$$PES = \frac{\%\Delta Qs}{\%\Delta P}$$
$$= \frac{20\%}{10\%} = 2$$

PES for foot massage services Singapore is 2, which means that supply is price elastic.

Exercise 10

If PES for wax candles is estimated at 1.4 and there is a 8% increase in price, calculate the response in quantity supplied.

Exercise 11

Calculate PES for baklava, a Middle-Eastern sweet, if local producers of baklava are able to increase weekly output from 5,500 pieces to 5,775 in the short run following an increase in price from €0.60 to €0.75.

Exercise 12

Explain, using diagrams and examples, why PED and PES of primary products is typically low and what effect this has on the observed short run instability of commodity prices.

Exercise 13

Why do you think business people would be very interested in knowing PED and YED for their goods or services? Why would they also like to know several XEDs for their products? Try to illustrate your answer with examples and diagrams.

Indirect taxes

- Indirect taxes are taxes on goods and services or on expenditure and may be imposed either on a per unit basis (specific) or as a percentage of the price (ad valorem).

- Such taxes are imposed to collect revenue and/or to decrease consumption of a good or service.

- Assuming typical demand and supply curves, an indirect tax increases the market price and decreases output and consumption of the good.

- It also decreases the revenue earned per unit by producers.

- The government collects tax revenue, the size of which depends on the size of the tax but also on PED and PES.

Example 1

Using diagrams explain why an indirect tax is analysed by a vertical shift up of the supply curve.

An indirect tax can be thought of as an increase in the production costs of firms. As a result, they will now be willing to offer each unit at whatever price they were originally willing to offer it **plus** the tax. Consider the diagram below assuming a specific tax of $3.00 per unit. Whereas the firms would have been willing to offer unit Q' at $6.00, now they will need to set a market price of at least $9.00 so that after the tax is paid they still earn the minimum $6.00 they require.

Equivalently for unit Q'', whereas they would have been willing to offer it for $8.00, now that the $3.00 tax has been imposed they will require at least $11.00. This analysis holds for all units so the effect of a specific tax is to shift supply vertically up by the amount of the tax to S (tax). Note that the segments (ab) and (fh) are equal to the $3.00 tax imposed.

If an ad valorem tax had been imposed, the logic would be exactly the same. The only difference is that the wedge between the original supply and the supply after the tax is imposed is not constant as the amount of tax increases at higher prices. Consider the diagram below.

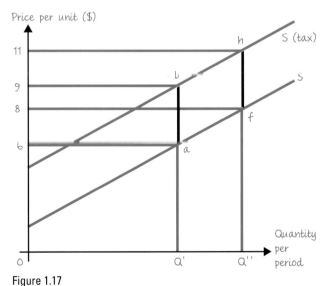

Figure 1.17

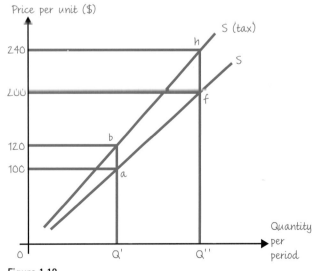

Figure 1.18

Assuming a VAT of 20%, whereas firms would have been willing to offer unit Q' at $100.00, they now require 20% more, i.e. they require the market price to be $120.00; and whereas they would have been willing to offer unit Q'' at $200, they now require the market price to be 20% more, i.e. $240.00. So segment (ab) = $20 and segment (fh) = $40. The shift is no longer parallel but the wedge increases because the amount of tax increases at higher prices.

Example 2

Using a diagram show the impact of a specific indirect tax on market outcomes.

Assume that initially equilibrium price in this market was Po and equilibrium quantity was Qo. If a specific tax is imposed then the new supply curve must decrease, shifting vertically up by the amount of the tax since it is as if production costs for the firms have increased. To be willing to offer each extra unit of output, the price must be higher by the amount of the tax.

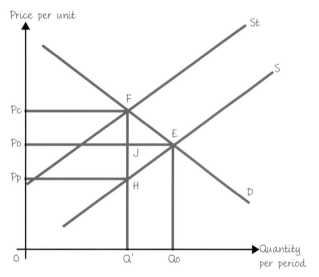

Figure 1.19

Given demand and the new supply St, the new market price is Pc and the new equilibrium quantity (produced and consumed) is Q'.

Consumers pay the price Pc for each unit but producers will not pocket the full amount. They will be earning less per unit because they now have to pay the tax to the government.

To determine the new price producers earn you must realize that what consumers pay is equal on the diagram to the segment (OPc), which is equal to the segment (Q'F). By subtracting from (Q'F) the tax (the vertical distance FH) that has to be paid, we arrive at line segment (Q'H) which is what is left for producers. This is equal to Pp on the price axis.

The tax has increased the price consumers pay for the good, has decreased production and consumption of the good, and has decreased the net of tax price that producers earn from selling each unit.

The government collects tax revenues equal to area (PpHFPc) which is found by multiplying the per unit tax (HF) by the amount sold (OQ') which is equal to (PpH).

HL ### Tip

To determine the incidence of an indirect tax you just need to remember that

$$\frac{\% \text{ of tax incidence on consumers}}{\% \text{ of tax incidence on producers}} = \frac{PES}{PED}$$

The table below summarizes all cases.

Since $\dfrac{\% \text{ of tax incidence on consumers}}{\% \text{ of tax incidence on producers}} = \dfrac{PES}{PED}$ then:	
Given PES: the lower the PED, the smaller the incidence on producers and the greater the incidence on consumers.	Given PED: the lower the PES, the smaller the incidence on consumers and the greater the incidence on producers.
If PES = 0 (vertical supply) then incidence will be 0% on consumers and 100% on producers.	If PED = 0 (vertical demand) then incidence will be 0% on producers and 100% on consumers.
If PES → ∞ then incidence will be 0% on producers and 100% on consumers.	If PED → ∞ then incidence will be 0% on consumers and 100% on producers.
If PED = PES then the left-hand side ratio in the formula at the top must also be equal to 1 so consumers and producers split the tax (50% each).	

(Remember that the sum of the two percentages is 100%.)

Tip

Since producers sell less and the net of price tax (their new revenue per unit) is smaller, they necessarily earn less revenue than before the tax. On the other hand, since consumers buy less at a higher price, whether they spend more or less depends on PED.

Tip

To deal with tax-related calculations remember that the tax creates a wedge between the price consumers pay (P^c) and the price producers receive (P^p): $P^c = (P^p + t)$ or $(P^c - P^p) = t$

How to approach questions with indirect taxes

If there is no indirect tax imposed in a competitive market, then to calculate the equilibrium price and output we have three equations and three unknowns.

   (1) $Qd = a - bP$
   (2) $Qs = c + dP$
   (3) $Qd = Qs$

Since (3) states that $Qd = Qs$, we substitute Q for Qd and Qs in (1) and (2). So we have two equations with two unknowns which we solve in whichever way is more convenient.

Now, a specific tax (or a subsidy) creates a wedge between the price consumers pay and the price producers receive.

Let Pc be the price consumers pay while Pp can be the price producers receive.

It follows that if a specific tax t is imposed:

   (4a) $Pp = (Pc - t)$ or (4b) $Pc = (Pp + t)$

and demand will now be expressed in terms of Pc while supply will now be expressed in terms of Pp. So, for example, equation (3) becomes

   $Qs = c + dPp$

Substituting (Pc – t) instead of Pp will permit you to use the equilibrium condition to solve for Pc and then find the new Q. Finally, using (4a) will yield Pp for you.

The examples below will help you solve any tax-related question.

Example 3

Assume a market originally described by the following demand and supply equations.

   (1) $Qd = 200 - P$
   (2) $Qs = 20 + 2P$, where the price is in euros and the quantity in units of the good.

1 Calculate the equilibrium price and quantity.

Step 1   Write the demand formula, the supply formula and the equilibrium condition.
   (1) $Qd = 200 - P$
   (2) $Qs = 20 + 2P$
   (3) $Qd = Qs$

Step 2   Substitute (1) and (2) into (3):
   $200 - P = 20 + 2P$

Step 3   Solve for P:
   $180 = 3P$
   $P = \dfrac{180}{3}$
   $P = 60$
   Answer: The equilibrium price is €60.

Step 4   Find Q by substituting the value of P in (2):
   $Q = 20 + (2 \times 60)$
   $Q = 140$

Step 5   Double-check by substituting the value of P in (1):
   $Q = 200 - 60$
   $Q = 140$
   Answer: the equilibrium quantity is 140 units.

2 Assume that an indirect tax of €15 per unit is imposed. Calculate the price now paid by consumers (i.e. the new market price), the price received by producers, and the new equilibrium quantity.

Step 1   Rewrite the demand and supply functions, but in the demand function use Pc instead of P (Pc is the price consumers pay) and in the supply function use Pp instead of P (Pp is the price producers earn net of tax). Also write the 'wedge' equation, i.e. that $Pp = (Pc - tax)$:
   (1) $Qd = 200 - Pc$
   (2) $Qs = 20 + 2Pp$
   (3) $Qd = Qs$
   (4) $Pp = (Pc - 15)$

Step 2   Substitute (1) and (2) into (3):
   (5) $200 - Pc = 20 + 2Pp$

Step 3   Substitute (4) into (5) and solving for Pc:
   $200 - Pc = 20 + 2(Pc - 15)$
   $200 - Pc = 20 + 2Pc - 30$
   $200 - 20 + 30 = 2Pc + Pc$
   $210 = 3Pc$
   $Pc = \dfrac{210}{3}$
   $Pc = 70$
   Answer: The new market price consumers pay is €70.

Step 4   Find Pp which is the new price (net of tax) producers receive.

Substitute the value for Pc (Pc = 70) into (4):

Pp = Pc − 15

Pp = 55

Answer: The price producers earn per unit (net of tax) is €55. This is their new revenue per unit (or average revenue).

Step 5   Find the new equilibrium quantity.

Either substitute Pc into (1):

Q = 200 − 70

Q = 130

or substitute Pp into (2):

Q = 20 + (2 × 55)

Q = 130

The new equilibrium quantity is 130 units.

3 What amount of the tax is paid by consumers? Also, what proportion of the tax is paid by consumers? (In other words, calculate the tax incidence on consumers.)

Step 1   Start with what you know about the initial situation.

The original pre-tax price was €60.

The new post-tax price that consumers pay is €70.

Step 2   So consumers pay €10 out of the €15 tax imposed, or $\frac{10}{15} = \frac{2}{3}$ of the tax. (This is the tax incidence on consumers.)

4 What amount of the tax is paid by producers? Also, what proportion of the tax is paid by producers? (In other words, calculate the tax incidence on producers.)

Step 1   Start with what you know about the initial situation.

The original pre-tax price was €60.

The new, post-tax price producers receive is €55.

In other words, the revenue earned per unit by producers was €60 while the new revenue per unit earned is €55.

Step 2   So producers earn €5 per unit less than they did; they are burdened with €5 out of the €15 tax imposed or $\frac{5}{15} = \frac{1}{3}$ of the tax. (This is the tax incidence on producers.)

5 How much tax revenue does the government collect?

Step 1   Start with what you know.

Since tax revenue earned by the government is given by:

(tax per unit) × (number of units bought)

then €15 × 130 units bought = €1,950.

Note: if the quantity was, say, in thousands of units, then tax revenues would be €1,950,000.

Step 2   To calculate the welfare loss we need to calculate the area of the welfare loss triangle (E_2E_1H) (sketch the relevant graph or see the diagram for question 9 on the next page).

Applying the formula for the area of a triangle $\frac{base \times height}{2}$, and realizing from a diagram that the height is the difference between the original and the post-tax equilibrium quantities ($\Delta Q = JE1$), while the base is the size of the tax (FE_2) we get:

$\Delta Q = 140 − 130 = 10$

Tax $t = €15$

Welfare loss $= \frac{(10 \times 15)}{2} = $ or €75

6 Calculate the initial total revenues (TR) producers earned, the new TR they earn after the imposition of the tax and the change in the TR collected.

Step 1   Start with what you know.

TR = (price per unit) × (number of units sold)

Note: If a tax has been imposed, to calculate total revenues that firms collect we need to use the price earned per unit **net of the tax** imposed.

This is our Pp.

Step 2   Original TR were:

€60.00 per unit × 140 units = €8,400.00

New, post-tax TR collected were:

€55.00 per unit × 130 units = €7,150.00

$\Delta TR = TR2 − TR1$

$\Delta TR = 7,150 − 8,400$

$\Delta TR = −€1,250.00$

As expected, the TR that firms collect after an indirect tax is imposed decrease, in this case by €1,250.00.

7 Calculate the initial total expenditures (TE) consumers make on the good, the new TE they make and the change in their TE.

Step 1 Start with what you know:
TE = (price per unit) × (number of units sold) (= total revenues)
Note: If an indirect tax has been imposed, the TE consumers make will no longer equal the TR firms earn.

Step 2 Original TE:
€60.00 per unit × 140 units = €8,400.00
New TE:
€70.00 per unit × 130 units = €9,100.00
$\Delta TE = TE2 - TE1$
$\Delta TE = 9100 - 8400$
$\Delta TE = €700.00$

In this case, TE consumers made increased by €700.00.

Since the new market price consumers pay is higher after the tax and the quantity bought is less, whether their TE increase or decrease depends on PED. Since in this case their spending increased following a price increase we can infer that demand is price inelastic. This is consistent with our finding that consumers pay a bigger proportion of the tax. Using the equation
$$\frac{\text{\% of tax incidence on consumers}}{\text{\% of tax incidence on producers}} = \frac{PES}{PED}$$
and since consumers pay $\frac{2}{3}$ (or 66.66%) of the tax while producers pay $\frac{1}{3}$ (or 33.33%) of the tax, we can find, by substituting these values for tax incidence on the left-hand side of the equation, that PED is half the value of PES.

8 Calculate PED for this good.

Step 1 Start with what you know.
$PED = \frac{\%\Delta Q}{\%\Delta P}$;
P1 = 60, P2 = 70; Q1 = 110, Q2 = 130.

Step 2 Calculate the percentage change in quantity demanded:
$\%\Delta Q = \frac{(Q2 - Q1)}{Q1}$
$= \frac{(130 - 140)}{140}$
$= -\frac{10}{140}$
$= -7.14\%$

Step 3 Calculate the percentage change in price:
$\%\Delta P = \frac{(P2 - P1)}{P1}$
$= \frac{(70 - 60)}{60}$
$= \frac{10}{60}$
$= 16.66\%$

Step 4 Substitute the above values into the PED equation:
$PED = \frac{-7.14\%}{+16.66\%} = -0.43$
Demand is price inelastic, confirming our previous results.

9 Draw (or plot) a diagram showing all of the numerical information available.

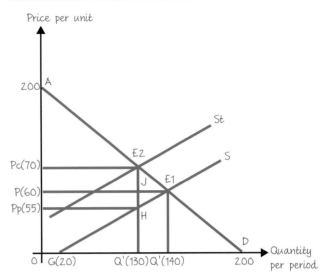

Figure 1.20

10 Calculate the effect on the consumer, the producer and social (or community) surplus.

Step 1 Start with what you know.
The consumer surplus is the area of the triangle below the demand curve and above the price line, while the producer surplus is the area above the supply curve and below the price line; the area of a triangle is $\frac{1}{2}$ (base × height); the area of a rectangle is length × width.

Step 2 Calculate the original consumer surplus, i.e. the area of (APE1):
$\frac{1}{2}$ (140 × (200 − 60)) = 9,800

Step 3 Calculate the new consumer surplus, i.e. the area of (PcE2A):
$\frac{1}{2}$ (130 × (200 − 70)) = 8,450
So consumer surplus decreased by €9,800 − €8,450 = €1,350.

Step 4 Calculate the original producer surplus, i.e. area (0GE1P).
In this case it is easier to find this area as the difference between area (0QE1P) and area (GQE1). This method of calculation reflects precisely what the producer surplus is: it is the difference between what firms own and the minimum

they require to offer some amount to the market. So:

$$(60 \times 140) - \frac{1}{2}((140 - 20) \times 60)$$
$$= 8,400 - 3,600 = €4,800$$

Step 5 Calculate the new producer surplus, i.e. area (OGHPp).

In this case it is easier to find this area as the difference between area (OQ'HPp) and area (GQ'H):

$$(55 \times 130) - \frac{1}{2}((130 - 20) \times 55)$$
$$= 7,150 - 3,025 = €4,125$$

So producer surplus decreased by 4,800 - 4,125 = €675.

Step 6 To calculate the initial, the new and the change in social surplus remember that social (or community) surplus is the sum of the consumer and the producer surplus.
Original social surplus =
9,800 + 4,800 = €14,600
New social surplus =
8,450 + 4,125 = €12,575
Social surplus decreased by
14,600 - 12,575 = €2,025, of which €75 is the 'deadweight loss' and €1,950 was transferred to the government (and could, in principle, be spent on roads and schools for example).

11 Construct a table summarizing all of the available information.

Initial, pre-tax situation	
Market (equilibrium) price (P)	€60 (this is also the revenue earned per unit by firms)
Market (equilibrium) quantity Q	140 units
Total revenues (TR) for firms (P × Q)	€60 per unit × 140 units = €8,400.00
Total expenditures (TE) consumers make (P × Q)	€60 per unit × 140 units = €8,400.00
Comments: TR and TE are of course the same as there is yet no tax to create a 'wedge' between the price consumers pay in the market and the price producers earn per unit (i.e. before the tax is imposed, price and average revenue (AR) are the same)	
New, post-tax situation	
Tax imposed per unit of output	€15
New market (equilibrium) price (Pc) that consumers pay	€70
Price net of tax that producers earn (Pp) (which is the AR for the firms)	€55
Tax incidence on consumers (and as a proportion of the tax)	€10 (or $\frac{10}{15} = \frac{2}{3}$ of the tax)
Tax incidence on producers (and as a proportion of the tax)	€5 (or $\frac{5}{15} = \frac{1}{3}$ of the tax)
New market (equilibrium) quantity	130 units
New TR firms collect	€55 per unit × 130 units = €7,150.00
Change in TR firms collect	€7,150.00 - €8,400.00 = -€1,250.00 (a decrease)
New TE consumers make	€70 per unit × 130 units = €9,100.00
Change in TE consumers make	€9,100.00 - €8,400.00 = €700.00 (an increase)
Tax revenues (collected by the government)	€15 per unit × 130 units = €1,950.00
PED	-0.43 (price inelastic)
Tax incidence versus elasticities formula: $\frac{\% \text{ of tax incidence on consumers}}{\% \text{ of tax incidence on producers}} = \frac{PES}{PED}$	$\frac{66.66\%}{33.33\%} = \frac{2}{1}$, so demand is less price elastic than supply
Original consumer surplus	9,800
Original producer surplus	4,800
Original social surplus	14,600
New post-tax consumer surplus	8,450
New post-tax producer surplus	4,125
New social surplus	12,575
Change in welfare	14,600 - 12,575 = 2,025, of which €75 is a 'deadweight loss' and €1,950 was transferred to the government (and so cannot be considered a deadweight loss)

Example 4

Assume a market originally described by the following demand and supply equations:
  (1) Qd = 500 – 10P
  (2) Qs = –100 + 50P, where the price is in euros and the quantity in units of the good.

1 Calculate the equilibrium price and quantity.
  P = 10
  Q = 400

2 Assume that an indirect tax of €3 per unit is imposed. Calculate the price now paid by consumers (i.e. the new market price), the price received by producers and the new equilibrium quantity.

Step 1 Rewrite the demand and supply functions but in the demand function use Pc instead of P (Pc is the price consumers pay), and in the supply function use Pp instead of P (Pp is the price producers earn net of tax).
This time, write the 'wedge' equation as Pp = (Pc – tax):
(1) Qd = 500 – 10Pc
(2) Qs = –100 + 50Pp
(3) Qd = Qs
(4) Pp = Pc – 3

Step 2 Substituting (1) and (2) into (3):
(5) 500 – 10Pc = –100 + 50Pp

Step 3 Substituting (4) into (5) and solving for Pc:
  500 – 10Pc = –100 + 50 × (Pc – 3)
  500 – 10Pc = –100 + 50Pc – 150
  500 + 100 + 150 = 50Pc + 10Pc
  750 = 60Pc
  $Pc = \frac{750}{60}$
  Pc = 12.5
Answer: The new post-tax price consumers pay will be €12.5. This is their new revenue per unit. This is the new market price.

Step 4 Find Pp which is the new price, net of tax, producers earn (their new revenue per unit).
Substitute the value for Pc you found (Pc = 12.5) in (4):
Pp = Pc – 3
Pp = 12.5 – 3
Pp = 9.5

Answer: the new price, net of tax, producers earn (their new revenue per unit) is €9.5.

Step 5 Find the new equilibrium quantity.
Either substitute Pc into (1):
Q = 500 – (10 × 12.5)
Q = 500 – 125
Q = 375
or substitute Pp into (2):
Q = –100 + 50Pp
Q = –100 + (50 × 9.5)
Q = –100 + 475
Q = 375
The new equilibrium quantity is 375 units.

3 What amount of the tax is paid by consumers? Also, what proportion of the tax is paid by consumers?) (In other words, calculate the tax incidence on consumers.)

Step 1 Start with what you know about the initial situation. The original pre-tax price was €10. The new post-tax price that consumers pay is €12.5.

Step 2 So, consumers pay €2.5 out of the €3 tax imposed, or $\frac{25}{30} = \frac{5}{6}$ of the tax.
(This is the consumer's tax incidence.)

4 What amount of the tax is paid by producers? Also, what proportion of the tax is paid by producers? (In other words, calculate the tax incidence on producers.)

Step 1 Start with what you know about the initial situation.
The original pre-tax price was €10.
The new post-tax price producers receive is €9.5.
In other words, the revenue earned per unit by producers was €10 while the new revenue per unit earned is €9.5.

Step 2 So, producers earn €0.5 per unit less than they did; they are burdened with €0.5 out of the €3 tax imposed or $\frac{5}{30} = \frac{1}{6}$ of the tax. (This is the tax incidence on producers.)

HL

Exercise 1

Assume a market originally described by the following demand and supply equations:

(1) $Qd = 120 - 4P$

(2) $Qs = 2P - 30$, where the price is in dollars and the quantity in thousands of units of the good.

1 Calculate the equilibrium price and quantity.

2 Assume that an indirect tax of $3.00 per unit is imposed. Calculate the price now paid by consumers (i.e. the new market price), the price received by producers and the new equilibrium quantity.

3 What amount of the tax is paid by consumers? Also, what proportion of the tax is paid by consumers? (In other words, calculate the tax incidence on consumers.)

4 What amount of the tax is paid by producers? Also, what proportion of the tax is paid by producers? (In other words, calculate the tax incidence on producers.)

5 How much tax revenue does the government collect? Remember that the units are in thousands.

6 Calculate the initial TR producers earned, the new TR they earn after the imposition of the tax and the change in the TR collected.

7 Calculate the initial TE consumers make on the good, the new TE they make and the change in their TE.

8 Calculate PED for this good.

9 Draw (or plot) a diagram showing all of the numerical information available.

10 Calculate the effect on consumer, producer and social (or community) surplus.

11 Construct a table summarizing all of the available information.

Exercise 2

Assume a market originally described by the following demand and supply equations:

(1) $Qd = 100 - 5P$

(2) $Qs = 5P$, where the price is in UK pounds sterling and the quantity is in millions of units of the good.

1 Calculate the equilibrium price and quantity.

2 Assume that an indirect tax of £2.00 per unit is imposed. Calculate the price now paid by consumers (i.e. the new market price), the price received by producers and the new equilibrium quantity.

3 What amount of the tax is paid by consumers (also, what proportion of the tax is paid by consumers?) (In other words, calculate the tax incidence on consumers.)

4 What amount of the tax is paid by producers? Also, what proportion of the tax is paid by producers? (In other words, calculate the tax incidence on producers.)

5 How much tax revenue does the government collect? (Remember that the units are in millions.)

6 Calculate the initial TR producers earned, the new TR they earn after the imposition of the tax and the change in the TR collected.

7 Calculate the initial TE consumers make on the good, the new TE they make and the change in their TE.

8 Calculate PED for this good.

9 Draw (or plot) a diagram showing all of the numerical information available.

10 Calculate the effect on consumer, producer and social (or community) surplus.

11 Construct a table summarizing all of the available information.

Subsidies

Remember

- Subsidies are granted to:
    - lower the cost of production for firms
    - lower the market price of a good or service
    - increase production and consumption of a good or service
    - increase the revenues firms earn.
- Assuming typical demand and supply curves, a subsidy decreases the market price (the price consumers pay), increases the price received by producers, increases output and consumption of the good, and increases TR to firms. It is not clear whether TE consumers make on the good increase or decrease as this depends on PED. If demand is price inelastic (elastic) then the fall in price will lead to a proportionately smaller (greater) increase in quantity demanded and so TE consumers make will decrease (increase).

- Total spending by the government on the subsidy is the product of the subsidy per unit times the number of units sold. The size of this expenditure depends not only on the size of the per unit subsidy granted but also on PED and PES.

- Both consumers and producers benefit from a subsidy.

HL

Remember

To determine how the benefit from a subsidy is split between the two groups the following relationship is helpful:

$$\frac{\% \text{ of benefit to consumers}}{\% \text{ of benefit to producers}} = \frac{PES}{PED}$$

For example, if the two elasticities are equal then they split the benefit 50-50; or, given PED, the more price inelastic supply is, the greater the benefit to producers.

How to approach questions with subsidies

If there is no subsidy granted in a competitive market, then to calculate the equilibrium price and output we have three equations and three unknowns:

(1) $Qd = a - bP$
(2) $Qs = c + dP$
(3) $Qd = Qs$

Since (3) states that $Qd = Qs$, we substitute Q for Qd and Qs in (1) and (2). So we have two equations with two unknowns which we solve in whichever way is more convenient.

Now, a per unit subsidy creates a wedge between the price consumers pay and the price producers receive.

Let Pc be the price consumers pay while Pp is the price producers receive.

It follows that if a per unit subsidy S is granted:

(4a) $Pp = Pc + S$ or (4b) $Pc = (Pp - S)$
(where S is the subsidy per unit)

and demand will now be expressed in terms of Pc, while supply will now be expressed in terms of Pp. So, for example, equation (3) becomes

$$Qs = c + dPp$$

Substituting Pc + S instead of Pp will allow you to use the equilibrium condition to solve for Pc and then find the new Q. Finally, using (4a) will yield Pp for you.

The examples below will help you solve any subsidy-related question.

Example 5

Assume that in the market described in the indirect tax example on page 43, the government offers producers a subsidy S of €15 per unit.

1 Calculate the price now paid by consumers (i.e. the new market price), the price received by producers and the new equilibrium quantity.

Step 1 Write the demand function, the supply function and the equilibrium condition. In the demand equation write Pc instead of P, and in the supply equation write Pp instead of P. Make sure you also write the 'wedge' equation, i.e. that $Pp = (Pc + S)$ or, equivalently, $Pc = (Pp - S)$ where S is the subsidy per unit.
(1) $Qd = 200 - Pc$
(2) $Qs = 20 + 2Pp$
(3) $Qd = Qs$
(4) $Pp = Pc + 15$

Step 2 Substituting (1) and (2) into (3):
(5) $200 - Pc = 20 + 2Pp$

Step 3 Substituting into (5) and solving for Pc:
$$200 - Pc = 20 + 2(Pc + 15)$$
$$200 - Pc = 20 + 2Pc + 30$$
$$200 - 20 - 30 = 2Pc + Pc$$
$$150 = 3Pc$$
$$Pc = 50$$
Answer: The price consumers will pay (the new post-subsidy market price) is €50.

Step 4 Substituting Pc into (4):
$$Pp = Pc + 15$$
$$Pp = 50 + 15$$
$$Pp = 65$$
Answer: The price producers earn per unit will be €50. This is their new revenue per unit.

Step 5 To find the new equilibrium quantity Q':
either substitute Pc into (1)
$$Q' = 200 - 50$$
$$Q' = 150$$
or substitute Pp into (2)
$$Q' = 20 + (2 \times 65)$$
$$Q' = 150$$

2 **What proportion of the subsidy is enjoyed by consumers?**

Step 1   Start with what you know about the initial situation.
The original pre-subsidy market price consumers paid was €60.
The new post-subsidy market price consumers pay is €50.

Step 2   The consumers' benefit is $\frac{10}{15}$ of the subsidy (or $\frac{2}{3}$ of it).

3 **What proportion of the subsidy is enjoyed by producers?**

Step 1   Start with what you know about the initial situation.
The original pre-subsidy price earned per unit by producers was €60.
The new post-subsidy price producers earn per unit = €65.
This is their new revenue per unit.

Step 2   The producers' benefit is $\frac{5}{15}$ of the subsidy (or $\frac{1}{3}$ of it).

4 **How much does the government spend on this subsidy? Also, calculate the resulting welfare loss.**

Step 1   Since spending on the subsidy by the government is given by:
(subsidy per unit) × (number of units bought) then
€15 × 150 units bought = €2,250.

Step 2   The welfare loss is the area of triangle (E1E2A) (see part 8 of this question or sketch a subsidy diagram); the height is the change in the resulting quantity $\Delta Q = 150 - 140 = 10$ units, while the base is the subsidy per unit (15); given that the area of a triangle is $\frac{1}{2}$ (base × height) we calculate that the welfare loss is equal to €75.

5 **Calculate the initial total revenues (TR) firms earn, the new TR they earn after the granting of the subsidy and the change in their TR.**

Step 1   Start with what you know.
TR = (price per unit) × (number of units sold)
Note: If a subsidy has been imposed, to calculate the new TR that firms collect we need to use the price earned per unit **inclusive of the subsidy granted**. This is our Pp.

Step 2   Original TR: area (0QE1P) (see part 8 for the diagram)
€60.00 per unit × 140 units = €8,400.00
New, post-subsidy, TR collected: area (0Q'HPp)
€65.00 per unit × 150 units = €9,750.00
$\Delta TR = TR2 - TR1$
$\Delta TR = 9750 - 8400$
$\Delta TR = + €1350.00$
As expected, the TR that firms collect after a subsidy has been paid to them increases, in this case by €1,350.00.

6 **Calculate the initial total expenditures (TE) consumers make on the good, the TE they make following the subsidy and the change in their TE.**

Step 1   Start with what you know:
TE = (price per unit) × (number of units sold) = TR
Note: If a subsidy has been granted, TE consumers make will no longer equal TR firms earn.

Step 2   Original TE:
€60.00 per unit × 140 units = €8,400.00
New TE:
€50.00 per unit × 150 units = €7,500.00
$\Delta TE = TE2 - TE1$
$\Delta TE = 7,500 - 8,400$
$\Delta TE = - €900.00$
In this case, TE consumers made decreased by €900.00.
Since the new post-subsidy market price consumers pay is lower and the quantity bought is greater, whether their TE increase or decrease depends on the PED. In this case, their spending decreased following a price decrease so we can infer that demand is price inelastic. This is consistent with our finding that consumers enjoy a bigger proportion of the subsidy. Using the
$$\frac{\text{\% of benefits to consumers}}{\text{\% of benefits to producers}} = \frac{PES}{PED}$$
relationship, and since consumers enjoy $\frac{2}{3}$ (or 66.66%) of the subsidy while producers enjoy $\frac{1}{3}$ (or 33.33%) of the subsidy, we can find, by substituting these values in the left-hand side of the equation, that PED is half the value of PES, or more price inelastic.

7 Calculate PED for the good.

Step 1 Start with what you know:
PED = %ΔQ/%ΔP; P1 = 60, P2 = 50;
Q1 = 140, Q2 = 150.

Step 2 Calculate the percentage change in quantity demanded:
$$\%\Delta Q = \frac{(Q2 - Q1)}{Q1}$$
$$= \frac{(150 - 140)}{140}$$
$$= \frac{10}{140}$$
$$= 7.14\%$$
Calculate the percentage change in price:
$$\%\Delta P = \frac{(P2 - P1)}{P1}$$
$$= \frac{(50 - 60)}{60}$$
$$= -\frac{10}{60}$$
$$= -16.66\%$$

Substitute the above values into the PED equation:
$$PED = \frac{+7.14\%}{-16.66\%} = -0.43$$
Demand is price inelastic, confirming our previous results.

8 Draw (or plot) a diagram showing all available numerical information.

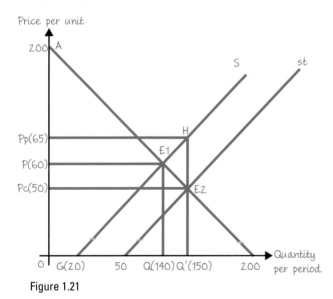

Figure 1.21

9 Calculate the effect of the subsidy on the consumer, producer and social (or community) surplus.

Step 1 Start with what you know.
The consumer surplus is the area of the triangle below the demand curve and above the price line, while the producer surplus is the area above the supply curve and below the price line; the area of a triangle is $\frac{1}{2}$ (base × height); the area of a rectangle is length × width.

Step 2 Calculate the original consumer surplus, i.e. the area of (APE1):
$$\frac{1}{2}(140 \times (200 - 60)) = €9,800$$

Step 3 Calculate the new consumer surplus, i.e. the area of (PcE₂A):
$$\frac{1}{2}(150 \times (200 - 50)) = 11,250$$
So consumer surplus increased by 11,250 − 9,800 = €1,450.

Step 4 Calculate the original producer surplus, i.e. area (OGE1P).
In this case it is easier to find this area as the difference between area (OQE1P) and area (GQE1). This method of calculation reflects precisely what the producer surplus is: it's the difference between what firms own and the minimum they require to offer some amount to the market. So:
$$(60 \times 140) - \frac{1}{2}((140 - 20) \times 60)$$
$$= 8,400 - 3,600 = €4,800$$

Step 5 Calculate the new producer surplus, i.e. area (OGHPp).
In this case it is easier to find this area as the difference between area (OQ'HPp) and area (GQ'H):
$$(65 \times 150) - \frac{1}{2}((150 - 20) \times 65)$$
$$= 9,750 - 4,225 = €5,525$$
So producer surplus increased by 5,525 − 4,800 = €725.

Step 6 To calculate the initial social (or community) surplus, the new social surplus and the change in social surplus, remember that social surplus is the sum of the consumer and the producer surplus.
Original social surplus
= 9,800 + 4,800 = €14,600
New social surplus = 11,250 + 5,525
= €16,775 − cost of subsidy
= €16,775 − €2,250 = €14,525
Social surplus increased by 16,775 − 14,600 = €2,175. This €2,175 increase in social surplus, though, came at the cost of a €2,250 subsidy. It follows that the subsidy led to a €75 'deadweight loss' for society as units QQ' (= 10 units) should not have been produced from society's point of view.

10 Construct a table summarizing all the available information.

Initial pre-subsidy situation	
Market (equilibrium) price (P)	€60 (this is also the revenue earned per unit by firms)
Market (equilibrium) quantity Q	140 units
Total revenues (TR) for firms (P × Q)	€60 per units × 140 units = €8,400.00
Total expenditures (TE) consumers make (P × Q)	€60 per units × 140 units = €8,400.00
Comments: TR and TE are of course the same as there is no subsidy yet to create a 'wedge' between the price consumers pay in the market and the price producers earn per unit (i.e. before the subsidy is paid, price and average revenue (AR) are the same)	
New post-subsidy situation	
Subsidy paid per unit of output	€15
New market (equilibrium) price (Pc) that consumers pay	€50
Price net of tax that producers earn (Pp) (which is the AR for the firms)	€65
Consumers' benefit from the subsidy (and as a proportion of it)	€10 (or $\frac{10}{15} = \frac{2}{3}$ of the tax)
Producers' benefit from the subsidy (and as a proportion of it)	€5 (or $\frac{5}{15} = \frac{1}{3}$ of the tax)
New market (equilibrium) quantity	150 units
New TR firms collect	€65 per unit × 150 units = €9,750.00
Change in TR firms collect	€9,750.00 − €8,400.00 = €1,350.00 (an increase)
New TE consumers make	€50 per unit × 150 units = €7,500.00
Change in TE consumers make	€7,500.00 − €8,400.00 = −€900.00 (a decrease)
Total cost of subsidy to government (eventually borne by taxpayers)	€15 per unit × 150 units = €2,250.00
PED	−0.43 (price inelastic)
Subsidy versus elasticities formula:	$\frac{66.66\%}{33.33\%} = \frac{1}{2}$, so demand is more price inelastic than supply
Original consumer surplus	€9,800
Original producer surplus	€4,800
Original social surplus	€14,600
New post-subsidy consumer surplus	€11,250
New post-subsidy producer surplus	€5,525
New social surplus	€16,775
Change in welfare	€16,775 − €14,600 = €2,175, at a cost of a €2,250 subsidy, resulting in a 'deadweight loss' of €75 as units QQ' are now produced even though they cost more in terms of sacrificed resources than they are valued by consumers.

Exercise 3

Assume a market originally described by the following demand and supply equations:

(1) Qd = 1,200 − 100P

(2) Qs = 100P, where the price is in euros and the quantity is in units of the good.

Let's say the government offers producers a subsidy S of €2 per unit.

1　Calculate the price now paid by consumers (i.e. the new market price), the price received by producers and the new equilibrium quantity.

2　What proportion of the subsidy is enjoyed by consumers?

3　What proportion of the subsidy is enjoyed by producers?

4　How much does the government spend on this subsidy? Also, calculate the resulting welfare loss.

5　Calculate the initial TR firms earn, the new TR they earn after the granting of the subsidy and the change in their TR.

6　Calculate the initial TE consumers make on the good, the TE they make following the subsidy and the change in their TE.

7　Calculate PED for the good.

8　Draw (or plot) a diagram showing all available numerical information.

9　Calculate the effect of the subsidy on the consumer, producer and social (or community) surplus.

10　Construct a table summarizing all the available information.

Exercise 4

Assume a market originally described by the following demand and supply equations:

(1) Qd = 200 − P

(2) Qs = 50 + P, where the price is in euros and the quantity is in units of the good.

Let's say the government offers producers a subsidy S of €10 per unit.

1　Calculate the price now paid by consumers (i.e. the new market price), the price received by producers and the new equilibrium quantity.

2　What proportion of the subsidy is enjoyed by consumers?

3　What proportion of the subsidy is enjoyed by producers?

4　How much does the government spend on this subsidy? Also, calculate the resulting welfare loss.

5　Calculate the initial TR firms earn, the new TR they earn after the granting of the subsidy and the change in their TR.

6　Calculate the initial TE consumers make on the good, the TE they make following the subsidy and the change in their TE.

7　Calculate PED for the good.

8　Draw (or plot) a diagram showing all available numerical information.

9　Calculate the effect of the subsidy on the consumer, producer and social (or community) surplus.

10　Construct a table summarizing all the available information.

Price controls

Remember

- An effective maximum price is set below the market (equilibrium) price while an effective minimum price is set above.

- An equilibrium price rations (distributes) the good efficiently, as whoever is willing and able to pay the price will end up with the good. When a price ceiling is set by the government, being willing and able to pay the price does not guarantee that one will enjoy the good because of the resulting shortage. This is why other mechanisms to ration the available amount are needed, such as 'first come, first served' and sellers' preferences, randomly (by ballot) or via coupons.

- Resource allocation is inefficient when the price is controlled. Less than the socially optimal amount is produced in the case of a maximum price whereas more than the socially optimal amount is produced in the case of a minimum price.

- In the case of a maximum price the costs of the government include the costs of enforcing the policy, while in the case of a minimum price the costs include the necessary expenditure to buy the surplus at the promised price (which eventually burdens taxpayers) and the costs of disposing of the surplus.

Tip

To avoid drawing incorrectly a maximum price above the equilibrium price (and a minimum price below), remember that the logic goes counter intuitively: maximum here is down and minimum is up!

Tip

When a maximum price is set, the probability of a black market resulting is greater, the more price inelastic demand is and the lower the maximum price is set compared with the free market price.

Tip

☐ The short end of the market always prevails: in the case of a price ceiling the amount of the good that will be traded (exchanged) is the quantity supplied at that price as it is less than the quantity demanded ($Q_s < Q_d$), while in the case of a price floor, the amount of the good that will be traded is the quantity demanded at that price as it is less than the quantity supplied ($Q_d < Q_s$).

☐ This point is important when trying to determine the effect on consumer and producer surplus of, for example, a price ceiling: remember to focus only on the new, lower quantity that will be traded.

Example 6

The diagram below illustrates the market for a particular basic product. Initially, the market is free from government intervention. A new administration, though, decides to intervene and impose a price ceiling. Answer the following questions using the diagram.

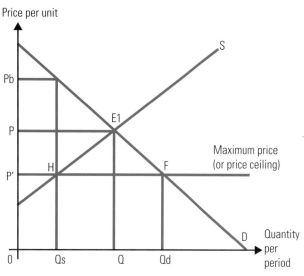

Figure 1.22

1 How does the free market price ration the good?

Given the demand and supply conditions illustrated above, the free market price is P. At this price, quantity demanded is equal to quantity supplied: there is enough quantity of the good offered by producers to satisfy whoever is willing and able to pay the price P.

2 What is the size of the shortage resulting at the maximum price P'?

At P', the quantity supplied Qs is less than the quantity demanded Qd. The line segment QsQd (= HF) illustrates this shortage.

3 Why is it that price P' cannot perform its rationing role anymore and so there is a need for other rationing mechanisms?

At price P' there are consumers willing and able to pay the price P' but their demand will not be satisfied as there is now a shortage in the market. Consumers who perhaps wait in line, or are regular customers, or are lucky, or who perhaps pay a higher price than P' in a parallel underground market will be able to obtain the good.

4 What is the amount of the good that is exchanged at P'?

The short end of the market always prevails, so since quantity supplied Qs is less than quantity demanded Qd, it will be only Qs units that will be exchanged.

5 What does price Pb illustrate?

Drawing a line from Qs (which is the last unit firms are willing to offer at the set price P') all the way to the demand curve shows the maximum most consumers are willing and able to pay for that unit. In the diagram this is Pb. If all units available were sold in an underground parallel market at a single price, this could be as high as Pb.

6 What were the TR of producers equal to before the maximum price was set?

These would be equal to the price received per unit multiplied by the number of units sold, or (OP) × (OQ) = area (OQE1P).

7 What were the TE of consumers equal to before the maximum price was set?

These would be equal to the price paid per unit multiplied by the number of units bought, or (OP) × (OQ) = area (OQE1P).

8   What are the new TR firms collect after the price ceiling is set?

These would be the maximum price set multiplied by the number of units sold, or (OP') × (OQs) = area (OQsHP'), assuming all units are sold at the legal price set.

9   What are the new TE consumers make after the price ceiling is set?

These would be the maximum price set multiplied by the number of units bought, or (OP') × (OQs) = area (OQsHP'), assuming no units are bought in a parallel underground market.

HL **Example 7**

Answer the following questions using the diagram below.

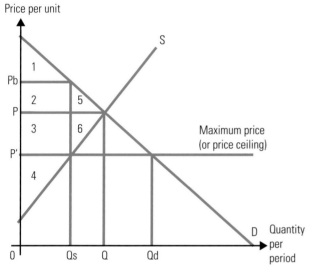

Figure 1.23

1   What was the consumer surplus equal to before the maximum price was set?

The consumer surplus is equal to the area below the demand curve and above the market price P **for the units that are exchanged**. Since Q units are exchanged, the surplus consumers enjoy is equal to area (1 + 2 + 5).

2   What was the producer surplus equal to before the maximum price was set?

The producer surplus is equal to the area above the supply curve and below the market price P **for the units that are exchanged**. Since Q units are exchanged, the surplus producers enjoy is equal to area (3 + 6 + 4).

3   What was the social (or community) surplus initially equal to?

The social (or community) surplus is equal to the sum of the consumer and the producer surplus. This is area (1 + 2 + 3 + 4 + 5 + 6).

4   What was the consumer surplus equal to **after** the maximum price was set?

It is equal to area (1 + 2 + 3). This is the area that lies below the demand curve and above the maximum price P' **for the units Q' that are exchanged** in the market.

5   What was the producer surplus equal to after the maximum price was set?

It is equal to area (4). This is the area that lies above the supply curve and below the maximum price P' **for the units Q' that are exchanged** in the market.

6   What happened to the producer surplus as a result of the maximum price? Are producers better off or worse off?

It decreased by area (3 + 6). This shows that producers are clearly worse off as a result of the price ceiling.

7   What happened to the consumer surplus as a result of the maximum price? Are consumers better off or worse off?

The consumer surplus decreased by area (6) but increased by area (3) which was originally enjoyed by producers. This shows that some consumers are better off as a result of the maximum price (those lucky enough to enjoy the available quantity at the now lower price) while others are worse off (those who would have enjoyed the good if the price had not been controlled but who now are left without the good).

8   What does area (5 + 6) represent?

Area (5 + 6) represents the resulting welfare loss and reflects the allocative inefficiency of a maximum price. Fewer units (units QsQ) are now produced and consumed which are valued by society more than what it would have cost society to produce. This means that there is under-allocation of scarce resources in this market. Note that the resulting welfare loss is bigger because at the controlled price the good is not necessarily enjoyed by those willing to pay the most, and because they may have to spend scarce resources to get the product (e.g. their scarce time waiting in line).

Example 8

Assume that the demand for olive oil is given by $Qd = 480 – 6P$ while supply is given by $Qs = 120 + 3P$, where the price is in euros and the quantity is in thousands of kilograms. Let's say the government sets a maximum price of €30 per kilogram.

1 What would the free market price and quantity of olive oil be equal to?

Step 1 $Qd = 480 - 6P$
$Qs = 120 + 3P$
$Qd = Qs$

Step 2 $480 - 6P = 120 + 3P$

Step 3 $480 - 120 = 3P + 6P$
$360 = 9P$
$P^* = 40$
Answer: The equilibrium price would have been €40 per kilogram.

Step 4 $Q^* = 480 - (6 \times 40)$
$Q^* = 480 - 240$
$Q^* = 240$

Step 5   To double-check this answer:
$Q^* = 120 + (3 \times 40)$
$Q^* = 120 + 120$
$Q^* = 240$
Answer: The equilibrium quantity would have been 240,000 kilograms.

2 Calculate the resulting shortage at the maximum price set by the government.

Step 1   Substitute the maximum price into the demand formula:
$Qd = 480 - 6P$
$Qd = 480 - (6 \times 30)$
$Qd = 480 - 180$
$Qd = 300$, or 300,000 kilograms.

Step 2   Substitute the maximum price into the supply formula:
$Qs = 120 + 3P$
$Qs = 120 + (3 \times 30)$
$Qs = 210$, or 210,000 kilograms.

Step 3   Calculate the resulting shortage:
$Shortage = Qd - Qs$
$Shortage = 210 - 300$
$Shortage = - 90$
Answer: 90,000 fewer kilograms of olive oil are supplied than demanded.

3 Determine the necessary subsidy that would have to be paid so that no shortage would result.

Step 1   To eliminate the shortage of 90 units at a price of €30, supply would have to increase at all prices (i.e. shift to the right) by 90 units. The new supply (after the subsidy was paid) would be
$Q's = Qs + 90$, or
$Q's = 120 + 3P + 90$
$Q's = 210 + 3P$
Substituting the price 30 into the new supply formula gives:
$Q's = 210 + (3 \times 30)$
$Q's = 300$, which is equal to Qd at that price.

Step 2   We need to calculate the price at which suppliers would have been willing to offer 300 units without a subsidy. To do that we substitute this quantity into the original supply formula and solve for the price:
$300 = 120 + 3P$
$3P = 300 - 120$
$P = 60$

Step 3   Using the subsidy 'wedge' equation we get: $Pc = Pp + S$
$S = Pc - Pp$
$S = 60 - 30$
$S = €30$

The necessary subsidy to eliminate the shortage would be equal to €30 per kilogram.

Step 4   To double-check this answer:
$Q's = 120 + 3 (P + 30)$
$Q's = 120 + 3P + 90$
$Q's = 210 + 3P$, which is the new supply we calculated above in step 1.

Example 9

Assume that the demand for a good is given by
Qd = 600 − 5P while supply is given by
Qs = 120 + 3P, where the price is in euros and the
quantity is in thousands of units. Let's say the
government sets a minimum price of €75 per unit.

1 What would the free market price and quantity
of this good be equal to?

Step 1   Qd = 600 − 5P
Qs = 120 + 3P
Qd = Qs

Step 2   600 − 5P = 120 + 3P

Step 3   600 − 120 = 3P + 5P
480 = 8P
P* = 60
Answer: The equilibrium price would
have been €60 per unit.

Step 4   Q* = 600 − (5 × 60)
Q* = 600 − 300
Q* = 300

Step 5   Double checking:
Q* = 120 + (3 × 60)
Q* = 120 + 180
Q* = 300
Answer: The equilibrium quantity would
have been 300,000 units.

2 Calculate the resulting surplus at the price floor
set by the government.

Step 1   Substitute the minimum price into the
demand formula:
Qd = 600 − 5P
Qd = 600 − (5 × 75)
Qd = 600 − 375
Qd = 225 or 225,000 units

Step 2   Substitute the minimum price into the
supply formula:
Qs = 120 + 3P
Qs = 120 + (3 × 75)
Qs = 120 + 225
Qs = 345, or 345,000 units

Step 3   Calculate the resulting surplus:
Surplus = Qs − Qd
Surplus = 345 − 225
Surplus = 120 or 120,000 more units
are supplied than demanded.

3 What must the government spend to support
this price?

The government must pay €75 per unit for each
of the 120,000 units it buys, spending:
€75 × 120,000 = €9,000,000

4 What TR will producers collect as a result of
the minimum price set?

They collect €75 per unit times the 345,000
units produced, or €25,875,000, of which
€9,000,000 is received from the government
and €16,875,000 from consumers.

(Consumers spend €75 per unit multiplied by
225,000 units they buy at that price.)

5 What amount of subsidy would be necessary
for producers to gain the same TR as they do
with the minimum price?

Step 1   Substituting the amount produced (345
units) in the demand curve would give us
the price at which consumers would buy
(absorb) all of that amount produced:
345 = 600 − 5P
− 255 = − 5P
$P = \frac{255}{5}$
P = €51

So if the price consumers paid was €51
then they would buy the 345 units
producers offered.

Step 2   Using the subsidy 'wedge' equation
Pc = Pp − S:
51 = 75 − S
S = €24
By paying producers a subsidy equal to
€24 per unit the government would
generate TR for producers equal to
€25,875,000.

Step 3 To double-check this answer: with a €9 subsidy the new supply formula Q's would be

$Q's = 120 + 3(Pc + 24)$

$Q's = 120 + 3Pc + 72$

$Q's = 192 + 3Pc$

Given the demand formula

$Qd = 600 - 5Pc$, the new market equilibrium price consumers would pay is:

$600 - 5Pc = 192 + 3Pc$

$600 - 192 = 3Pc + 5Pc$

$408 = 8Pc$

$Pc = \dfrac{408}{8}$

$Pc = €51$

6 Which of the two policies would be cheaper for the government?

Step 1 The cost to the government of the €75 minimum price was calculated above to equal €9,000,000.

The cost of the subsidy would equal to the subsidy paid per unit (€24) times the number of units produced (345,000) or $24 \times 345,000 = €8,280,000$.

Step 2 It follows that the minimum price policy would be more expensive by:

€9,000,000 - €8,280,000 = €720,000

Exercise 5

Rewrite the following statements filling in the blanks by using the terms provided below. Some terms may be used more than once, others might not be used at all.

taxpayers	demanded	producers
floor	less	above
higher	surplus	agricultural
collapse	much	supplied
over-allocation	consumers	allocative
farmers	demand	

A minimum price, also known as a price (1)_____, must be set (2)_____ the free market equilibrium price to be effective. As a result of quantity (3)_____ being greater than quantity

(4)_____, a (5)_____ is created. If the government did not buy this (6)_____ then the price would (7)_____. Effectively, buying it artificially increases (8)_____ for the good. The expenditures the government makes eventually burden (9)_____. Minimum prices are often set in (10)_____ markets to protect (1)_____. A consequence of minimum prices is that too (12)_____ of the good is produced, leading to (13)_____ of scarce resources and thus (14)_____ inefficiency. (15)_____ are better off while (16)_____ are worse off. The latter enjoy (17)_____ of the good at a (18)_____ price.

Exercise 6

Determine whether the following statements are true or false. Explain your answers. Use a diagram to illustrate if possible.

1 A minimum price benefits the producers of the good.
2 All consumers are better off if a maximum price is imposed.
3 Since, as a result of a price floor, production of the good increases, society is better off.
4 Rationing a good on a random basis is efficient.
5 Given PED and PES , the lower a maximum price is set with respect to the free market price, the greater the resulting surplus.
6 Ceteris paribus, when prices are controlled, resource misallocation is greater and the more price elastic are demand and supply.

7 In the long run, the quality of rent-controlled apartments improves.
8 In markets for unskilled labour, a minimum wage law may increase unemployment.
9 When governments set the price for tickets for soccer games below the market clearing price, members of soccer clubs are typically better off.
10 Price floors and price ceilings, although inefficient, are often an attempt by governments to create equity or fairness in some markets.
11 A price ceiling of €12.00 when the equilibrium price is €10.00 will cause a shortage.
12 Queues will form in gas stations if a maximum price of $2.00 per gallon of gasoline is set when the market price is $1.70.

HL Exercise 7

Explain the types of price control available to governments and discuss the effectiveness of these controls in achieving their goals.

Exercise 8

Explain why queues may form when markets are not allowed to operate freely.

Exercise 9

Assume that the demand for apartments is given by $Qd = 4800 - 35P$ while supply of apartments is given by $Qs = 160 + 5P$ where the price is in euros and the quantity is in thousands of units. Let's say the government introduces a rent control policy which makes it illegal for landlords to ask for rents above €100 per apartment.

1   How much would apartments rent for in the absence of rent control?
2   What is the size of the shortage of apartments resulting under the rent control policy?
3   Calculate the necessary subsidy that would decrease the shortage of apartments by half.

Exercise 10

Assume that demand for a good is given by $Qd = 800 - 4P$ while supply by $Qs = 200 + 2P$, where the price is in Brazilian real (BRL) and quantity is in thousands of units. Let's say the government introduces a policy for minimum price whereby price is set at BRL120.

1   What was the market price and quantity before the price support scheme was introduced?
2   What is the resulting surplus once the price floor is set?
3   How much did total consumer expenditures change by as a result of the minimum price?

4   What does this suggest about the PED for this good?
5   Calculate the PED.
6   How much did total revenues for producers change by a result of the price floor?
7   How much would this policy cost taxpayers?
8   What is the size of the necessary subsidy to guarantee producers the same revenues?
9   Which policy choice is cheaper for the government?

Exercise 11

Explain, using appropriate diagrams, the consequences of rent controls on market outcomes and discuss their possible effect on stakeholders.

Exercise 12

Explain, using appropriate diagrams, the consequences of a minimum wage being set by a government and discuss its effect on workers, firms, the government and society.

The meaning of market failure

Remember

- Allocative efficiency is achieved if neither too much nor too little quantity of a good is produced and consumed from society's point of view, and so neither too many nor too few resources are allocated in that market. It follows that a market fails if market forces lead to over-provision of a good (and so over-allocation of resources) or to under-provision of a good (and so under-allocation of resources).

- Markets can fail:
  - when externalities are present,
  - in the case of common-access resources,
  - in the case of public, merit and demerit goods,
  - when firms have monopoly power,
  - as well as in the case where asymmetric information is present.

Externalities

Example 1

Provide examples where the MSB are greater, equal and smaller than the MPB of consuming a good or service, or of engaging in an activity.

MSB > MPB	■ If Aled gets vaccinated against flu, not only does he benefit but also all others that come into contact with him, as their probability of catching flu from him is lower. By getting vaccinated, the prevalence of the disease decreases. ■ If Elena paints her house and improves her yard, not only does she benefit but also all her neighbours, as the value of their property increases.
MSB = MPB	■ If Herry buys a Mont Blanc pen to sign her cheques, no one else benefits or is hurt by her buying and using it. ■ If Manuel buys and drinks skimmed milk for breakfast, no one else benefits or is hurt by him buying and drinking it.
MSB < MPB	■ If Zachary lights up a cigar in the restaurant, his action imposes health costs on others in the restaurant. ■ If Rachel decides to drive to work rather than taking the train, she may benefit, but her decision imposes costs on all others in the form of additional traffic congestion and pollution.

Example 2

Explain why we consider a market to have failed if the MSB are not equal to the MSC.

Here one would first have to explain what exactly the two terms mean. An easy way to proceed is to consider, using a diagram such as the one below, how many units of a good society would like to have produced and consumed.

Tip

The welfare loss triangle (assuming straight line demand and supply curves) is the triangle that 'points' to the socially optimal amount.

For example, this triangle ▶ points to the right, whereas this triangle ◀ points to the left.

To make sure the welfare loss triangle is correct take any point inbetween the market determined output and the socially optimal output and bring a line up: in the case of negative externalities the marginal social costs (MSC) must be greater than the marginal social benefits (MSB), whereas in the case of positive externalities the MSB must be greater than the MSC.

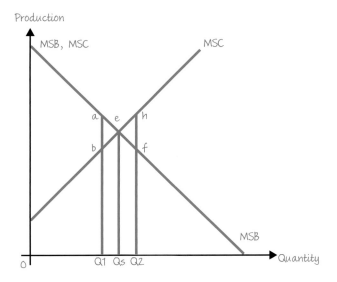

Figure 1.24

Society would like to enjoy all units which are worth more to it than what they cost it (in terms of sacrificed resources) up until that unit for which the two are equal. For example, society would want to have unit Q1 produced and consumed because it is worth to society Q1a (the size of the MSB enjoyed) while it would cost society only Q1b, so a net benefit to society equal to ab would be enjoyed. This holds true for all units up to (at the limit) unit Qs. If more of the good were produced then society would incur a net loss (i.e. a decrease in social welfare).

For example, unit Q2 is worth to society Q2f (so there are benefits from producing and consuming it) but it would cost society Q2h. In other words, society would incur a net loss from producing and consuming the good equal to fh. This holds for all units past unit Qs.

From the above it follows that any market outcome other than Qs for which MSB = MSC should be considered a market failure. Any amount less than Qs implies that the market forces did not produce all units society values more than their cost, while any amount more than Qs implies that market forces led to the production of units which cost more to society than they were worth.

Example 3

Discuss, using examples, the options available to governments to deal with the free market outcome resulting in the case of demerit goods.

Demerit goods are goods that are considered harmful and for that reason governments would like to limit their consumption. Not only are the consumers of such goods harmed but so are others

around them as consumption of such goods creates significant negative externalities. The typical examples include tobacco and alcohol consumption (smoking and drinking). The market outcome is suboptimal in that it leads to 'too much' of these goods produced and consumed. A market failure is the result. In the diagram below the MSB from consuming the good are less than the MPB because of the external costs of consumption created. In the case of smoking these external costs may include the elevated health risks of passive smokers, while in the case of alcohol they may include the unacceptable behaviour often associated with alcohol consumption (for example drunk driving and violence).

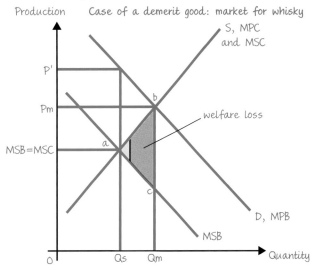

Figure 1.25

The market forces, demand and supply, will lead to Qm units produced and consumed at a market price Pm. The socially optimal amount is less and equal to Qs, as at Qs the MSB equals the MSC. For units QsQm, the MSC of producing the good exceeds the MSB of consuming the good so these units should not have been produced and consumed. Since they are, a welfare loss equal to the shaded triangle (abc) results.

For consumption to be limited to Qs units per period the market price should be at P'. An indirect tax equal to the external cost of consumption (bc) could do the trick. There are, though, some associated problems: first, it is difficult to estimate the size of the external cost and so the size of the necessary tax. The tax should be substantial as demand for these goods is typically price inelastic, but indirect taxes are regressive in nature meaning that they burden lower-income consumers proportionately more.

Most importantly, a chain of substitutions may be initiated as consumers, especially poorer individuals, will switch to cheaper but lower-quality substitutes that may entail higher health risks and other risks. Direct regulation may prove helpful (for example, prohibiting smoking in offices and restaurants) as at least the external effect of tobacco inhaling is minimized. In the case of alcohol, prohibiting the sale to minors (individuals under a certain age) has not been as effective to curtail consumption. Education (through advertising) may prove the most effective long-term option but this should be targeted towards the very young as older people may already be addicted.

Exercise 1

Explain why each of the following examples may give rise to an externality. Determine the good or the activity that creates the external effects, the type of externality that arises, whether at the market determined outcome the MSB is greater or smaller than the MSC, whether there is over- or under-allocation of resources, and propose one type of solution discussing its relative merits and shortcomings.

1 Banks providing funds for their employees to obtain specialized training
2 Smoke from smokers in restaurants
3 Home improvement loans in a city
4 A power plant using fossil fuels to generate electricity.

Exercise 2

Determine whether the following statements are true or false. Explain your answers. Use a diagram to illustrate if possible.

1 Whenever a negative externality is present, market forces produce a greater quantity of the good than the socially desirable amount.
2 When an activity creates external benefits then markets left on their own lead to more of the good being produced than is socially desirable.

3 Efficiency occurs when competitive firms internalize any external production costs, forcing consumers of pollution-causing goods to pay these costs.
4 Issuing and selling pollution permits takes advantage of the market mechanism to reduce pollution-related externalities.

Exercise 3

Rewrite the following statements and fill in the blanks by using the terms provided below. Some terms may be used more than once or not at all.

positive	regulation	output
emissions	last	optimal
polluter	third	legislation
education	cost	Pigovian
social	pollution	cap
under-allocation	trade	more

If external costs are present, then markets lead to (1)_____ units of the good being produced and consumed than the socially (2)_____ amount. In such a case the market price is too low in the sense that it does not reflect the marginal (3)_____ of producing or of consuming the (4)_____ unit of the good. On the other hand, in the case of (5)_____ externalities, i.e. situations when the production or consumption of a good creates benefits to (6)_____ parties then there is

(7)_____ of resources as less than the socially optimal amount is produced or consumed and thus fewer resources than the socially optimal amount are employed in the market.

A (8)_____ tax internalizes the external (9)_____ forcing the (10)_____ to pay. When tradable (11)_____ permits are employed the maximum level of permissible pollution is set (the (12)_____) by the government and then permits or licences are issued to firms with the right to (13)_____ them in the open market. Direct government (14)_____ may include requiring firms to limit their level of (15)_____ or to limit the amount of polluting (16)_____. Subsidies in the case of (17)_____ externalities are a possible solution as they lower the price and result in a greater level of output but governments may also through (18)_____ attempt to increase consumption or production of such externalities. For example in many countries (19)_____ is compulsory up to a certain level.

Public goods

Remember

The key concepts to be able to deal with questions about public goods are:

- non-excludability
- non-rivalry
- free rider including those able to enjoy the good because it is non-excludable
- the marginal cost of an extra user, which is zero or near zero because of non-rivalry.

Tip

Examples of public goods include national defense, lighthouses, traffic lights, law and order in a city, and off-the-air TV and radio broadcasting. Price stability may also be considered an example of a public good.

Example 4

Determine whether the following statements are true or false. Explain your answers. Use a diagram to illustrate if possible.

1 Goods provided by government are public goods.

False. To determine whether a good is a public good or not you must always check whether it is non-excludable and non-rival. Governments have provided and may provide a number of goods and services that are neither non-excludable nor non-rival. For example, in some countries, parts of the food industry are nationalized with several food products provided by the government. Telephone services were (and in some countries still are) provided by the government but these are excludable.

2 Since in schools for the general public every child has the right to attend it follows that education is non-excludable

False. Education, especially primary and secondary education, creates massive positive externalities so that provision by the free market alone would lead to under-consumption and under-allocation of resource. Governments ensure that education is available for all by offering schools for the general public often operating alongside private schools. The mere fact that private schools exist implies that the service is excludable.

Exercise 4

Determine whether the following statements are true or false. Explain your answers. Use a diagram to illustrate if possible.

1 If Prabha plants beautiful flowers by her street then this may be considered an example of a public good.
2 Market forces fail when positive externalities are present, because they under-produce the good associated with the positive externality.
3 If Ansar can be prevented from using a good he did not pay for then we can conclude that consumption of this good is rival.
4 The Barcelona versus Manchester United soccer game is an example of an excludable service which is non-rival up to a point (the capacity of Camp Nou stadium).
5 Natalie is a free rider if she benefits from a good without paying for it.

Exercise 5

Using examples explain the attributes that define what a pure public good is.

Make sure that you explain why the free market typically fails.

Exercise 6

In what ways do public goods create externalities.

Exercise 7

Rewrite the following statements and fill in the blanks by using the terms provided below. Some terms may be used more than once or not at all.

rival	decrease
congestion	free rider
private	excludable
advertising	marginal cost

Once a highway is built, the (1) _____ of an extra user is zero up until (2)_____ costs arise. The lack of incentive for individuals to contribute to a public good is known as the (3)_____ problem. The incentive to contribute towards its provision (4)_____ as more is contributed by others. Off-the-air TV and radio broadcasting is an interesting example of a pure public good that is provided by (5)_____, profit-oriented firms as TV and radio channels do not sell the programmes broadcast but (6)_____ time which is both (7)_____ and (8)_____.

Common access resources and the threat to sustainability

Remember

- Common-access (or common pool) resources share two characteristics, which are:
  - the difficulty in excluding individuals from benefiting from a good
  - the subtractability of the benefit enjoyed by one individual from those available to others; this is also referred to as rivalry in consumption.
- The benefits of using the common-access (or pooled) resources accrue to the user while the costs are spread to all.
- Do not forget the work of Elinor Ostrom (awarded the Nobel Prize, 2009) who has shown that there are many ways of organizing institutions that enable people to use common-access resources together and to use them in a renewable way over time; people can find rules, adjust their behaviour over time and they have to grow trust in one another. The simplistic logic of the 'tragedy of the commons' may prove more disastrous. Watch her 'sustainable development and the tragedy of the commons' 8 minute lecture on the Internet.
- Poverty often forces poorer communities to over-exploit land in order to produce more and more food and this is a threat to sustainability.

Tip

The easiest way to remember the characteristics of common-access resources is to think of the ocean and the fish: any fishing boat benefits from a catch but the more fish it catches the fewer fish are available for all other fishing boats.

Example 5

Determine whether the following statements are true or false. Explain your answers. Use a diagram to illustrate if possible.

1 Property held in common by a community tends to be used efficiently.

False (but think of Ostrom's work). Efficient use requires that the user enjoys all the benefits but also suffers all the costs. If property is communal than there is the risk that users will enjoy the benefit but the costs will be shared.

2 There is an incentive to use resources efficiently if property rights are clearly defined.

True. If property rights over an asset exist then there is an incentive to preserve its value. For example, if Chrissie owns a piece of land and has her cows graze on it then she will make sure that the she will be able to continue this as the extra benefits are for her to enjoy but the extra costs generated are also for her to pay.

3 Common-access resources entail negative externalities.

True. When people use a common-access resource they impose a cost on others as the amount available for other users decreases. The cost of depleting the resource is not taken into account.

Example 6

Provide examples of common-access resources, explaining your choices.

Typical examples of common-access resources include: fisheries, forests, pastures and grazing systems, lakes, oceans and the Earth's atmosphere.

Each of the above has characteristics that define the CPRs, namely that it is difficult to exclude one from using these and the subtractability of the benefits enjoyed (their consumption is rival).

For example, it is difficult to exclude fishing in the ocean (as no one owns the ocean) and the more fish one fishing company catches, the fewer are available for others to catch. Each fishing boat imposes a negative externality on all other fishing boats. This externality leads to over-fishing.

Exercise 8

Explain why open software programs or weather forecasts, despite having common-access characteristics, are not a threat to sustainability.

HL Abuse of monopoly power

> **Remember**
>
> ■ A monopoly firm faces the negatively sloped market demand curve for the product and is in a position to restrict output (supply) and so raise its price.
>
> ■ Firms with monopoly power typically create a 'deadweight loss' to society as the output rate they choose is less than the socially optimal.

Example 7

Explain why the existence of monopoly power in a market leads to market failure. Use a diagram to illustrate your answer.

Start from what you know: you know that a market is (allocatively) efficient if just the right amount of the good is produced and consumed from society's point of view. This requires that all units worth more than what they cost are indeed produced. Or, in other words, that for the last unit produced and consumed, the extra benefit enjoyed (MB) from consuming it is equal to the extra cost (MC) incurred of producing it (note that we are assuming away externalities).

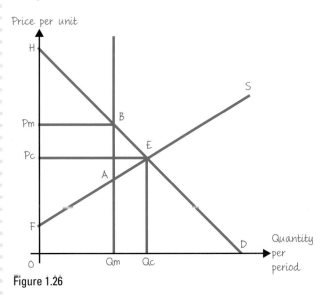

Figure 1.26

This condition is satisfied in competitive markets and it means that social (community) surplus (the sum of the consumer surplus and the producer surplus) is maximized. In the diagram below a competitive market will lead to Qc units being produced (and consumed) at a price Pc.

Consumer surplus is equal to area (PcEH), producer surplus is equal to area (FEPc) and social (or community) surplus is equal to area (FEH).

The monopoly firm is able to restrict output to Qm as it faces the market demand curve D. By restricting output the price at which the good can be sold increases to Pm. In the diagram above, distance QmB shows how much consumers value the last unit Qm (MB) while distance QmA shows the marginal cost of producing that unit (MC). Society would have wanted to enjoy units QmQc because each of these is worth more than what it costs to produce. The monopoly firm does not produce these units so we say that the market fails. Fewer resources are therefore allocated in the production of this good than the socially optimal level. Social welfare has also decreased by area (AEB). This area represents net value that society does not attain or enjoy because of the presence of monopoly power.

Example 8

What solutions could governments adopt to limit excessive monopoly power?

Government can enact legislation aimed at ensuring that competitive conditions prevail in markets. Certain business behaviour considered anti-competitive may be prohibited, for example in:

■ market sharing agreements (where firms divide up markets either geographically or based on some other criterion and agree not to compete in each other's territory)

■ collusive tendering (when, say, in a government contest to award the construction of a new airport, competitors agree that they will all bid high prices)

■ predatory pricing (when a firm sells at a very low price to drive out competitors and assume a monopoly position in the market).

Legislation may also be passed that requires the breaking up of a large monopoly into smaller units (but lawmakers must keep an eye on any economies of scale that may be sacrificed).

Governments can regulate the behaviour of firms with significant monopoly power. They can require, for example, that prices are set lower and closer to the competitive ideal so that output increases and approaches the socially optimal level.

In certain circumstances, governments may even assume ownership of the monopoly firm. This has been the case, especially in the past, in the provision of telephone services, water and electricity services as well as postal services. The goal is to set price close to the competitive ideal even if this implies operating at a loss, as in the case of postal services since service to rural, low population-density areas is often guaranteed.

Lastly, an effective way to lower the monopoly power of domestic firms is to expose them to foreign competition by decreasing trade barriers such as any taxes on imports (tariffs). Imports increase the supply of the good made available in the domestic markets so price will be squeezed.

Exercise 9

Answer the following questions using the diagram below.

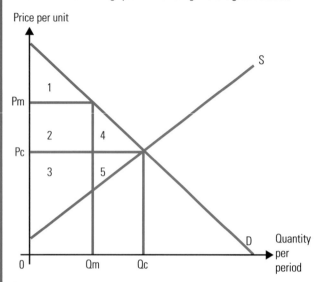

Figure 1.27

1 Assuming the market above was competitive, what is the consumer surplus equal to?

2 Assuming the market above was competitive, what is the producer surplus equal to?

3 Assuming the market above was competitive, what is the social (or community) surplus equal to?

4 Assuming the market above is monopolized and the monopolist chooses to offer Qm units per period at the price Pm, what is the new consumer surplus?

5 What is the change in consumer surplus?

6 What is the new producer surplus?

7 What is the change in the producer surplus?

8 In area (2), what is the new social (or community) surplus equal to?

9 What is the change in social (or community) surplus?

10 Explain why the monopolization of this competitive market results in allocative inefficiency and therefore is a market failure.

Asymmetric information

Remember

- Asymmetric information exists when one side of a market knows more than the other side does. There are two types of such informational failures: one is referred to as the 'moral hazard' problem while the other is referred to as 'adverse selection'.

- Moral hazard arises when one party to a contract alters his or her behaviour in ways that is costly to the other party with the limited information.

- Adverse selection arises when the seller knows more about the characteristics of the good being sold than the buyer does. The 'market for lemons' example is the best known and as a result of adverse selection 'bad cars will drive good cars out of the market'.

Example 9

Determine whether the following statements are true or false. Explain your answer.

1 In the 'market for lemons' the adverse selection issue is that as the price falls, the proportion of low-quality goods offered for sale increases.

True. Sellers with cars of higher than average quality will be turned off and withdraw their cars from the market, increasing the proportion of low-quality cars in the market.

2 If a car company offers a guarantee then consumers correctly believe that the car must be good because if it were not the company would pay the cost of honouring the guarantee.

True. Any additional cost that such companies incur (guarantees, advertising, expensive premises, etc.) are signals to prospective buyers that cars sold must be good.

3 If Jakub drives carelessly because he just got car insurance then this is an adverse selection problem.

False. This is a moral hazard problem where Jakub has an incentive to change his behaviour as a result of the contract he signed.

4 Costly advertising undertaken by a firm is used to signal quality.

True. The logic is that otherwise the company would not be willing to undertake the additional expense.

Exercise 10

Determine whether the following statements are true or false. Explain your answer.

1 If by law HIV patients are not obliged to reveal their medical condition to health insurance companies the adverse selection problem is intensified.

2 As car insurance premiums increase, drivers least likely to have an accident drop out of the market.

3 A brand name designer in the world of fashion may not cut prices fearing that its customers may infer that it no longer has the incentive to maintain its reputation.

4 Actions taken by sellers to persuade buyers that their goods are of high quality are referred to as screening.

Exercise 11

Explain, providing examples, what is meant by the terms 'moral hazard' and 'adverse selection'. In what sense will markets fail if either is present? What are some possible market responses and what can governments do to correct these problems?

Exercise 12

Several respected sites and publications routinely test digital cameras and other electronic products and report on their quality. Explain why this practice will tend to increase the prices of high-quality products.

HL Production in the short run

Remember

- The short run period in production implies the existence of at least one fixed factor. In the long run there are no fixed factors — all factors are considered variable.

Tip

It is the existence of a fixed factor that gives rise to the law of diminishing marginal (and average) returns.

Example 1

Explain the relationship between marginal and average variables, for example between MP and AP.

The easiest way to explain the relationship is to think of the following example. Consider any course you are taking, say IB Economics. Assume that your teacher has announced a series of 10 tests that will determine your grade for the term. Test grades are from zero to 100. Say that after having taken five tests, your average is 60 points. If on the next test (the 'extra' test, the marginal test, i.e. on the 6th test) you score 70 points (your average points were 60 while your marginal points are 70), then your average will increase:

if MP > AP then AP↑

If, though, you had scored 50 points on your 6th test (remember, these are your extra points earned, your marginal points), then your average would unfortunately fall. So:

if MP < AP then AP↓

It should be pretty clear that if on the 6th test you earned a 60, as much as your average to that point, then your average would remain a 60.

If MP = AP then AP remains constant.

It is an easy step to think of MP and AP not as marginal and average points from test taking at school but as MP and AP in the theory of production (and, later, as marginal and average costs).

Now, if the MP and AP functions are continuous functions (so that when you draw them you do not lift your pencil from the paper) then when average is at a maximum (or at a minimum) marginal must be equal to average, as shown in the diagram opposite.

1. AP is continuous, first rising and then dropping.
2. When MP>AP, AP rises while when MP<AP, AP drops. It follows that when MP=AP, AP must be at a maximum.

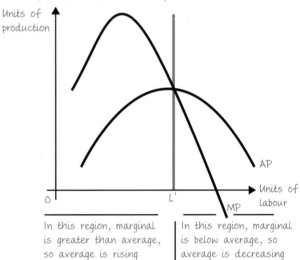

In this region, marginal is greater than average, so average is rising

In this region, marginal is below average, so average is decreasing

Figure 1.28

Example 2

The table below provides information on some production process.

Labour or number of workers (L)	Output (Q) or total product TP(L)	Average product AP(L)	Marginal product MP(L)
0	0	—	—
1	10	**(1)**	10
2	**(2)**	**(3)**	15
3	45	**(4)**	**(5)**
4	**(6)**	18.75	**(7)**
5	**(8)**	**(9)**	25
6	120	**(10)**	**(11)**
7	**(12)**	**(13)**	15
8	145	**(14)**	**(15)**
9	**(16)**	**(17)**	5
10	150	**(18)**	**(19)**
11	145	**(20)**	**(21)**
12	**(22)**	**(23)**	−10

1 Fill in the missing cells.

To complete the table remember the following three points:

- $MP_L = \dfrac{\Delta Q}{\Delta L} = \dfrac{(Q_2 - Q_1)}{(L_2 - L_1)}$ and since in this case the number of workers increases by 1, $\Delta L = 1$

- $AP_L = \dfrac{Q}{L}$

- TP (of n workers) = TP (of (n − 1) workers) + MP (of the nth worker) → see (2) below.

(1): $\dfrac{10}{1}$ = 10 units of output

(2): TP(2) = TP(1) + MP(2)
    = 10 + 15 = 25 units (note: TP(2) means the total product when two workers are employed and MP(2) is the marginal product of the 2nd worker)

(3): AP(2) = $\dfrac{TP(2)}{2}$ = $\dfrac{25}{2}$ = 12.5 units

(4): AP(3) = $\dfrac{TP(3)}{3}$ = $\dfrac{45}{3}$ = 15 units

(5): MP(3) = TP(3) − TP(2)
    = 45 − 25 = 20 units

(6): TP(4) = AP(4) × 4
    = 18.75 × 4 = 75 units

(7): MP(4) = TP(4) − TP(3)
    = 75 − 45 = 30 units

(8): TP(5) = TP(4) + MP(5)
    = 75 + 25 = 100 units

(9): AP(5) = $\dfrac{TP(5)}{5}$ = $\dfrac{100}{5}$ = 20 units

(10): AP(6) = $\dfrac{TP(6)}{6}$ = $\dfrac{120}{6}$ = 20 units

(11): MP(6) = TP(6) − TP(5)
    = 120 − 100 = 20 units

(12): TP(7) = TP(6) + MP(7)
    = 120 + 15 = 135 units

(13): AP(7) = $\dfrac{TP(7)}{7}$ = $\dfrac{135}{7}$ = 19.29 units

(14): AP(8) = $\dfrac{TP(8)}{8}$ = $\dfrac{145}{8}$ = 18.13 units

(15): MP(8) = TP(8) − TP(7)
    = 145 − 135 = 10 units

(16): TP(9) = TP(8) + MP(9)
    = 145 + 5 = 150 units

(17): AP(9) = $\dfrac{TP(9)}{9}$ = $\dfrac{150}{9}$ = 16.67 units

(18): AP(10) = $\dfrac{TP(10)}{10}$ = $\dfrac{150}{10}$ = 15 units

(19): MP(10) = TP(10) − TP(9)
    = 150 − 150 = 0 units

(20): AP(11) = $\dfrac{TP(11)}{11}$ = $\dfrac{145}{11}$ = 13.18 units

(21): MP(11) = TP(11) − TP(10)
    = 145 − 150 = − 5 units

(22): TP(12) = TP(11) + MP(12) = 145 + (−10) = 135 units

(23): AP(12) = $\dfrac{TP(12)}{12}$ = $\dfrac{135}{12}$ = 11.25 units

2 Diminishing marginal returns set in after the addition of which worker?

Since up until the 5th worker MP increases, but the MP of the 6th worker (20 units) is less than that of the 5th worker (25 units), it follows that diminishing marginal returns start with the 6th worker employed.

Example 3

The TP curve for a particular production process is illustrated below. Sketch the MP and AP curves below it.

Remember that $MP_L = \dfrac{\Delta Q}{\Delta L}$, which is the slope of the TP curve. $AP_L = \dfrac{Q}{L}$, which is the slope of the ray from the origin to various points on the TP curve.

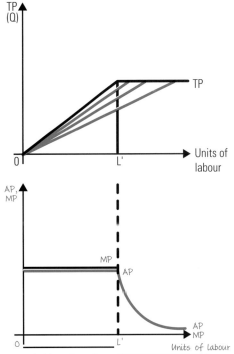

Between 0 and L' units of labour the slope of the TP curve above is positive and constant so MP is constant at some positive level. Since AP is the slope of the ray from the origin to points on TP, this is constant and coincides with the slope of TP:MP and AP are equal up to L'.

Past L' units of labour the slope of TP is zero so MP is zero (coinciding with the horizontal axis). The slope of the rays from the origin to the points of the TP (blue lines on top diagram) continuously decrease, so AP decreases approaching zero.

Figure 1.29

Exercise 1

1 Complete the blanks in the table below.

Labour or number of workers (L)	Output (Q) or total product TP(L)	Average product AP(L)	Marginal product MP(L)
0	0	–	–
1			120
2		150	
3			200
4	640		
5		135	
6			0

2 Diminishing marginal returns set in after the addition of which worker?

Exercise 2

Explain using appropriate diagrams the law of diminishing marginal and average returns.

Costs in the short run

Remember

- In economics, because resources are scarce, we care about every resource that is sacrificed in the production of a good, whether the firm makes or does not make an explicit payment for its use. This explains why economic costs are not just explicit costs but also implicit costs.

- The behaviour of cost curves in the short run is the flip side of the behaviour of product curves. Costs behave the way they do in the short run because of the law of diminishing marginal (and average) returns in production.

Tip

In economics, whenever you see the word 'marginal' substitute the word 'extra' or the word 'change' for it.

Tip

To draw marginal costs (MC) and average (total) costs (ATC) curves together in one diagram, first draw a shallow U-shaped ATC and then the MC curve shaped like the 'Nike-swoosh', making sure that the latter cuts the ATC at its minimum.

Tip

To draw ATC and AVC (average variable costs) curves in one diagram, first draw a shallow U-shaped ATC and then, below it, draw a shallow U-shaped AVC, making sure that the vertical distance between the two curves decreases as output increases.

Example 4

Why are marginal costs (MC) U-shaped (or shaped like the 'Nike-swoosh') in the short run?

The shape of cost curves in the short run reflects what happens in the production process. In the short run the behaviour of output is a result of the operation of the law of diminishing marginal (and average) returns. The law states that as a result of the existence of a fixed factor (typically capital), there is a point beyond which the MP of labour will start to decrease. However, if the contribution of each extra unit of labour decreases then it becomes more and more costly to produce each extra unit of output. It follows that if MP increases then MC must decrease and if MP is decreasing (i.e. when diminishing marginal returns set in) then MC increase.

Opposite is a slightly technical but very easy way to see this.

You know that MC are the change in TC over the change in output, or:

$$MC = \frac{\Delta(TC)}{\Delta Q} \quad (1)$$

TC in the short run are equal to FC — that, by definition, do not change when output changes — and variable costs (VC) — that do change when output changes:

So (1) becomes: $TC = (FC + VC)$

$$MC = \frac{\Delta(FC + VC)}{\Delta Q} \quad (2)$$

But, since FC do not change when output Q changes:

$$MC = \frac{\Delta(VC)}{\Delta Q} \quad (3)$$

If labour is the only variable input, then VC are the wage costs the firm pays, which are equal to the wage per worker (a constant for the firm as it is determined in the labour market) multiplied by the number of workers employed, or:

$$VC = \varpi \times L$$

So (3) becomes:

$$MC = \frac{\Delta(\varpi \times L)}{\Delta Q} = \frac{\varpi \times \Delta L}{\Delta Q} = \varpi \times \left[\frac{\Delta L}{\Delta Q}\right]$$

(as the wage rate ϖ is a constant) (4)

But MP is defined as the change in output over the change in labour (i.e. $MP = \frac{\Delta Q}{\Delta L}$) so equation (4) can be written as:

$$MC = \varpi \times \left[\frac{1}{MP}\right] \quad (5)$$

Equation (5) shows that MC and MP are inversely related: when MP increases, MC decrease but once MP starts to decline (i.e. diminishing marginal returns begin) then MC start to increase, giving rise to the 'Nike-swoosh' shape of the MC curve.

The shape of the MC curve is therefore a reflection of the behaviour of MP. It is the law of diminishing marginal returns that is responsible for the shape of the MC curve in the short run.

Example 5

The diagram below illustrates the ATC and the AVC curves of a firm. Explain why it is incorrectly drawn.

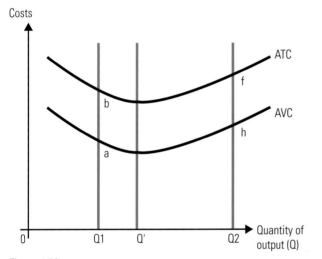

Figure 1.30

ATC include AVC plus AFC. So the following equations hold: ATC = AVC + AFC or ATC − AVC = AFC. The last equation states that if we subtract AVC from ATC then what will be left is AFC. On Figure 1.30, for each level of output Q, the AFC is the vertical distance between ATC and AVC for that level of output. For example, at output level Q1, ATC = Q1b, while AVC = Q1a; so, their difference ab is AFC for that level of output.

But AFC are defined as FC over output (Q) and it follows that as Q increases the ratio will decrease. For example, if FC for a firm are $2,000 per month (say, the rent for the premises it occupies) then if it produces 200 units of output per month its AFC will be equal to $\frac{2,000}{200}$ or $10 per unit of output. If it produces 2,000 units of output per month

then its AFC will be equal to $\frac{2,000}{2,000}$ or $1 per unit of output; and if it produces 20,000 units of output per month then its AFC will be equal to $\frac{2,000}{20,000}$ or $0.10 (10 cents) per unit of output. It should have become clear that AFC continuously decrease as Q increases, approaching zero for very large output rates.

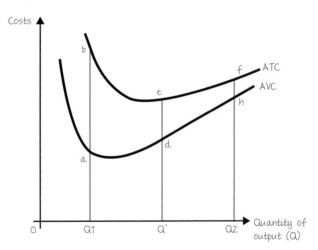

Figure 1.31

In Figure 1.30 though, the AVC and the ATC curves do not seem to approach each other. Their vertical distance which is AFC should have been decreasing but it is not. It seems that distance (ab) is pretty much equal to distance (hf) even though output Q2 is significantly bigger than output Q1. This means that the two curves are drawn incorrectly. They should have tended to touch one another but they do not. In Figure 1.31, the vertical distance between ATC and AVC decreases as Q increases, illustrating correctly that AFC become smaller and smaller.

Example 6

Determine whether the following statements are true or false. Explain your answers.

1 Variable costs (VC) increase as output increases.

True. To produce more of a good or service a firm needs to employ more inputs. If more inputs are employed then VC the firm has to pay increase. On a slightly more technical level, if $Q2 > Q1 \rightarrow VC(Q2) > VC(Q1)$, as more inputs are needed to produce Q2 than Q1.

2 Costs that never change are known as fixed costs (FC).

False. The statement is too broad: FC can change (for example, rents may be renegotiated at a higher or lower level) but they do not change when output changes. FC are costs that remain the same whatever the firm's output level: they remain constant when output varies.

3 If MC are falling throughout then AC must also be falling.

True. If your test grades are continuously falling (i.e. the extra points you score on each extra test are lower and lower) your average in the course is necessarily continuously decreasing.

4 If AC are falling throughout then MC must also be falling.

False. For AC to be falling, MC must be less than average, but they do not have to be continuously falling. For example, if after four tests your average in a course is 60 points and in the 5th test you score 10, then your average will fall to 50. If you do better in the next (6th) test scoring, say, 20 points (i.e. your marginal points increased), your average will still fall (to 45%).

Exercise 3

The following are cost items for Simply Burgers, a fast food restaurant specializing in hamburgers. Determine whether the following costs should be considered fixed or variable. Explain your choices.

Cost item	Amount
Ground meat	$1.23/kg
Insurance	$600/month
Delivery personnel	$5.00/hour
Electricity	$0.20/kWh
Store manager	$28,000/year
Potatoes	$0.60/kg
Hamburger buns	$0.05/bun
Lettuce	$0.30/head
Property taxes	$1,800/year
Grill assistants	$4.90/hour

Exercise 4

Fill in the blanks in the table below.

Q	FC	VC	ATC	AFC	AVC
0	500				
1		20			
2			300		
3					133.33
4		1,100			

Production in the long run

Remember

- In the long run, all factors of production are considered variable: the firm can change its size or its scale of production.

Tip

The word 'scale' implies the long run.

Tip

A firm's production process may be characterized at the same time by increasing returns to scale and diminishing marginal returns to a factor (say, labour). The former relates to what happens in the long run if the scale of production increases (i.e. if the use of all inputs increases), whereas the latter relates to what happens in the short run, when the scale of production is given (so capital is constant) but the number of workers increases.

Example 7

Study the table below and determine whether the statements below are true or false. Explain your answers.

Capital (K) Number of machines	Units of output (Q)			
4	920	1,760	2,500	3,200
3	660	1,260	1,800	2,280
2	420	800	1,140	1,440
1	200	380	540	680
	1	2	3	4
	Labour (L) Number of workers			

1 When the firm employs 3 units of capital, the marginal product (MP) of the 4th worker is 480 units of output.

True. Reading along the row where K = 3 we see that Q rises from 1,800 to 2,280 units when the 4th worker is added so that worker's MP was indeed 480 units.

2 When the firm employs 4 workers and increases its capital from 3 to 4 machines the MP of capital is 720 extra units of output.

False. Reading the column where 4 workers are employed the MP of capital increases from 2,280 to 3,200 units so the MP of the 4th machine is 920 units.

3 When the firm employs 2 machines and increases labour from 2 to 3 workers the MP of the 3rd worker is 340 units of output.

True. Reading along the row where K = 2 we see that Q rises from 800 to 1,140 units when the 3rd worker is added so that worker's MP was indeed 340 units.

4 The production technology employed by this firm exhibits increasing returns to scale.

True. When the firm doubles its scale, output more than doubles and when it triples its scale, output more than triples. More specifically, with one machine and one worker the firm produces 200 units but with 2 machines and 2 workers output more than doubles to 800 units. And when the firm triples in size employing 3 machines and 3 workers output more than triples, rising to 1800 units.

5 There are decreasing marginal returns to labour.

True. Reading across each row for each amount of capital employed it is revealed that the extra output from extra labour decreases. For example, when the firm employs 2 machines, MP of labour decreases from 380 to 340 to 300 units.

6 There are decreasing marginal returns to capital.

False. Reading vertically for each amount of labour employed it is revealed that the extra output from employing an additional unit of capital increases. For example, when the firm employs 2 workers, MP of capital increases from 420 to 460 to 500 units.

Exercise 5

Study the table below.

Capital (K) Number of machines	Labour (L) Number of workers	Output (Q) Number of units of the good
6	12	200
6	13	220
6	14	235
12	24	600
12	25	660
12	26	710

1 Does this firm experience constant return to scale? Explain your answer.
2 Does the law of diminishing marginal returns hold? Explain your answer.

Costs in the long run

Remember

- Defining the long run average cost (LRAC) curve properly is crucial. For each output level (Q) the LRAC curve shows the minimum average cost with which it can be produced in the long run, i.e. when the firm is able to vary all factors of production (both K and L) so that any desired scale of plant can be built.

Tip

The behaviour of costs in the long run is a reflection of the characteristics of production in the long run (when all factors are variable).

Tip

Remember the 'three Cs' when discussing diseconomies of scale: costs arising from communication, coordination and control problems that large size may be responsible for.

Example 8

Explain how the diagram below illustrates the idea of economies of scale.

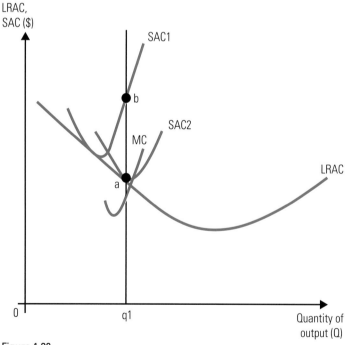

Figure 1.32

Tip

The smallest size with which a firm can achieve minimum LRAC is referred to as the minimum efficient scale of minimum optimal size and it is important in determining whether an industry will comprise one, few or many firms.

In the diagram above the LRAC of a firm is illustrated as well as two short run average costs (SRAC), labelled SAC1 and SAC2, each associated with a different scale of operation. Curve SAC1 is the SRAC curve when the firm employs some level of capital (say, K = K1) whereas curve SAC2 is the SRAC curve when the firm is larger in size, employing some level of capital K2 which is greater than K1. You can visualize K1 as representing a factory and K2 a larger factory.

If this firm were to produce q1 units of output it could do so employing either K1 or K2 units of capital (or, more simply, with either factory). However, it is able to produce q1 units cheaper (with an average cost of q1a instead of an average cost of q1b on the diagram) when it is larger in size: it enjoys economies of scale; its AC decrease as its scale of operation increases. Production is therefore characterized by increasing returns to scale.

Notice though that given its size K2 (i.e. with capital fixed at K2 units), the firm's MC curve is rising so it is experiencing diminishing marginal returns to labour.

Exercise 6

Outline the relationship between SRAC and LRAC.

Exercise 7

Explain, using a diagram, the reason for the typical shape of the LRAC curve of a firm.

Exercise 8

Describe factors giving rise to both economies of scale and diseconomies of scale.

Exercise 9

Discuss the statement: 'Small firms are always less efficient than large ones.'

Revenues

Remember

- If a firm can sell as much as it wants at the same price then the extra revenue it earns (i.e. its marginal revenue or MR) will be equal to the price: AR (= P) = MR.

- If, though, to sell more per period it must lower the price then the extra revenue it earns from an extra unit it sells (its MR) will be less than the price: AR (=P) > MR.

Tip

The AR a firm earns is the price per unit consumers pay; only if there is an indirect tax or a subsidy will AR and price per unit differ (by the amount of the tax or the amount of the subsidy).

Example 9

Explain why the demand curve is also the AR curve.

The demand curve a firm faces is typically negatively sloped, implying that the market will absorb greater quantities per period at lower prices. AR is defined as revenue per unit, so the AR collected when Q units are sold is equal to $\frac{TR}{Q}$. Since TR are (P × Q) it follows that:

$$AR(Q) = \frac{TR(Q)}{Q} = \frac{(P \times Q)}{Q} = P$$

Look at the demand curve opposite, reading it vertically.

Quantity Q1 will be absorbed by the market at price P1. Since all units are sold at the same price it follows that the revenue earned per unit (AR) is P1. The same holds for output Q2: this quantity will be absorbed by consumers at a price per unit of P2. Since all units are sold at the same price, AR(Q2) = P2.

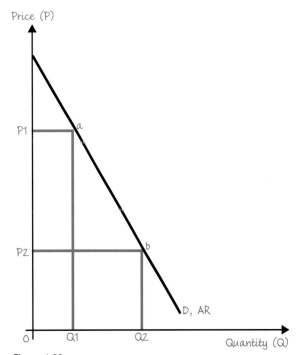

Figure 1.33

Example 10

Explain why MR will lie below a negatively sloped demand curve.

To understand this without the mathematics (which HL and SL Methods students know) we have to rely on the laws governing the behaviour of marginal and average magnitudes (product, costs and now revenue).

If, as Figure 1.33, the AR curve is continuously decreasing, then extra revenue (MR) must at all levels of output be less than AR:

if AR↓, then MR must be less than AR

It follows that the MR curve will lie below the AR curve (which is also the demand curve the firm faces).

Alternatively, a numerical example can suggest why MR is less than price and AR.

Let's say a cinema sells 60 tickets per show at \$12. AR is \$12 and its total revenues (TR) are \$720.

Assume that for it to sell 61 tickets per show it must lower the price to \$11.90. AR is \$11.90 and TR now increase to \$725.90 (61 × \$11.90).

The extra revenue (= MR) from selling one more ticket per show is only \$5.90:

MR (=\$5.90) < AR (=\$12)

Why? Because the cinema collects the \$11.90 from selling that extra (61st) ticket but that new price applies to all tickets sold in each show. The cinema owner is earning \$0.10 less per ticket from all tickets previously being sold at \$12.00. So:

MR (from the 61st ticket)
= TR (from selling 61 tickets) − TR (from selling 60 tickets)
= \$5.90

or

MR (from the 61st ticket)
= \$11.90 − (60 × \$0.10) = \$11.90 − \$6.00
= \$5.90.

More generally, if the demand curve a firm faces is negatively sloped then for all levels of output Q:

P (=AR) > MR

Exercise 10

Copy the table below and fill in the blank cells. What can you infer about the PED faced up to the 7th unit sold?

Q	P	TR	MR	AR
0	160	0	–	–
1	**(1)**	150	**(2)**	**(3)**
2	140	**(4)**	**(5)**	**(6)**
3	**(7)**	**(8)**	110	**(9)**
4	**(10)**	**(11)**	90	**(12)**
5	**(13)**	**(14)**	**(15)**	110
6	**(16)**	**(17)**	**(18)**	100
7	**(19)**	**(20)**	30	**(21)**
8	**(22)**	**(23)**	10	**(24)**
9	**(25)**	630	**(26)**	**(27)**
10	**(28)**	**(29)**	−30	**(30)**

All necessary calculations are based on the following:

$P = AR$; $AR = \dfrac{TR}{Q}$; $MR = \dfrac{\Delta TR}{\Delta Q}$;

TR(nth + 1 unit)
= TR(nth) + MR(nth +1)

So, for example, TR from selling 6 units are equal to the TR from selling 5 units plus the MR from the sale of the 6th unit.

Starting the exercise:

(1) and (3): $AR = P = \dfrac{TR}{Q} = \dfrac{150}{1} = 150$

(2): $MR = \dfrac{\Delta TR}{\Delta Q} = \dfrac{(150 - 0)}{1} = 150$
(since ΔQ is always 1 here, we can ignore it)

(4): $TR = P \times Q = 140 \times 2 = 280$

(5): $MR = \dfrac{\Delta TR}{\Delta Q} = 280 - 150 = 130$

(6): $AR = P = 140$

(8): Since TR(3) = TR(2) + MR(3rd), so TR = 280 + 110 = 390, etc.

Exercise 11

A bookstore is selling an old edition of an economics textbook at €20 per copy but decides to offer schools which buy it a 5 % discount if they order at least 50 copies. Calculate the MR collected from the 50th copy.

Profit

Remember

- Normal profits are defined as the minimum return needed to keep a firm operating and reflect the opportunity cost of entrepreneurship, a scarce factor of production.

- Entrepreneurs risk some (financial) capital so they require as a return at least what they would have earned by investing this (financial) capital in risk-free assets (such as in government bonds) plus enough to compensate them for the risk they take by setting up the firm. Without the entrepreneur and the (financial) capital this person ties up in a firm, there would be no firm. It is in this sense that normal profit is considered an element of cost.

- The firm just earns normal profits if economic profits are zero (as normal profits have been included in costs). In this situation, the firm will continue operating as it is making the minimum it requires (it is making normal profits).

- If economic profits are positive then the firm is earning more than normal (which is referred to as supernormal or abnormal profits).

- A firm is breaking even if it is making zero economic profits, i.e. if total revenues equal total costs: TR = TC.

Tip

- By setting total revenues (TR) equal to total costs (TC) and solving for Q you can find the break-even level of **output**, i.e. the output for which zero economic profits are earned.

- The break-even **price** for a perfectly competitive firm is the price that is equal to its minimum average total costs (ATC).

- In the long run, the break-even price (P = min ATC) is also the shut-down price for a perfectly competitive firm.

Example 11

Using the information provided below, determine the level of profits at levels of output Q1, Q2 and Q3. (Figures are in pounds sterling.)

	Price per unit	Average total cost (ATC)
At Q1 = 100 units	15	10
At Q2 = 220 units	8	8
At Q1 = 300 units	3	12

To calculate profits we need to calculate for each level of output the total revenues (TR) collected and the total costs (TC) incurred, as

$$\pi(Q) = TR(Q) - TC(Q).$$

	TR	TC
At Q1 = 100 units	1,500	1,000
At Q2 = 220 units	1,760	1,760
At Q1 = 300 units	900	3,600

Subtracting TC incurred from TR collected we arrive at the profit figures:

	Profits (π)
At Q1 = 100 units	500
At Q2 = 220 units	0
At Q1 = 300 units	−2,700

The firm is making positive economic profits also referred to as supernormal profits equal to £500 when it produces 100 units per period, it is breaking even when it produces 220 units of output and it incurs economic losses equal to £2,700 if it produces 300 units per period.

Alternatively, we could calculate for each level of output the average profit earned and multiply it by the number of units produced and sold.

	Price per unit	ATC	Per unit profit $\left[\dfrac{\pi}{Q}\right]$	Profits (π)
At Q1 = 100 units	15	10	5	500
At Q2 = 220 units	8	8	0	0
At Q1 = 300 units	3	12	−9	−2,700

Example 12

Using the diagram below, determine the level of profits at levels of output Q1, Q2 and Q3. All figures are in pounds sterling. (This is similar to the example above, the only difference being that the information is provided in a diagram.)

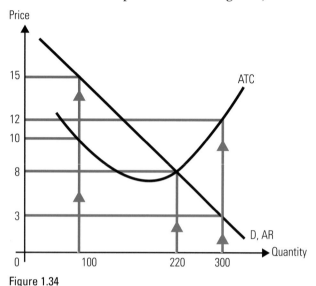

Figure 1.34

We read these diagrams vertically, as we want to find for each level of output Q the price at which the market will absorb it (and, at the same time, the AR) as well as the ATC of producing it. So, for each Q, say for 100 units, we follow the arrows towards the demand and the ATC curves and find that 100 units will be absorbed by the market at P = £15 (which is also the AR collected) and that the ATC of producing 100 units is £10.

(See above for the answers; note that at Q = 220 units, the firm is breaking even if π = 0.)

Exercise 12

Explain why a firm making zero economic profits would bother operating.

Exercise 13

Rewrite the following statements and fill in the blanks by using the terms provided below.

sacrifice	opportunity cost
normal	financial
investing	supernormal
15%	

Assume that Nikhita, a young budding entrepreneur, has the choice between (1) _____ in a chain of cosmetics outlets and in a chain of supermarkets, having equal knowledge of both industries. If Nikhita can achieve a 10 & rate of return if she invests her (2) _____ capital in a chain of cosmetics outlets, while she could achieve 15 % in a chain of supermarkets, the (3) _____ profit, or opportunity cost of getting involved in chain of cosmetics outlets, would be (4) _____. In this case, Nikhita (5) _____ profit. If, instead, the return in a chain of cosmetics outlets was 20 %, Nikhita achieves more than the (6) _____ of getting involved in the supermarket business, which is still the next best alternative to resource extraction. The difference can now be called (7) _____ profit.

Goals of firms

Remember

- If MR > MC, then revenues are rising faster than costs so it pays the firm to increase output as in this way it will increase profits or decrease losses.

- If MR < MC, then costs are rising faster than revenues so it pays to decrease output as in this way the firm will increase profits or decrease losses.

  It follows that if MR = MC (and, assuming that MC is rising) then there is no reason for the firm to change the level of output as if it does it will decrease profits or increase losses. The firm's best output is therefore where MR = MC (assuming MC rises) as there it is either maximizing profits or minimizing losses.

- Revenue (or sales) maximization requires that the firm chooses that output level Q for which MR = 0.

Example 13

Rewrite the following statements filling in the blanks by using the terms provided below. Some terms may be used more than once or not at all.

staff	profits	utility
sales	managerial	salaries
shareholders	maximizing	
objectives	share	

Managers may not aim at (1) _____ profits as their interests and the interests of the owners (or the (2) _____ of the firm) may not coincide. Williamson's (3)_____ utility maximization theory argues that managers often pursue their own (4)_____ seeking to maximize their own (5)_____. These managerial objectives may include their own (6) _____, more perks and perhaps a bigger (7) _____.

On the other hand, since Baumol's (8) _____ maximization theory argues that revenues are important as they are typically positively associated with (9)_____, they are more easily measured and because a firm's performance is often measured by its (10)_____ of the market.

(1) maximizing, (2) shareholder, (3) managerial, (4) objectives, (5) utility, (6) salaries, (7) staff, (8) sales, (9) profits, (10) share

Example 14

Explain, using a diagram, why profits are maximized (or losses are minimized) at that level of output at which MR = MC (and MC is rising).

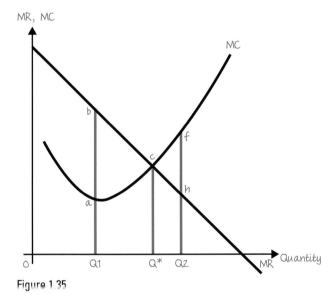

Figure 1.35

Figure 1.36

Figure 1.35 illustrates a firm facing a negatively sloped demand curve while Figure 1.36 reflects a firm facing a perfectly elastic (horizontal) demand curve. (Later, you will see that Figure 1.36 illustrates a perfectly competitive firm while the LHS diagram illustrates a monopoly or an imperfect competitor).

In either case at Q1, MR exceeds MC (Q1b > Q1a). Reading this a bit differently we see that the extra revenue from selling one more unit is bigger than the extra cost of producing it, so the firm's profits will increase (by ab) or its losses will decrease (by ab). Thus, if MR > MC, the firm should produce more to increase profits or decrease losses.

At Q2 , MR is less than MC (Q2h < Q2f). Reading this a bit differently we see that by not producing unit Q2 the firm will sacrifice less in revenue than the cost it will avoid paying. So, by producing less it will increase its profits or decrease its losses. If MR < MC, the firm should produce less to increase profits or decrease its losses.

It follows that to maximize profits (minimize losses) it should produce more when it is located to the left of Q* and less when it is located to the right of Q*, then at Q* it should neither increase nor decrease output as it is achieving its goal.

Exercise 14

Rewrite the following statements and fill in the blanks by using the terms provided below. Some terms may be used more than once or not at all.

profits	stakeholders	management
satisficing	objective	risk
pricing	information	share
corporate social	targets	
growth	economies	

According to Herbert Simon, firms do not have the necessary (1) _____ to aim at maximizing any (2) _____. Modern corporations are very complex organizational structures with a multitude of (3) _____ having different

(4) _____. They aim instead at (5) _____, achieving in other words some minimum satisfactory rate of return.

(6) _____ maximization of the firm is an alternative behavioural assumption that was proposed by R. Marris. This hypothesis has the advantage that it may incorporate and satisfy the interests of both (7) _____ and ownership. A large firm could benefit from (8) _____ of scale and lower (9) _____ as it could expand into more markets selling more products, increasing market and thus (10) _____ power. Both (11) _____ and market (12) _____ could increase.

Creating and maintaining an ethical and environmentally responsible image is the prime objective of what is referred to as (13) _____ responsibility.

Exercise 15

Describe Baumol's sales maximization and Marris' growth maximization objectives, and contrast these to Simon's satisficing theory.

Exercise 16

Why do you think 'corporate social responsibility' has become more important in recent years? Why could profits and sales increase for environmentally conscious firms?

Perfect competition

Remember

- A perfectly competitive market has very many small firms, each too small to affect the market price. An easy way to visualize the insignificance of a perfectly competitive firm is to think of the market as a sandy beach and each firm as a grain of sand. Whether a perfectly competitive firm produces more or less, the market will not be affected in the same way that a beach will not be affected if a grain of sand is blown away or doubles in size.

- It's easy to understand why a perfectly competitive firm cannot increase price above the market determined level: no rational consumers would ever buy even a single unit as they could get exactly the same good from very many other firms at a lower price.

- It is not as easy to understand why such a firm doesn't sell at a lower price. The answer is that it has no incentive to do so: it is so small compared with the market (remember the analogy of the beach and a grain of sand) that its output decisions (how much it produces and offers) do not affect the market price. So, if it can sell all it wants at the going market price why would it ever want to sell at a lower price?

- Perfect competition requires very many small firms, a homogeneous product and no barriers, as well as perfect information and factor mobility.

Tip

When discussing perfect competition you usually need to draw two diagrams side by side, one illustrating the market (i.e. market demand and market supply) and one the typical firm.

Tip

If you multiply any per unit variable (such as average revenue or average variable cost) by the number of units you arrive at the total of the same variable, i.e. at total revenues or total variable costs.

Tip

To determine the profit-maximizing level of output for a perfectly competitive firm from data provided in a table, you need to determine MC and then find the greatest output level for which MC is equal to price (which in perfect competition is MR), assuming that MC is rising.

At this output level the firm is making either maximum profits or minimum losses. To determine which of the two it is you need to examine the relationship between price (= AR) and ATC or between TR and TC.

Example 15

Assume that a perfectly competitive firm faces fixed costs equal to €100 per month and that its average variable cost (AVC) of production is given below.

Q	AVC in €
10	10
20	11
30	12
40	13
50	14
60	15
70	16

1 Is this firm operating in the long run?

No, it is operating in the short run as there are fixed costs and so fixed factors of production.

2 What is the profit maximizing level of output for this firm if market demand and supply conditions determine the market price at €16?

To determine this we need first to find MC. These costs are defined as the change in total or variable costs (VC) divided by the change in output. It is easy to calculate (total) VC from the information: multiply AVC by Q.

Q	AVC in €	VC
10	10	10 × 10 = 100
20	11	220
30	12	360
40	13	520
50	14	700
60	15	900
70	16	1,120

Since VC for zero units rise from €0 to €100 when output rises from 0 to 10 units, it follows that $MC = \dfrac{\Delta VC}{\Delta Q} = \dfrac{100}{10} = €10$. *Using the same formula we derive MC for all levels of output:*

Q	AVC in €	VC	$MC = \dfrac{\Delta VC}{\Delta Q}$
10	10	100	10
20	11	220	12
30	12	360	14
40	13	520	16
50	14	700	18
60	15	900	20
70	16	1,120	22

If the market price is €16 then the greatest level of output for which price is equal to marginal cost is 40 units. MC is €16 for each extra unit produced when output rises from 30 to 40 units.

3 Calculate the level of profits π at this profit-maximizing output rate.

To calculate the level of profits π when Q = 40 we need to calculate TR when 40 units are sold and TC of producing 40 units.

TR(40) = price quantity = €16 × 40 = €640

TC(40) = FC + VC(40) = €100 + €520 = €620

π(40) = TR(40) − TC(40) = €640 − €620 = €20

4 What is the lowest price that will permit a firm to remain in the business in the short run?

In the short run a loss-making firm will continue to produce as long as it covers its variable costs (VC) or, equivalently, as long as price (P) is at least equal to minimum average VC. From the table above, minimum AVC is €10 so this is the lowest price that will permit the firm to continue operations. At any price less than €10, it will exit the market.

Example 16

The diagram below represents the demand and cost conditions a firm faces.

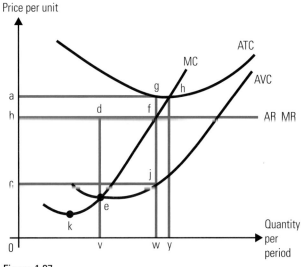

Figure 1.37

1 Is this firm a perfectly competitive firm?

Yes, it is. It is facing a constant MR curve: the extra revenue collected from selling one more unit is constant. This is possible only if the firm is very small (remember the analogy of a grain of sand) and sells a homogeneous product, which are characteristics only of perfect competition.

2 Is this firm operating in the short run or the long run?

It is operating in the short run as the firm faces fixed costs and so at least one fixed factor of production exists. This is evident from the diagram as there is a difference between average total and average variable costs. This difference reflects the average fixed costs (which decrease as output increases).

3 Why is the AR curve identical to the MR curve?

Remember that AR collected from selling any amount of output Q is the price at which that amount of output Q was sold, as:

$$AR(Q) = \frac{TR(Q)}{Q} = \frac{P \times Q}{Q} = P$$

If AR (=P) is constant, then the extra revenue (MR) collected from selling an extra unit will also be constant and equal to price. You may recall from the laws on marginal and average quantities that if marginal is equal to average then average is constant.

Remember that the AR curve is always the demand curve a firm faces.

4 If this perfectly competitive firm is a profit maximizer what output rate will it choose? Why?

It will choose to produce and sell that output level at which MR = MC and MC is rising. MR intersects MC at point f, right above output level w (and MC is rising). Output w is therefore the best choice for this firm, i.e. its optimum output.

5 Is this firm making positive economic profits?

No. It is making negative economic profits (losses) equal to area (bfga).

To find the profit area one has subtract the TC incurred from the TR collected. TR are equal to price (or AR) × quantity, i.e.
(Ob) × (Ow) = area (Owfb).

TC are equal to ATC for the quantity chosen times the quantity, i.e.
(wg) × (Ow) = area (Owga). Since the total cost area is bigger than the total revenue area, the firm is incurring losses equal to the difference, or area (bfga).

You could have instead found the profit per unit (in this case loss per unit) as the difference between AR and ATC and multiplied it by the level of output chosen:
(gf) × (Ow) = (gf) × bf) = area (bfge)

6 Since this firm is making economic losses should it perhaps shut down?

No. Remember it is operating in the short run so it has to pay its fixed costs even of output Q = 0. To determine whether it makes sense or not to shut down we must determine whether its revenues are enough to cover its variable (operating) costs. The firm should shut down if TR < TVC, or if (dividing both sides of the inequality by Q):

P (= AR) < AVC

At the optimum (best) output level w, TR are area (Owfb) while TVC are area (Owjc). Revenues collected exceed operating costs by area (cjfb) but these are insufficient to cover al the fixed costs which are equal to area (cjga). Alternatively, the firm should not shut down as P (= AR) > AVC: (Ob) > (Oc).

7 'All the points on this firm's MC curve that are above point k are the firm's supply curve.' Do you agree?

No. The perfectly competitive firm's short run supply curve is its MC curve above the minimum AVC curve. This is because at any price below the minimum AVC the firm will not supply any quantity — it will shut down. Only the section of the MC above point e is the firm's supply curve.

Example 17

Determine whether the following statements are true or false. Explain your answers. Use a diagram to illustrate if possible.

1 A lump-sum tax will not affect the output of a perfectly competitive firm unless profits are driven below zero.

True. The profit-maximizing output level is determined where MR = MC. MC is the extra cost of producing an extra unit. Since a lump sum tax is equivalent to an increase in fixed costs it will not affect MC and so it will not affect the choice of output. If, though, payment of the tax forces the firm to make losses then the output choice will be zero.

2 A per unit (i.e. specific) tax may increase the level of output that a perfectly competitive profit-maximizing firm will produce since in this way it will maintain profitability.

False. We have analysed specific taxes earlier and we have determined that such a tax decreases supply. Now we know that essentially the specific tax imposed increases the cost of producing an extra unit (the MC of the firm) shifting the MC curve (which is the supply curve of the firm above minimum AVC) vertically up by the amount of the tax from MC to MC'. The diagram below illustrates that such a tax will decrease the profit-maximizing output (from q to q').

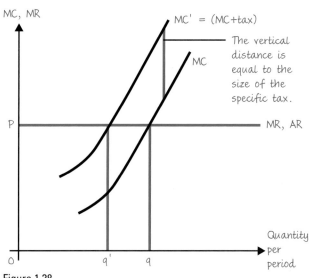

Figure 1.38

Example 18

The following information pertains to the current position of a firm.

Q	P	MC	MR	AVC	ATC
100	€0.60	€0.50	€0.60	€0.30	€0.65

1 Is this a perfectly competitive firm?

Yes, it is. Price is always equal to AR but only in perfect competition is price equal to MR. Here, P = MR (both are €0.60) so the firm is a perfectly competitive firm.

2 Is this firm maximizing its profits? If not, should it increase or decrease output? Why?

A firm is maximizing profits if MR = MC. Here, MR > MC, so it is not maximizing profits. Since the extra revenue (MR) it collects from selling one more unit exceeds the extra cost incurred (MC) from producing it, it pays to increase output as this way it will increase whatever profits it was making or decrease its losses.

3 Calculate the firm's total revenues.

Since TR = P × Q it follows that total revenues are equal to €0.60 × 100 = €60.00.

4 Calculate the firm's total costs.

TC are equal to average TC times output or ATC Q = €0.65 × 100 = €765.00.

5 Is this firm breaking even?

For a firm to be breaking even, AR (price) must equal ATC. Here, AR < ATC, so it is making losses.

6 Should this firm shut down?

This firm is operating in the short run as there are fixed costs to be paid. We know this because ATC > AVC. To determine whether it is a good idea to shut down we need to compare P to AVC (or TR to VC) and if P (which is always equal to AR) is less than AVC, then it should shut down. Here P exceeds AVC: €0.60 > €0.30, so it would not be a good idea to shut down. If it continues producing it will be losing €5.00 per period whereas if it shuts down it will need to pay the fixed costs per period. The fixed costs per period are equal to (ATC − AVC) × Q or (€0.65 − €0.30) × 100 = €0.35 × 100 = €35.00. Once all factors are variable the firm will need to re-evaluate and decide whether to shut down.

7 Draw a diagram illustrating its current output level and the above values.

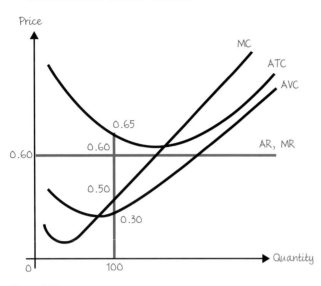

Figure 1.39

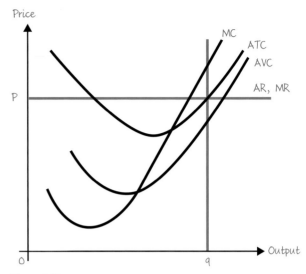

Figure 1.40

Example 19

A firm has chosen to produce a level of output q at which:

$$MC > ATC = P = AR = MR > AVC$$

1 Is this firm a perfectly competitive firm?

Yes it is as P = MR.

2 Is this firm maximizing its profits? If not, should it increase or decrease output? Why?

No, it is not, as MR ≠ MC. Since MC > MR, this firm should decrease output to maximize profits.

3 Is this firm breaking even?

Yes, at the current output choice it is breaking even as AR = ATC so π = 0.

4 Is it operating in the short run or in the long run?

It is operating in the short run. Since ATC > AVC, it is facing fixed costs.

5 Draw the appropriate diagram to illustrate its output choice q.

Example 20

How would the short run supply curve of a perfectly competitive firm be affected if fixed costs increased?

The short run supply curve of a perfectly competitive firm is that section of its MC that lies above the minimum of its AVC curve. Since neither MC nor AVC are affected by a change in fixed costs it follows that the firm's short run supply curve will not be affected by an increase in its fixed costs.

Example 21

Explain, using appropriate diagrams, the 'shut-down' rule or price for a perfectly competitive firm.

The shut-down rule or price pertains to a loss-making firm and the question of whether or not it should shut down.

A firm in the long run, the time period when all adjustments are possible and when all factors are considered variable, will shut down if it is making losses. A firm not earning as much as it could earn in its next best alternative has the incentive to shut down and move on to this alternative. The firm should shut down in the long run at any price P below its ATC.

Conversely, the firm will be willing to produce if the price (AR) is at least equal to the minimum AC incurred.

Remember that the AC curve is 'U'-shaped and that AR for a perfect competitor is constant and horizontal. This implies that for the firm to be willing to produce, the price (the AR curve) can fall as low as the minimum of the ATC curve but not any lower. This is shown in Figure 1.41.

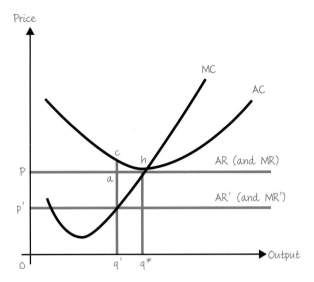

Figure 1.41

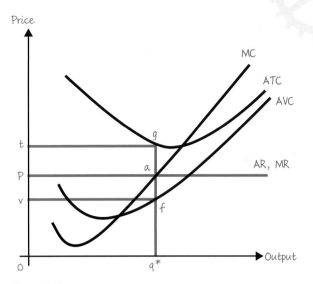

Figure 1.42

If the price is P, then AR (which is also in perfect competition MR) is tangent to the lowest point (minimum) of the firm's AC curve. If the firm produces q* units, it is maximizing profits and these profits are equal to zero: the firm is making normal profits — it is making the minimum it requires to remain in this line of business. The entrepreneur is satisfied and has no reason to shut down as the individual earns as much as he or she would earn in the next best alternative. But this will not be the case at any price less than the minimum AC: at price P' the profit-maximizing level of output is q' and the firm would make losses equal to ac per unit. It would shut down and resources would be re-allocated elsewhere.

In the short run, though, it is not necessary that a loss-making firm shuts down as there is at least one fixed factor involved and so there are fixed costs that the firm will have to pay even if output is zero, i.e. even if it shuts down. It will have to make a decision about whether it pays to continue despite the losses or whether it pays to shut down. If by producing goods the firm more than covers its entire variable (i.e. operating) costs then by continuing operations it is losing less than the amount of FC which it would have to pay in full if it shut down. So, despite losses, it will not shut down. If, though, its revenues are not enough to cover its variable (operating) costs then there is no point in operating. It will shut down as by shutting down it will have to pay only for its FC (for as long as, say, the rental agreement for the premises it occupies exists).

For example, in Figure 1.42, the firm is making losses equal to area (Pagt) but since its FC (found by multiplying AFC, the difference between ATC and AVC, by the chosen level of output) are bigger (they are equal to area (vfgt)) it will not shut down: by operating it is at least covering part of these, whereas if it shut down it would face the entire amount.

If P is the price then the profit maximizing output is at q* as it is for this level of output that MR = MC (and MC is rising). The ATC at q* is greater than AR (q*g > q*a) so the firm is losing per period, area (agtP). But fixed costs are equal to area (fgtv) which is larger, so it would make no sense to shut down: for as long as these fixed costs have to be paid, the firm would be losing more by shutting down than if it continued to operate.

The lowest price that would be acceptable is the one corresponding to the minimum of its AVC.

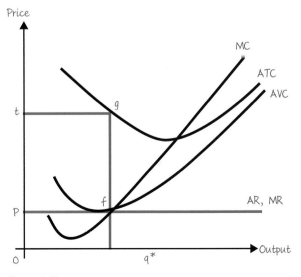

Figure 1.43

85

In Figure 1.43, the minimum of AVC is $q*f = OP$. At a price equal to P the firm by producing would lose area (fgtP) which is exactly equal to the fixed costs it would have to pay anyway, whether it continued operating or shut down. Thus, the firm should shut down in the short run at any price P below the minimum of its AVC.

Here is a more technical but very easy way to understand the short run shut down rule.

In the short run, do not shut down if:

(1) Loss < fixed costs; dividing now both sides by Q

(2) $\left| \frac{loss}{Q} \right| < (AFC)$; since the loss per unit is (ATC−AR) or (ATC−P)

(3) $(ATC−P) < AFC$

(4) $ATC < AFC < P$

(5) $AVC < P$

Below is a summary of the short run and long run rule to remember:

Short run shut-down rule	Long run shut-down rule
Shut down at any price below min AVC	Shut down at any price below min ATC

Example 22

Explain, using appropriate diagrams, the difference between the shut-down price and the break-even price for a perfectly competitive firm.

In the short run, a perfectly competitive firm will shut down if P < min AVC.

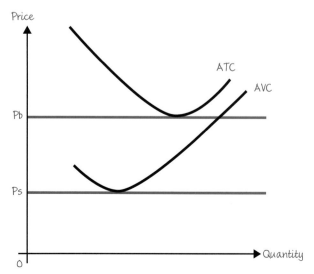

Figure 1.44

In Figure 1.44, this price is Ps. The break-even price for a perfectly competitive firm is that price for which economic profits are zero so that P = min ATC. This is the case at price Pb in the diagram above.

So, below is the situation for a perfectly competitive firm.

Short run	
Break-even price	P = min ATC
Shut-down price	P = min AVC
Long run	
Break-even price and Shut-down price	P = min ATC

Example 23

A perfectly competitive firm faces average fixed costs equal to €80.00 when producing 5 units of output, and its total revenues when selling 8 units are equal to €2,400.00. The table below provides cost and output data for this firm.

Output (per period)	Variable costs (VC) of production
1	300
2	550
3	750
4	900
5	1,100
6	1,350
7	1,650
8	2,000

1   Assuming the goal is to achieve maximum profit, what rate of output should this firm choose?

To determine the profit-maximizing level of profit we must determine the MR and the MC of this firm. Since it is a perfect competitor, MR is equal to P which in turn is equal to AR. The latter can be calculated by dividing the TR by output, or €2,400 ÷ 8 = €300.00. So P = €300.00

MC is the increase in variable (or total) cost when one more unit is produced. For example, the marginal cost of the fifth unit is the difference between the variable cost of producing 5 units and of producing 4 units of output or €1,100 − €900 = €200. The table below gives MC for different quantities produced.

Output (per period)	VC	MC
1	300	300
2	550	250
3	750	200
4	900	150
5	1100	200
6	1350	250
7	1650	300
8	2000	350

Since profit maximization requires MR = MC and MC rising and since MC is initially falling, the profit-maximizing level of output is 7 units. (MR and MC are equal for 1 unit also but MC is falling there.)

2 Calculate the level of profits attained.

This requires to determine TR and TC at Q = 7 units.

Remember that TC is the sum of VC and fixed costs (FC). Since AFC is €80.00 when producing 5 units it follows that

FC = €400.00.
TR(7) = 300 × 7 = €2,100.00
TC(7) = FC + VC(7) = €400.00 + €1,650.00
= €2,050.00
π(7) = €50.00

3 What is the shut-down price for this firm?

To calculate the shut-down price in the short run, information about the firm's AVC is required.

Output (per period)	VC	AVC
1	300	300
2	550	275
3	750	250
4	900	225
5	1,100	220
6	1,350	225
7	1,650	235.71
8	2,000	250

The minimum average variable cost for this firm is €220.00. It follows that at any price below €220.00 the firm would shut down.

Exercise 17

The data below refer to a perfectly competitive firm. All costs are in Indian rupees. Assume that FC are Rp1,000 and that the market price is Rp1,400.

Output (Q)	VC
1	1,200
2	2,200
3	3,000
4	3,600
5	4,400
6	5,400
7	6,600
8	8,000
9	9,600
10	11,400
11	13,400

1 What is the profit maximizing level of output? (Choose the highest Q for which the condition is satisfied.)
2 Calculate profits.
3 What is the shut-down price equal to?
4 Answer the same questions assuming that FC increase to Rp5,000. Explain why some answers do not change.
5 Answer all of the above assuming market price increased to Rp1,800.

Exercise 18

The following information pertains to the current position of a firm.

Q	P	MC	MR	AVC	ATC
1000	€1.50	€0.80	€0.90	€1.40	€1.80

1 Is this firm a perfectly competitive firm?
2 Is this firm maximizing its profits? If not, should it increase or decrease output? Why?
3 Calculate the firm's total revenues (TR).
4 Calculate the firm's total costs (TC).
5 Is this firm breaking even?
6 Should it perhaps shut down?

Exercise 19

Explain how profit is determined in perfect competition. Do firms necessarily strive to maximize profits?

Exercise 20

Explain, using appropriate diagrams, why profits are competed away in the long run in perfect competition. What if firms are making losses?

Monopoly

Remember

- A monopoly firm faces the (negatively sloped) market demand curve which is also its average revenue (AR) curve. As a result, marginal revenue (MR) lies below this and so P (= AR) > MR.

- If demand is linear then MR is also linear and has the same vertical intercept and double the slope. Also, at that Q at which MR is zero, PED is 1 (so, it is the mid-point of the demand (and AR) curve. That is the output that a revenue maximizing firm will choose since maximization of revenue requires that MR = 0.

- Barriers are defined as anything that deters entry. They can be natural (or structural), strategic (or created by firms) or created by the state: for example,

massive economies of scale are a natural barrier, advertising and brand names are barriers created by firms and patents are a state-created barrier.

- Monopoly is both allocatively and productively inefficient but may prove dynamically efficient.

- Firms with significant monopoly power are a cause for market failure: governments try to curb their market power, for example by regulating their behaviour, by breaking them up and by liberalizing trade so they face competition from abroad.

- A natural monopoly is the result of very significant scale economies for the relevant output range. One firm can therefore produce any relevant rate of output at a lower unit cost than two firms could.

Tip

When drawing the monopoly equilibrium position diagram, a very common mistake is to get the price charged by the monopolist wrong. To avoid making this error, find the profit-maximizing output where MR = MC and then go all the way up to the demand curve to find the price. Some candidates think that the price is much lower, where MR intersects MC.

Tip

- A profit-maximizing monopoly firm never chooses an output level Q corresponding to the inelastic portion of the demand curve it faces.

- A revenue-maximizing monopoly firm produces more and so charges less.

- A monopoly firm does not have a supply curve: only perfectly competitive firms and markets have supply curves.

Tip

You cannot compare a perfectly competitive firm with a monopoly firm: you can only compare a perfectly competitive market with a monopoly market. So, diagrammatically, start off with a perfectly competitive market (simply, a linear demand–supply diagram) and then assume that this market is monopolized: just draw an MR curve with double the slope of the demand curve.

Tip

Since the defining characteristic of a natural monopoly is the existence of very significant economies of scale within the relevant output range, make sure that you draw a steeply falling LRAC curve.

Tip

The existence of entry barriers means that the short run and long run equilibrium position of a monopoly firm does not differ.

Example 24

Show using an appropriate diagram, why monopoly worsens income distribution.

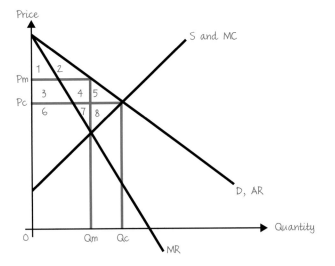

Figure 1.45

The question refers to the transfer of surplus from consumers to producers that occurs when a competitive industry is monopolized, assuming that the production technology and so MC remain unchanged.

The competitive industry will produce Qc units at Pc (where D intersects the supply curve).

The monopoly firm will choose Qm units and sell them at Pm as it is able to restrict output and raise the price. At Qm, MR = MC.

Remember that the consumer surplus is the area below the demand curve and above the price for the relevant output range, while producer surplus is the area below the price and above supply (i.e. MC) for the relevant output range. The relevant output range when the industry is competitive is (0,Qc) whereas it becomes (0,Qm) when it is monopolized. The table below summarizes the changes.

	If the market is perfectly competitive	If the market is a monopoly
Consumer surplus	Area (1, 2, 3, 4, 5)	Area (1, 2)
Producer surplus	Area (6, 7, 8)	Area (6, 7, 3, 4)

Consumers lose area (3, 4, 5) of which area (3) and area (4) are transferred to the monopolist.

The monopolist gains from consumers area (3) and area (4) and loses area (8).

Thus income is transferred from consumers to producers. Consumers were buying units 0Qm at a lower price Pc. Now they are paying (Pm — Pc) more for each of these units because of the monopoly power.

Note that area (5) which consumers lose and area (8) which the monopolist loses are gained by no-one: their sum is the welfare loss society suffers as a result of the monopoly power.

Example 25

The table below provides data on demand and cost conditions for a monopoly firm facing fixed costs equal to $100.00. All monetary figures are in dollars.

Q	P	VC
1	200	100
2	190	175
3	180	225
4	170	265
5	150	310
6	140	360
7	130	420
8	110	510
9	90	595
10	70	685
11	100	780
12	90	880
13	80	985
14	70	1,095

1 Determine the firm's best output choice and the price it will set assuming it is a profit-maximizing firm.

To determine the optimal output and price we need to calculate MR and MC. Thus we first need to calculate from the data TR. Since fixed costs do not affect MC, we do not need to calculate TC at this point.

Q	P	TR	MR	MC
1	200	200		
2	190	380	180	75
3	180	540	160	50
4	170	680	140	40
5	160	800	120	45
6	150	900	100	50
7	140	980	80	60
8	130	1,040	60	90
9	120	1,080	40	85
10	110	1,100	20	90
11	100	1,100	0	95
12	90	1,080	−20	100
13	80	1,040	−40	105
14	70	980	−60	110

The last unit for which MR exceeds MC (and so, by producing and selling it, the firm will increase whatever profits it was making per period) is unit 7. For that unit, MR = $80 whereas MC = $60, so by producing and selling it the firm adds 20 dollars to its profits. If, though, it produced unit 8 it would enjoy lower profits per period as the MR for the unit 8 is $60 and the MC of the eighth unit is $90: it would be lowering the per period profits by $30.

2 What are profits equal to?

We need to calculate the TR from selling 7 units and the TC of producing 7 units. The TR collected are the product of the price per unit multiplied by the number of units sold, or $7.00 × 140 = $980.00. The total costs incurred are the sum of the variable costs for 7 units ($420.00) plus the fixed costs of $100.00, or $520.00. Economic profits are therefore TR(7) − TC(7) = $460.00.

3 If the goal was to maximize revenue would it increase output? What would happen to price?

Revenue maximization requires producing and selling all units for which MR is positive up until that unit for which MR = 0. The table above shows that MR is zero for unit 11. Since output is higher the price at which it will be absorbed by the market must be lower: 11 units per period would be absorbed at a market price of $100.00 per unit.

Example 26

The diagram below illustrates the various output choices for a monopoly firm.

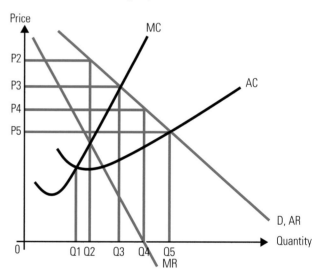

Figure 1.46

1 At what output rate will profits be maximized? Why?

At Q = Q2, as at that output MC = MR (and MC is rising).

2 At what output rate will revenues be maximized? Why?

At Q = Q4, as at that output MR = 0.

3 At what output rate will society suffer no welfare loss? Why?

At Q = Q3, as at that output P = MC so allocative efficiency would have been achieved.

4 At what output rate will technical efficiency be achieved? Why?

At Q = Q1, as at that output MC = AC and so AC is at a minimum.

5 At what output rate will the monopolist break even?

At Q = Q5, as breaking even requires zero profits and, at Q5, AR = AC.

Example 27

The following information pertains to the current position of a firm. All monetary figures are in euros.

Q	P	MC	MR	AC
25,000	190.00	80.00	80.00	150.00

1 Is this firm a perfectly competitive firm?

No, since P ≠ MR. Here P (= €190.00) > MR (= €80.00) which implies that the firm is facing a negatively sloped demand curve.

2 Is this firm maximizing its profits? If not, should it increase or decrease output? Why?

Yes it is, since at the chosen output rate MR = MC.

3 Is it making non-negative profits?

For profits to be non-negative P (= AR) must be at least equal to AC. Here, P is bigger than AC (€190.00 > €150.00).

4 Calculate the firm's total revenue.

$$TR(25,000) = P \times Q$$
$$= 190 \times 25,000$$
$$= 4,750,000$$

5 Calculate the firm's total cost.

$$TC(25,000) = ATC(25,000) \times Q$$
$$= 150 \times 25,000$$
$$= 3,750,000$$

6 Calculate the profits earned

$$\pi(25,000) = TR(25,000) - TC(25,000)$$
$$= 4,750,000 - 3,750,000$$
$$= 1,000,000$$

7 Illustrate the current position of this firm.

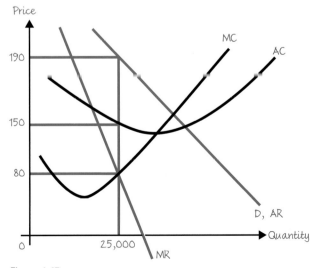

Figure 1.47

Example 28

The following information pertains to the current position of a firm. All monetary figures are in euros.

Q	AR	MC	MR	AC
111,000	50.00	111.00	– 25.00	70.00

1 Is this firm a perfectly competitive firm?

No, since P ≠ MR. (Remember that P is always the same as AR.)

2 Is this firm maximizing its profits? If not, should it increase or decrease output? Why?

This firm is not maximizing profits as MR ≠ MC. Since MR > MC, the firm should decrease output to maximize profits. (Remember that MR can be negative as it is the change in revenues if output per period increases by one unit; this implies that revenues for this firm would increase if it lowered output.)

3 Is this firm making non-negative profits?

No. It is making negative profits (losses) as AR is less than AC.

4 Calculate its economic profits.

$$TR(111,000) = P \times Q$$
$$= 50 \times 111,000$$
$$= 5,550,000$$
$$TC(111,000) = ATC(111,000) \times Q$$
$$= 70 \times 111,000$$
$$= 7,770,000$$
$$\pi(111,000) = TR(111,000) - TC(111,000)$$
$$= 5,550,000 - 7,770,000$$
$$= -2,220,000 \text{ (i.e. losses)}$$

5 Draw a diagram illustrating its current output level and the above values.

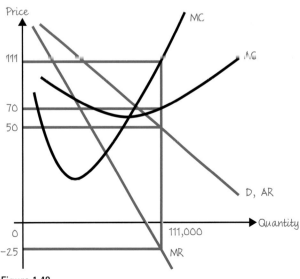

Figure 1.48

6 Draw a diagram illustrating its current position.

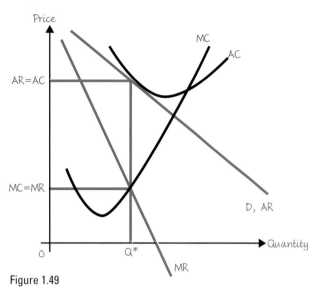

Figure 1.49

Example 29

The table below provides data on demand and cost conditions for a monopoly firm.

Output (Q)	P (per unit)	TR	MR	ATC	TC	MC
100,000	100			20		
200,000	80			15		
300,000	60			$16\frac{2}{3}$		
400,000	40			$23\frac{1}{2}$		
500,000	20			30		

1 Complete the table.

Remember that $TR = P \times Q$; $MR = \frac{\Delta(TR)}{\Delta Q}$ (in this case you need to find the change in Q as output does not increase by one unit at a time); $TC = ATC \times Q$; $MC = \frac{\Delta(TC)}{\Delta Q}$ (here, you also need to calculate the change in Q).

Output (Q)	P (per unit)	TR	MR	ATC	TC	MC
100,000	100	10,000,000		20	2,000,000	
200,000	80	16,000,000	60	15	3,000,000	10
300,000	60	18,000,000	20	$16\frac{2}{3}$	5,000,000	20
400,000	40	16,000,000	-20	$23\frac{1}{2}$	9,400,000	44
500,000	20	10,000,000	-60	30	15,000,000	56

2 Determine the profit-maximizing level of output for this firm.

Maximum profits occur at $Q = 300,000$ units (which will be sold at $P = 60$) as at that Q, $MR = MC = 20$.

Exercise 21

The diagram below illustrates the demand and costs of a firm. Using the information presented in the diagram answer the questions that follow.

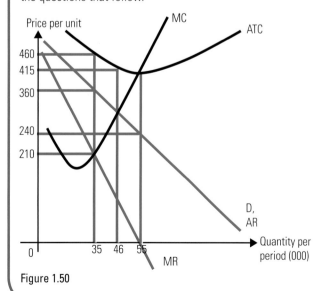

Figure 1.50

1 Is this a perfectly competitive firm? Explain.
2 Determine the profit-maximizing level of output. Explain.
3 Calculate the maximum level of profits earned.
4 Determine the revenue-maximizing level of output. Explain.
5 Calculate the maximum revenues earned.
6 Will this firm immediately exit? What does its decision depend on?

Exercise 22

Assume a firm producing an output rate Q for which:

AC	P	MR	MC
45	60	– 30	60

Figures are in the currency of your choice.

1 Is this a perfectly competitive firm? Why?
2 Is it making positive economic profits? Why?
3 Has this firm chosen the best output rate if its goal is to maximize profits? Why?

4 Would you recommend it to increase or decrease output? Why?
5 Is it productively efficient? Why?
6 Is allocative efficiency achieved? Why?
7 If it decreases output will unit costs decrease or increase? Why?
8 Should it produce more or less to maximize revenues instead? Why?
9 Should it produce more or less to break even? Why?
10 Illustrate its position on an appropriate diagram.

Exercise 23

Evaluate the view that a perfectly competitive market is more efficient than a monopoly market. Can monopolies benefit society? Illustrate your answer using appropriate diagrams.

Exercise 24

Using an appropriate diagram and examples, explain the concept of a natural monopoly. What problem will such a firm face if asked by the regulator to price its output efficiently (i.e. to set price equal to marginal cost)?

Exercise 25

Explain how is it possible for a firm to continue operating in the short run, even if revenues are insufficient to cover all of its costs.

Exercise 26

Discuss whether a monopoly (or, more generally, firms with significant market power and the ability to maintain supernormal profits in the long run) may benefit the public.

Exercise 27

Explain why, for a monopoly firm (and more generally any firm facing a negatively sloped demand curve), the MR curve is not identical to the AR curve.

Exercise 28

Explain why breaking up a monopoly into smaller firms may not always be a good idea. What other solutions can governments adopt to check monopoly power?

Monopolistic competition

Remember

- Product differentiation is what distinguishes monopolistic competition from perfect competition.

- If the product a firm is selling is considered by consumers to be even slightly different from what its competitors are selling, then if it decides to increase price it will not lose all of its customers. It therefore faces a negatively sloped demand for its product and has a tiny degree of monopoly power.

- Since in monopolistic competition there is nothing to deter entry of new firms into the market, it follows that whenever there are supernormal profits they will be competed away. The short run diagram may be identical to the typical monopoly diagram but the long run diagram must show zero economic profits and so the AC curve is tangent to the AR curve.

Example 30

Determine whether the following statements are true or false. Explain your answers.

1 Firms in monopolistic competition have monopoly power and are large in size.

False. Even though some degree of monopoly power is present, the large number of firms in the market implies that the share of each is small. The market power each firm has is very limited as each one has many competing firms selling very close substitutes.

2 In the monopolistically competitive model firms can earn supernormal profits in the long run.

False. Freedom of entry drives any supernormal profits to zero. If supernormal profits exist, new firms enter. As a result, the demand that each firm faces 'shrinks and tilts' meaning that it decreases and becomes more price elastic as more and closer substitutes are available to consumers. Entry continues until there is no more incentive for it to take place, i.e. until profits become zero and each firm earns normal profits.

3 As more and more firms enter a monopolistically competitive market the demand each firm faces will eventually become perfectly elastic.

False. The goods available to consumers may be extremely close substitutes but are not considered identical, i.e. perfect substitutes. Only if consumers considered the goods available as perfect substitutes would the demand each firm faced become perfectly elastic. In that case, the model would have become perfectly competitive.

4 In monopolistic competition firms are forced to produce with minimum unit costs.

False. Since demand is not perfectly elastic but negatively sloped, it must be tangent to the U-shaped AC curve at the left of its minimum. Firms in monopolistic competition produce with excess capacity.

5 Since there is a huge variety of a breakfast cereal available to consumers in some countries, it follows that the breakfast cereal industry is a good example of monopolistic competition.

False. There may be many different kinds of cereal but the market is dominated by a handful of firms (such as Kellogg's and Nestlé). These firms produce a huge variety of cereals to make it difficult for new firms to enter the industry (i.e. as a strategic, firm-created entry barrier).

Example 31

Explain how the profits and the demand curve a monopolistically competitive firm faces are affected by the entry of new firms. Use a diagram to illustrate if possible.

As more firms enter a monopolistically competitive market, the demand that each firm faces decreases: each enjoys a smaller market share. Diagrammatically, the demand curve that each firm faces shifts left (or 'shrinks'). However, as consumers will have even more and closer substitutes available to choose from, the PED increases ('tilts'). Entry continues until economic profits become zero, i.e. each firm earns as much as it would earn in the next best alternative with the same risk (normal profits). The process is illustrated in the diagram below: demand decreases from D1 to D2 to D3 and 'tilts' becoming more price elastic. At D3, economic profits are zero as demand (which is also AR curve) is at a tangent to AC.

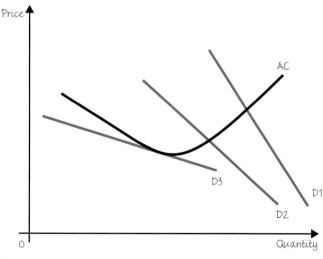

Figure 1.51

Example 32

What are the most important points to mention in a comparison of monopolistic competition with perfect competition?

- Both markets assume many firms as well as no entry barriers.
- As a result, firms are typically small in size and in the long run economic profits are driven to down to zero in both models.
- However, in perfect competition the product is homogeneous while in monopolistic it is differentiated, so the perfect competitor is a price taker whereas the monopolistic competitor is a price setter.
- Consumers may benefit from the variety that exists in monopolistically competitive markets and the greater probability of finding a product that better satisfies their needs or wants.
- On the other hand, this variety may be responsible for the higher than minimum average costs characterizing monopolistically competitive firms, the resulting excess capacity and the technical (productive) inefficiency.
- In perfect competition allocative efficiency, on top of productive efficiency, is achieved (but neither is achieved in monopolistic competition), and neither market structure permits significant economies of scale, the funding of R&D or leads to technological innovations.
- Lastly, in monopolistic competition, firms resort to non-price competition while in perfect competition not only are firms price takers (atomistic competition) but other forms of competition are absent.

Example 33

What are the most important points to mention in a comparison of monopolistic competition with monopoly?

- In monopoly entry barriers are present while in monopolistic competition these are absent.
- Positive consequences of the absence of barriers include that entry will drive profits down to normal, drive price close to marginal cost and also exert downward pressure on costs, forcing the least efficient firms to fold.
- Positive consequences of the existence of barriers include that firms will be able to maintain supernormal profits that could be used to finance expensive R&D projects leading to technological innovations.

- Assuming that barriers are not prohibitive then these large (dominating) firms with monopoly power will be forced to innovate to maintain their dominance.
- Both structures fail to achieve allocative efficiency but, since in monopolistic competition any monopoly power decreases dramatically as a result of entry and product differentiation, the price charged will not be much higher than the marginal cost of producing the last unit.
- Both structures fail to achieve productive efficiency, but in monopolistic competition the existence of many other similar firms forces these firms to decrease costs whereas in monopoly this is not the case.
- Then again, monopoly firms that are large in size may be able to employ technologies that create significant economies of scale (rendering the static efficiencies meaningless).
- Remember also that the non-price competition in which monopolistically competitive firms engage (and which is absent from monopoly structures) may entail significant benefits for consumers.

Example 34

The diagram below illustrates the demand and costs of a firm. Using the information presented in the diagram to answer the questions that follow.

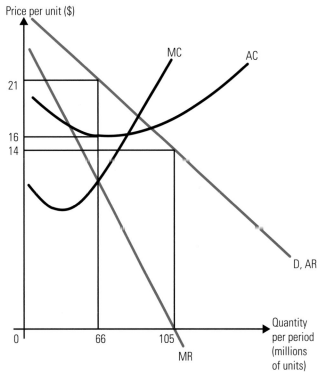

Figure 1.52

1 Is this firm a perfectly competitive firm? Explain.

This firm is not a perfectly competitive firm as it faces a negatively sloped demand curve.

2 What is the profit-maximizing level of output for this firm? Why?

The profit-maximizing level of output is determined at that level at which MR = MC (and MC is upward sloping). This is the case at 66 million units per period.

3 Calculate the economic profits this firm is making. Explain every step of your answer.

To calculate economic profits, first we have to calculate total revenues collected, total costs incurred and then subtract the total costs of the firm from the total revenues.

Total revenues are found by multiplying the price per unit (or, equivalently, the average revenue) by the number of units. The price at which this market will absorb 66 million units per period is equal to $21 per unit so:

TR = 21 × 66
    = 1,386 million dollars,
    or 1.386 billion dollars

Total costs are found by multiplying the output chosen (66 million units) by the average cost of producing this quantity (the cost per unit) which is $16 per unit so:

TC = 66 × 16
    = 1,056 million dollars,
    or 1.056 billion dollars

It follows that:

π = TR − TC
  = 1,386 − 1,056
  = 330 million dollars per period

4 Calculate the size of this firm's sales revenues if it decides to increase output to 105 million units.

Since the market will absorb 105 million units per period at a market price of $14 per unit, total revenues will equal:

TR = P × Q
   = 14 × 105
   = 1,470 million dollars or, 1.47 billion dollars per period

5 Could this firm increase its sales revenues if it increased output? Explain.

No, it could not as sales revenue maximization occurs at that level of output at which marginal revenue is zero and this (MR = 0) occurs at 105 million units per period. Any deviation (increase or decrease in output from this level) will lead to a decrease in total revenues collected for this firm.

6 Could this be a short run or a long run equilibrium position? Explain your answer.

Whether this is a short run or a long run equilibrium position depends upon whether or not there are barriers to entry into this market. It could be a long run equilibrium position only if entry barriers are present. In such a case, the illustrated firm could be either a monopoly or an oligopolist. If the illustrated firm is a monopolistic competitor then this equilibrium could not be a long run equilibrium position as the supernormal profits enjoyed would induce entry into this market.

Exercise 29

What possible advantages are there for consumers in monopolistic competition?

Exercise 30

Using appropriate diagrams, compare and contrast monopolistic competition with both perfect competition and monopoly.

Oligopoly

Remember

- The defining characteristic of oligopoly is interdependence. If the outcome to an action that a firm takes depends on the reaction of the other firms then the market is oligopolistic.

- Game theory is used to best illustrate the interdependence in oligopolistic structures.

- Competition is typically restricted to non-price methods because of the risk of a price war. Non-price competition may be in the form of advertising and brand name creation, product differentiation and innovation, offering volume discounts, offering gifts or coupons, offering extended guarantees or after-sales service, etc.

- In the prisoners' dilemma game the dominant strategy for both players is to cheat even though it leads to a solution where both players are worse off: both parties end up worse off by independently pursuing their own self-interest. When an agreement in this context cannot be enforced, it collapses. If the game is repeated then simple rules may be arrived at which induce collusion, for example 'tit for tat'.

- The n firm concentration ratio (CR) is nothing but the proportion of industry sales accounted for by the largest n firms of the industry. Typically the CR is calculated for the largest 4, 8 or 20 largest firms or for the 3, 5 or 10 largest firms of the industry.

Example 35

Determine whether the following statements are true or false. Explain your answers.

1 In the prisoners' dilemma game, each player's best strategy would be the same one they would choose if they behaved cooperatively.

   False. The main point of this game is that the cooperative (best for both players) solution cannot be reached because confessing (or cheating) is the dominant strategy.

2 In the kinked demand curve model, an increase in variable costs will lead to a higher price but not a change in fixed costs.

   False. It is true that a change in fixed costs will not affect output in any profit-maximizing situation (unless revenues do not even cover variable costs) but the whole point of the kinked demand curve model is that a change in variable (and so marginal) costs will not affect the price (assuming that the resulting change in marginal cost is within the discontinuity of the MR curve).

3 A CR measures the proportion of total sales in an industry produced by the largest firms.

   True. It is typically the sales of the largest n firms divided by the total industry sales. Instead of the sales (turnover) of the largest n firms, a CR can focus on the capital employed or employment. If the industry is perfectly competitive then the CR will be close to zero while in a monopoly it is equal to 1.

4 In the price leadership model it is assumed that firms adjust their pricing decisions to match the price of the dominant firm.

   True. There is a dominant firm, usually the largest or the most successful in the past to predict market swings, which sets the price while the others act as price takers adjusting their prices accordingly.

Tip

- Use a simple monopoly diagram to illustrate a cartel or tacit collusion and joint profit maximization.

- Use the kinked demand curve to show price rigidity in non-collusive oligopoly in the face of changes in marginal cost.

- Use a simple prisoners' dilemma setup to illustrate strategic interdependence and that lack of coordination leads to sub-optimal solutions.

Tip

Firms in the kinked demand curve model are still considered profit-maximizing firms: do not change the behavioural assumption to revenue maximization.

Tip

To construct the pay-off matrix for a prisoners' dilemma game you must make sure of the following:

- The pay-offs in cell II and cell III below are symmetric (mirror images) where one player does **very** well (the best) and the other **very** poorly (the worst).

- In both outcomes I and IV each player does as well as the other player.

- Pay-offs in outcome I are better than payoffs in outcome IV for both players.

Cell I	Cell II
Cell III	Cell IV

Example 36

Explain how strategic interdependence is illustrated in the game below and determine the dominant strategy, explaining your choice.

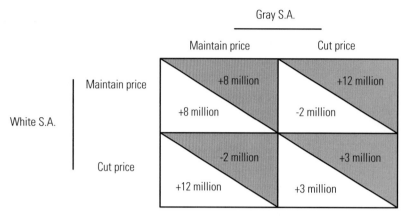

Figure 1.53

The game illustrates two duopolists (an oligopoly consisting of two rival firms): Gray and White. Each firm has two options, to maintain the price charged or to cut the price. Each firm realizes that the outcome of any action it decides to take depends on how its rival will react. For example, White cannot be sure whether maintaining the price (say, in dollars) will lead to supernormal profits equal to 8 million or to a loss of 2 million. Equivalently, if White chooses to cut price, it could either make 12 million if Gray maintains the price, or make 3 million if Gray also cuts the price. The outcome of either decision depends on the reaction of Gray.

To determine the dominant strategy, White's chief executive thinks:

'If my rival, Gray, cuts price, then I will make 3 million if I also cut price but I will lose 2 million if I am the "sucker" and I maintain the price. So, if he cuts price my best response is also to cut price.

If my rival, Gray, maintains price, then I will make 8 million if I also maintain price, but I will make 12 million if I "defect" and cut price. So, if he maintains price my best response is to cut price.

In other words, no matter what Gray does, I am better off if I cut price: cutting price is the best strategy for White. Symmetrically, it is the best strategy for Gray. So, cutting price is the dominant strategy.'

The firms will each make only 3 million which is less than the 8 million each would make if they maintained price.

Example 37

The table below shows the annual sales (turnover) of the 20 supermarket chains that existed in Greece in 2005. Joey, a junior analyst at Analytica, is trying to determine whether the industry was oligopolistic or not. Help him to reach a valid conclusion.

Firm	Annual sales
Carrefour Marinopoloulos	1,775,167,212
AB – Vasilopoulos	880,342,000
Sklavenitis	806,618,814
Veropoulos	588,577,792
Atlantic	560,871,018
Metro	499,827,469
Masoutis	477,611,243
Dia	354,771,108
Galaxias	320,703,016
Arvanitidis	206,167,091
Alfa Delta	155,731,144
INKA Chanion	113,126,837
Chalkiadakis	96,943,578
Balis	73,238,026
Market In	71,505,593
Xynos	69,016,546
Bazaar	68,697,754
Super Market Larissa	58,872,472
Extra	48,851,585
Doukas	42,867,233

The industry was not a monopoly as the largest firm did not dominate, having a market share of only 24%. Since both perfect and monopolistic competition require the existence of very many small firms, each being able to act independently of the rest, it seems safe for Joey to rule out both these market structures. This leaves him with oligopoly, but he should calculate the 5 and 10 firm CRs to determine the extent of concentration in the industry.

Remember that the 5CR = $\dfrac{\sum\limits_{1}^{5} s_i}{\sum\limits_{1}^{n} s_i}$ or, the proportion

of total industry sales accounted for by the five largest firms. Here, the sum of the sales of the five largest was almost 4,612 million euros (4,611,576,836 to be exact) while the total industry sales were almost 7,270 million euros (7,269,507,531 to be exact). Their share was 63% of the total.

The 10CR calculates the share of the 10 largest firms and is equal to 89% of the total. It seems therefore that the industry should be considered an oligopoly. If Joey dug deeper and examined market shares pertaining to specific geographic regions, then the shares of the largest firms in specific markets may be even bigger.

Example 38

The table below shows the annual sales (turnover) of the five largest banks and of the five largest insurance companies in Ugamiland. In an analysis of these companies, why could using CRs prove misleading?

Firm's name	Banking industry
	Market share
A	23%
B	19%
C	21%
D	17%
E	20%

Firm's name	Insurance industry
	Market share
A	88%
B	3%
C	3%
D	3%
E	3%

Calculating the 5CR reveals that these firms in both markets control 100% of sales. If an analyst did not have access to firm-level data but only the 5CR figure, he or she could argue that both markets are oligopolistic. In fact, only the banking industry is an oligopoly as the insurance market is dominated by firm A which controls 88% of the total market share. CRs should therefore be used with caution as they may not reveal the true picture. There are other statistics that may be used to arrive at a clearer picture, such as the Hirschman–Herfindahl index (not in the syllabus), which takes the sum of the squared market share of each firm.

Exercise 31

Determine whether the following statements are true or false. Explain your answers. Use a diagram to illustrate if possible.

1 In a duopoly, if firm A expects firm B to follow a price decrease and not to follow a price increase then demand is price inelastic below the current price.

2 In the kinked demand curve model it is assumed that each firm believes that other firms will join in a price increase but not in a price decrease.

3 Each member of a cartel has the incentive to expand output beyond the quota agreed upon.

4 In an oligopoly, each firm faces a demand for its product that is independent of the behaviour of rival sellers.

5 In a cartel, firms coordinate their behaviour to act as a monopoly.

Exercise 32

'In an oligopoly, only the firms benefit; consumers invariably lose.' Discuss.

Exercise 33

'One benefit of oligopolistic markets is that the market price does not fluctuate with every change in demand or in cost conditions the way it does in a perfectly competitive market.' Discuss.

Exercise 34

Explain the dilemma that a firm in an oligopolistic market faces.

Price discrimination

Remember

- A firm must have some monopoly power to price discriminate. It must also be able to prevent resale of the good from one market to the other and, for some reason, consumers in one market must be prepared to pay more (in other words price elasticities of demand across markets must differ).

- If a firm sells in market A at a price that is 10 & higher than the price in market B, because it costs the firm 10 & more to market the product in market B, then this is not a case of price discrimination. The price ratios in the two markets must differ from ratios of production costs or provision costs in the two markets to qualify as price discrimination.

Tip

There are two popular diagrams used to illustrate price discrimination. 'Occam's razor' is a line of reasoning that suggests you use the simplest method that drives the point home. In this case it is the 'back-to-back' diagram, where we assume for simplicity that marginal costs are constant. Drawing two demand (and MR) linear curves with different slopes will lead you to the desired result that in third degree price discrimination the highest price is charged in the market with the relatively inelastic demand.

Example 39

Rewrite the following statements and fill in the blanks by using the terms provided below. Some terms may be used more than once or not at all.

monopoly power	marginal cost	higher	pricing
fewer	ability	consumer	
profits	perfectly	inelastic	

Price discrimination is a (1)_____ policy that many firms often adopt to further increase their (2)_____. Simply, they manage to appropriate part of the (3)_____ surplus by charging different prices to different consumers. Consumers with a greater willingness and (4)_____ to pay will be charged more as they face (5)_____ substitutes or have a (6)_____ income. In either case, their demand will be more price (7)_____.

The price-discriminating firm must enjoy some degree of (8)_____, defined as the ability of some firms to set price above (9)_____. This really just means that (10)_____ competitive firms cannot adopt such a policy.

(1) pricing, (2) profits, (3) consumer, (4) ability,
(5) fewer, (6) higher, (7) inelastic, (8) monopoly power,
(9) marginal cost, (10) perfectly

Exercise 35

Explain using examples the conditions that need to be satisfied for a firm to be able to practise price discrimination successfully, illustrating its pricing decision with an appropriate diagram. Are all consumers always necessarily worse off when such a pricing policy is adopted by a firm?

2.1 The level of overall macroeconomic activity

Economic activity

Remember

- 'Domestic' refers to the boundaries of a country whereas 'national' refers to the nationality of the factors of production.

  The difference between GDP and GNI is that GNI includes incomes earned abroad by nationals of the country while it excludes incomes earned domestically by foreign factors (which are paid abroad).

- A 'nominal' variable (such as nominal GDP) refers to a variable without having isolated or adjusted for changing prices so it is measured at current prices.

  But a 'real' variable (such as real GDP) refers to a variable measured at constant prices of some base year; real GDP and real GNP focus on the volume and not the value of output produced.

- Per capita means per person, so to arrive at a 'per capita' figure just divide that figure by the population of the country. For example, per capita GDP is arrived at by simply dividing real GDP of a country by its total population.

- 'Green GDP' refers to output after factoring in the detrimental effect of the production process on the environment. Specifically:

  green GDP
  = GDP − cost of natural resource depletion − cost of environmental depletion.

Example 1

Why is it important to measure national income (or output)?

We cannot evaluate the performance of an economy if we have no measurements available. We cannot determine whether an economy is doing better or worse this year compared with last year or five years ago if there is no measurement of economic activity. We cannot compare the performance of one economy against other economies at a point in time or over some period if we do not know how total output and income have behaved. If performance has been judged unsatisfactory then policy makers will need measurements to devise and implement policies to improve performance and also to later judge the effectiveness of their policy choices.

National income statistics therefore help in evaluating economic performance through time, across countries as well as in devising and evaluating policies.

Note though that the term 'performance' is rather general and may mean different things to different people, so conclusions about 'performance' may be misleading. For example, if based on the use of GDP figures it is determined that an economy has grown rapidly over the past decade,

is it safe to conclude that its performance has improved? What if this increase in output and incomes has come at a terrible environmental cost? Green GDP statistics may help in such assessments as the environmental cost is accounted for in such statistic. Still, such statistics are aggregates and may not reveal important information so they have to be used with extra care.

Example 2

Rewrite the following statements and fill in the blanks by using the terms provided below.

base	value
incomes	living standards
firms	boundaries
real	circular flow
non-marketed	households
goods and services	constant prices
nominal	output
green	factors of production
final	land, labour, capital and entrepreneurship
rent, wages, interest and profits	

The inner circle of the (1) _____ diagram illustrates the economic links between (2) _____ and (3) _____. There is a flow of (4) _____ from households to firms and, in the opposite direction, a flow of (5) _____ from firms to households. These are considered (6) _____ flows whereas in the opposite direction there is a money flow which refers to the (7) _____ paid by firms to households for use of the factors supplied. The factors of production include (8) _____ and their rewards or payments are the sum of (9) _____.

GDP is a measure of the total (10) _____ of an economy in a year. More specifically it is the (11) _____ of all (12) _____ goods and services produced within the (13) _____ of an economy over a period of time, typically a year.

(14) _____GDP measures output at current prices, i.e. the price prevailing each year. Real GDP measures output valued at (15) _____, i.e. the prices prevailing during the (16) _____ year.

If the deleterious effect of many production processes on the environment is accounted for, then we will arrive at an estimate of (17) _____ GDP.

Using national income statistics to make inferences about (18) _____ is fraught with problems. For example, subsistence agriculture in developing nations and, more generally, (19) _____ output is not included even though these are income-generating activities.

(1) base, (2) households, (3) firms, (4) factor of production, (5) goods and services, (6) real, (7) incomes, (8) land, labour, capital and entrepreneurship, (9) rent, wages, interest and profits, (10) output, (11) value, (12) final, (13) boundaries, (14) nominal, (15) constant prices, (16) base, (17) green, (18) living, (19) non-marketed

Example 3

National income figures are often used to compare living standards across countries and through time. Explain the problems associated with this practice.

Bear in mind first of all that if any such attempt is made it is better to use GNI rather than GDP figures, as GNI focuses on incomes earned by the nationals of a country while GDP focuses on output produced inside the country. But such a figure must be divided by the population to adjust for the size of the country. And, if comparisons are made through time, then real and not nominal figures must be used to adjust for changing prices.

The major argument in favour of using per capita income as a measure of living standards is that if it is higher it implies that people command more output, and more output is considered better than less output.

If per capita income is used as a measure of living standards we should bear these points in mind:

■ It is just an average income figure providing no information on its distribution.

■ It reveals nothing about its composition.

■ It does not include the value of leisure.

■ It does not include non-marketed output such as the output and income of a parent helping his or her child with homework, or of subsistence agricultural output in a developing country.

■ It does not include parallel market activity that goes unrecorded.

■ It does not account for pollution and other negative externalities that the production process often creates.

These are just some of the most important issues to be aware of when national income statistics are used to assess living standards.

HL
Calculations

To calculate nominal GDP from expenditure data you just need to add together consumption, investment, government expenditure and net exports or:

nominal GDP = C + I + G + (X − M)

- To calculate GNP/GNI you will be given (or you will have computed) GDP values, and then you just need to add net factor (or property) income from abroad which is the difference between income earned abroad minus income paid abroad. Remember that, in GDP, 'domestic' refers to whatever economic activity takes place inside the borders of a country, whereas, in GNI, 'national' focuses on the nationality of the factors of production involved irrespective of where the activity takes place. So once we have GDP figures we need to add incomes that domestic factors earned abroad (say, profits and wages) but subtract incomes that foreign factors earned domestically (again, for example, profits and wages). The difference is mostly a result of so-called multinational corporations and is a large amount for only a few countries.

- To calculate real GDP from nominal GDP data you need to divide the nominal GDP data by the price index for that year and multiply your result by 100. A price index is an average of the prices of goods and services expressed as an index number, i.e. as a pure number without units of measurement. A year (period) is chosen as the base (reference) year and the value of the index in all other years is expressed as a percentage of that in the base year (period). Typically, to calculate real GDP we use the so-called GDP deflator as the price index of choice (see more on the GDP deflator later).

Example 1

The following data refer to Fictionland in 2011.

Type of expenditure	Amount ($ billion)
Consumption expenditures (C)	35.86
Investment expenditures (I)	6.52
Government expenditures (G)	22.82
Export revenues (X)	8.6
Import expenditures (M)	9.8

Calculate nominal GDP from the expenditure approach.

Nominal GDP can be calculated from expenditure data using the relationship:
nominal GDP = C + I + G + (X − M)
So:
nominal GDP
= 35.86 + 6.52 + 22.82 + (8.6 − 9.8)
= $64.1 billion

Example 5

Assume that there are only two countries in the world, Fictionland and Fairyland. In 2011 there were a number of active Fairyland-owned corporations in Fictionland as well as many Fictionland-owned corporations operating successfully in Fairyland. If Fairyland-owned factors earned $1.3 billion in Fictionland whereas Fictionland-owned factors earned $1.1 billion in Fairyland, calculate Fictionland's GNP/GNI for 2011 (given that its GDP was estimated at $64.1 billion). What will the relationship between Fairyland's GDP and GNP/GNI be and why?

To calculate Fictionland's GNP/GNI we need to add net factor (or property) income from abroad to its GDP figure. This is equal to income earned abroad ($1.1 billion) minus income paid abroad ($1.3 billion):
1.1 − 1.3 = − $0.2 billion.

It follows that in 2011 Fictionland's GNP/GNI was
64.1 − 0.2 = $63.9 billion.

Since there are only two countries in the world it follows that net factor income for Fairyland was positive so its GNP/GNI was higher (by $0.2 billion) than whatever its GDP was.

Example 6

The table below provides nominal GDP figures for Freedmania between 2007 and 2011 as well as the price index for each year (2008 is the base year). Calculate the level of real GDP of Freedmania.

Year	Nominal GDP (€ billion)	Price index (2006 = 100)
2007	45.5	97.0
2008	49.3	100
2009	54.3	104.3
2010	60.4	107.4
2011	62.1	110.1

To calculate real GDP from nominal GDP figures you need to divide nominal GDP by a price index and multiply the result by 100.

Year	Calculation	Real GDP (7 billion) (2008 prices)
2007	$\dfrac{45.5}{97.0} \times 100$	46.91
2008	$\dfrac{49.3}{100} \times 100$	49.30
2009	$\dfrac{54.3}{104.3} \times 100$	52.06
2010	$\dfrac{60.4}{107.4} \times 100$	56.24
2011	$\dfrac{62.1}{110.1} \times 100$	56.40

Exercise 1

Explain why, if GDP of country A is double that of country B, it is potentially very misleading to conclude that living standards in country A are twice as high as living standards in country B.

Exercise 2

Explain why it is increasingly important for countries to measure green GDP alongside conventional GDP.

Exercise 3

The following data represent the GDP of a country at current prices in millions of euros and a comprehensive price index (a price deflator).

Year	2000	2001	2002	2003	2004	2005	2006	2007	2008	2009
Nominal GDP	136,281	146,428	156,615	172,431	185,266	194,819	209,919	225,539	235,679	233,046
Price index	100	103.12	103.40	103.92	102.95	102.81	103.12	103.06	103.20	101.20

Calculate real GDP for this economy.

The business cycle

Remember

- The short-term fluctuation of real GDP around its trend path is referred to as the business or trade cycle. The long-term trend is often referred to as the potential GDP of a country.

Tip

Be careful labelling or reading labels of business cycle diagrams. It makes a big difference whether the vertical axis measures the level of real GDP or the percentage change in real GDP. The horizontal axis measures time (not Q!).

If real GDP decreases then there is a recession. If growth decreases (but continues to be positive) there is no recession as real GDP continues to increase but at a slower rate.

Example 7

Match each term or concept with the appropriate definition or explanation.

1 Long-term trend
2 Recession
3 Expansion
4 Trough
5 Peak

a The maximum GDP recorded immediately before a downturn starts

b When real GDP increases

c The real GDP recorded immediately before recovery begins

d Potential GDP

e When real GDP falls for at least two consecutive quarters

(1, d), (2, e), (3, b), (4, c), (5, a)

Example 8

Answer the following questions based on the business cycle diagram below.

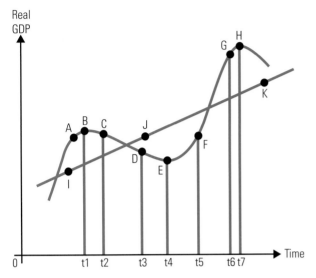

Figure 2.1

1 Technically when can we say that a recession starts?

An economy is in recession if real GDP decreases. A popular definition requires that this drop in output is at least for two consecutive quarters; in reality, calling a particular economic situation a recession is a much more complicated issue that experts decide. On the diagram, real GDP starts to fall immediately after time t1 and time t7.

2 Which points are known as 'peaks'?

Peaks are shown at Points B and H, which are immediately before real GDP starts to fall.

3 On the above diagram where can one say that growth is slowing down?

As long as growth is positive it means that real GDP is rising. A slowdown refers to decreasing but positive growth rates so points immediately before a peak are good candidates, such as points A and G (bear in mind that an alternative definition of a recession is that it is when growth is below the long-term trend rate).

4 Which levels of real GDP are equal to this economy's potential output?

These are any points on the long-term trend line such as I, J and K.

5 Which point is known as the trough of the cycle?

Point E would be called the trough as it represents the lowest level of real GDP immediately before it starts to increase.

6 What about points C, D and F?

At point C (time period t2) the economy is still operating above its long-term trend but economic activity is shrinking, whereas at point D it is below its potential and shrinking. At point F (time period t5) the economy continues to operate below its potential but economic activity is picking up.

7 If we define as natural unemployment the unemployment that exists when output is at its potential rate, then what can be said about unemployment at points (A, B, C) and (D, E, F) of the business cycle?

When output is greater than its potential rate (points A, B and C) then actual unemployment must be below its natural rate, while when the economy is operating below its potential rate (points D, E and F) then actual unemployment is above its natural rate.

Exercise 4

Use the diagram below to determine whether the following statements are true or false.

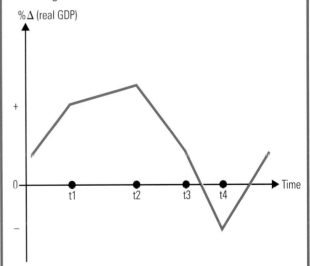

Figure 2.2

1 Economic growth is slowing down between time t1 and time t2.

2 The economy is in recession after time t2.

3 Real GDP is lower at time t2 than at time t1.

4 The economy was in recession in time t4.

5 Real GDP was lower at time t3 than it was at time t2.

6 Recovery begins after time t4.

Aggregate demand

Remember

■ Aggregate demand (AD) is not negatively sloped for the same reason that the demand for, say, pizza is negatively sloped: if the price of pizza rises then all other goods become relatively cheaper so buyers will substitute other goods for pizza. If all prices are rising (i.e. the **general** price level is increasing) such a substitution effect is not possible.

AD slopes downwards because of the 'wit' effects: wealth, interest rate and trade effects.

■ Often there is confusion because AD is the sum of C + I + G + NX which is the same as GDP measured from the expenditure approach. The crucial difference is that GDP is **actual** output that has been produced within an economy, while AD shows the **planned** level of spending at different possible average price levels by households, firms, the government and the rest of the world on domestic output. The key word is 'planned'.

■ As is the case with any function there can be no shift of AD when either of the variables represented on the two axes changes. Changes in the price level will lead to a movement along the AD curve while changes in national income cannot initiate an increase or decrease in AD. Once some other non-income factor induces a change in any of the components of AD, then AD will shift.

Example 1

Explain how each of the following entries may affect AD. Assume that the ceteris paribus clause holds.

1 Household and firm debt levels rise significantly.

This means that what households and firms owe to banks and other lending institutions has increased. Such a development may force both households and firms to cut down on their spending. The decrease in C and I will tend to decrease AD and shift it to the left.

2 Households become more optimistic.

Consumer confidence is a major driving force of household expenditures. Optimism and a positive outlook tend to induce greater spending, especially on durables such as cars, furniture and appliances. AD will tend to increase and shift to the right.

3 The exchange rate appreciates.

The exchange rate is the price of a currency expressed in terms of another currency. For example, €1.00 = $1.40. If the euro becomes more expensive (say, €1.00 = $1.50) then eurozone products will become more expensive in the USA and US goods cheaper in the eurozone. An appreciation will therefore tend to decrease net exports, and so AD, shifting it to the left.

4 The government decides to overhaul all infrastructure such as highways and bridges.

This is tantamount to saying that government expenditure, a component of AD, increases, so this would increase AD and shift it to the right.

5 The central bank decreases interest rates.

The central bank of a country is responsible for conducting monetary policy, including changing interest rates. The interest rate can be thought of as the cost of borrowing (or the reward for saving). If the central bank decreases interest rates then cheaper borrowing will induce more spending, leading to an increase in AD and a shift to the right.

6 Households demand more money to make the same transactions as a result of a higher price level and the resulting increase in the interest rate lowers their spending.

This will not shift AD as it is the average price level (represented on the vertical axis of the AD diagram) that initiates the change in spending. What is described above is the interest rate effect, one of the three reasons, together with the wealth and trade effects, responsible for the negative slope of AD. In any diagram, changes in the level of whatever variables are measured on the two axes of the diagram cannot shift the function illustrated.

7 A major trading partner resorts to increased levels of trade protection.

Trade protection is a term that refers to policies which aim to block imports from entering a country. The imports of a major trading partner are a country's exports so what the statement is really saying is that the country's exports will decrease. This will decrease AD and shift it to the left as exports are a component of AD.

8 Personal taxation increases.

If the government increases personal taxation then disposable income, defined as national income less direct taxes, will decrease. This will force households to cut down on their spending. AD will tend to decrease, shifting to the left.

9 Our major trading partner enters a severe recession.

A recession is defined as a period of time during which economic activity shrinks, i.e. real GDP and so incomes decrease. If, for some reason, that is the case for our trading partner then its spending will decrease. Part of its spending was on our goods and services. Since domestic goods and services sold abroad are a country's exports then the recession of our trading partner will tend to decrease our AD, shifting it to the left. This chain of events is referred to as the international transmission mechanism of the business cycle.

10 Expectations concerning continued growth increase share prices and so household wealth.

Here, increased wealth is a result of optimism concerning the future path of the economy. Consumption will tend to increase and so will AD, shifting it to the right.

11 Real wealth decreases as a result of a rising price level.

Here, it is the rise in the average price level that is responsible for the change in real wealth so there will be no shift in AD but only a movement along as people will tend to cut down on their spending.

Example 2

Define the term consumption expenditures. Briefly explain three important factors that may affect their level.

The term refers to spending by households on durable and non-durable goods as well as on services. Interest rates, the extent of household indebtedness and the degree of consumer confidence are major factors influencing consumption expenditures.

Interest rates determine the cost of borrowing from banks as well as the size of the reward for saving (defined as income not consumed). An increase in interest rates makes it more expensive to borrow and more attractive to save. Both effects will tend to lower household spending.

If a household has in the past borrowed heavily to finance spending sprees on goods and services, then a big proportion of its monthly income will have to be used to repay banks for the capital and interest on these loans. This will mean that less income will remain to spend on current output.

Even if interest rates are low and a household is not in large debt, individuals will think twice before they spend, especially on expensive durables, when they feel insecure and pessimistic about the future. If people are laid off or made redundant and unemployment is rising, even the ones lucky enough to have a job will cut down on their spending as a result of the rising uncertainty.

Exercise 1

Define the term investment expenditures. Explain three important factors that may affect their level. Provide examples to illustrate your answer.

Exercise 2

Explain two important factors that may affect the level of government expenditures. Provide examples to illustrate your answer.

Exercise 3

Explain three important factors that may affect the level of net exports of a country. Provide examples to illustrate your answer.

Aggregate supply

Remember

- Aggregate supply (AS) is not real GDP. AS shows how much firms are planning to offer at different average price levels per period of time.
- It is the 'stickiness' of money (nominal) wages that is responsible for short run AS sloping upward.
- According to the monetarist or new classical perspective it is the assumed flexibility of money wages and prices that is responsible for long run AS being vertical at the level of potential (full employment) output.
- The Keynesian model is effectively a short run model of national income determination as there is no guarantee that money wages and prices would adjust to restore full employment.

To accommodate the idea of natural unemployment in the Keynesian AS model, define potential output a little to the left of the vertical (third) section of the Keynesian AS curve. In this way, the Keynesian idea of full employment being a 'wall' beyond which output cannot increase can co-exist with the idea that there is always some unemployment in an economy (natural unemployment) at the potential output level.

It is a mistake to write about the 'long run Keynesian AS' curve. Remember that according to Keynes, 'in the long run we are all dead' so the distinction is meaningless. It suffices to write the 'Keynesian AS' curve.

Example 3

Explain factors that may cause the short run AS curve to shift.

Across the board, changes in the production costs of the firms of a country will shift its short run AS. Most importantly this includes changes in the level of money wages. But any factor that changes production costs will have the same effect, for example, changes in the prices for imported raw materials or a change in VAT or in subsidies.

Temporary (adverse or positive) non-economic factors may also create supply shocks.

A natural disaster (a hurricane, a tsunami or an earthquake) could decrease AS at least temporarily until destroyed infrastructure and capital is rebuilt. A bumper crop year for an economy with a large primary sector could increase short run AS.

As long as there is no change in the quantity or quality of available factors of production, of technology or of the institutional framework, supply-side changes affect only short run AS. Changes in the quantity and quality of available resources, in technology or in the institutional framework affect the long run but also the short run AS curves.

Example 4

Explain why the monetarist or new classical long run AS (LRAS) curve is vertical at the level of potential (full employment) output.

Potential output is defined as the level of output that an economy would produce if all prices and money (nominal) wages were flexible. Assume an economy in long run equilibrium located, say, at point A1 in the diagram below, where the average price level is P1 and real output is at its potential level Yp. If for some reason the average price level increases to P2, then the economy will move along the short run AS shown as SRAS1 because of the assumption that money wages are fixed in the short run. Firms will witness lower costs as the real wage (the ratio of the money wage over the price level) is lower. Output will increase to Y', above the potential output level Yp (point A2).

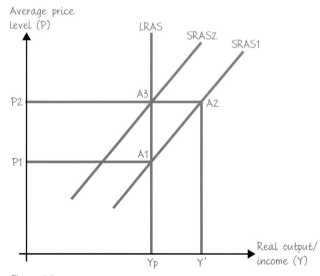

Figure 2.3

In the long run though, money wages will also increase to match (by assumption) the rise in prices. The higher money wages will shift short run AS to the left until it reaches SRAS2, so that the real wage as well as firms' profitability return to their previous level. Consequently, real output will return to Yp: firms have no reason to produce more when money wages have risen as much as prices. Output will remain at its potential level but the price level will be higher at P2 (point A3).

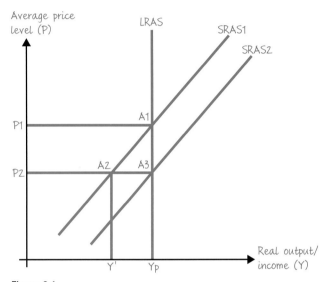

Figure 2.4

Now let's see what happens if, symmetrically, the average price level drops: start from a point on the LRAS, say point A1, where the economy is producing the potential output Yp and the average price level is P1. If the average price level falls to P2 then the economy will move along the short run AS curve SRAS1 because of the assumption that money wages are fixed in the short run. Firms will witness increased costs as the real wage (the ratio of the money wage over the price level) is higher. Output will decrease to Y', below the potential output level Yp (point A2).

In the long run though, money wages will also decrease to match (by assumption) the decrease in prices. The lower money wages will shift short run AS to the right until it reaches SRAS2, so that the real wage as well as firms' profitability return to their previous level. Consequently, real output will return to Yp: firms will produce more when money wages have dropped as much as prices. Output will return to its potential level but the average price level will be lower at P2.

This means that any deviation from potential output will be temporary. The assumed flexibility of money wages guarantees that the economy will return to its potential output. LRAS is vertical at the potential level of output as the latter is independent of the level of prices.

Example 5

Explain the horizontal section of the typical Keynesian AS curve making explicit reference to the downward 'stickiness' of money wages.

According to the (extreme) Keynesian model, money wages do not adjust downwards (because of labour unions, contracts, minimum wage laws, etc.) to lower the real wage rate for firms, so firms are forced to lower output. As long as money wages do not adjust, the economy can get stuck at a lower output than its potential output with unemployment therefore higher than natural.

Example 6

Explain the role of 'bottlenecks' in the production process while explaining the rising section of the typical Keynesian AS curve.

The meaning of 'bottlenecks' is instrumental in explaining the rising section (the second section) in Keynesian AS. After some level of total output, as real GDP continues to increase, wages will start to increase because of 'bottlenecks': unemployment will have decreased to such levels that firms can only find workers by offering higher wages. Picture how the neck of a bottle becomes narrower so that less liquid can flow through it.

However, if production costs increase then firms will be willing to offer more output only at higher prices. So the average price level rises. A direct relationship has been established between the average price level and the level of real output of an economy. This is region 2 (the positively sloped section) of the Keynesian AS curve.

Exercise 4

Explain three factors that may increase the long run AS of an economy employing the monetarist or new classical approach. Would these factors also shift the Keynesian AS curve to the right? Use appropriate diagrams to illustrate your answer.

Exercise 5

Explain why the monetarist or new classical perspective considers labour unions, government regulation in labour markets and lack of competition in product markets as impediments to full employment.

Equilibrium

Remember

- Long run equilibrium in the monetarist or new classical model will always be at the potential (full employment) level of output. At that level of real output, on a diagram, AD intersects SRAS and LRAS.

- Short run equilibrium output in the monetarist or new classical model can be either below or above the economy's potential (full employment) output, but only temporarily. The assumed flexibility of money wages will guarantee that the economy will return to its long run potential output.

- In the Keynesian model, the economy can get stuck at a level of output below potential (full employment) output as wages and prices are assumed to be 'sticky' downwards: insufficient AD will force a decrease in output and a rise in unemployment with no automatic adjustment mechanism present to restore full employment. There is a need for government intervention.

- Whether discussing the monetarist or new classical approach, or in the Keynesian approach, if equilibrium real output is below the potential (full employment) level of output then the economy experiences a recessionary (deflationary) gap, while if equilibrium real output is greater than the potential (full employment) level of output then the economy experiences an inflationary gap.

Tip

Poor labelling in AD/AS diagrams is the biggest source of errors on macro questions in exams. Keep these tips in mind.

- Do not cut corners: fully label the vertical axis 'average price level' and the horizontal axis 'real output/income' ('real GDP' is also accepted even though it is not strictly correct).

- If you label the vertical axis with only a 'P' you run the serious risk of discussing macro issues as if they were micro issues: candidates very often refer in exams to 'the price' of the good increasing, forgetting that they are analysing movements in the general (average) price level.

- Avoid labelling the horizontal using the letter 'Q'. Once again, candidates get thrown off and start discussing 'the quantity of the good rising' as if the question was about the market for, say, corn. Using the label 'Yr' is preferable (or perhaps 'real GDP').

- Proper labels (especially fully descriptive labels) will help you stay focused on a macro analysis.

Example 7

Explain, using appropriate diagrams, how full employment equilibrium is restored if a recessionary (deflationary) gap exists within the monetarist or new classical model.

Assume an economy in long run equilibrium producing the potential (full employment) level of output Yp with an average price level P1. This is illustrated in Figure 2.5 at point a1, the intersection of AD1 with SRAS1 on the LRAS curve. Let AD, for some reason, decrease to AD2. The average price level decreases to P' but since, in the short run, money wages are assumed fixed, the real wage has increased and forced firms to cut back production so that total output will be less at Y'. The economy will have moved along SRAS1 to point a'. A recessionary (deflationary) gap will result, equal to the line segment Y'Yp.

Tip

At this level of theoretical sophistication there are plenty of 'grey' areas in macro. This is unavoidable. You must deal with these issues keeping in mind the 'pillars' of each perspective. These include the following.

- For the Keynesians, real output is demand-determined and economies can get stuck at a lower than full employment level of equilibrium. Wages are 'sticky' downwards so there is no automatic mechanism available to restore full employment. Increasing AD can increase output towards full employment.

- For the monetarists or new classical school, real output in an economy is whatever its resources, technology and institutional framework permit it to produce. If prices and wages are flexible it will gravitate towards this potential level of output. Increases in AD may increase output only temporarily (in the short run) until money wages adjust and the economy returns to its potential, long run equilibrium with a higher price level.

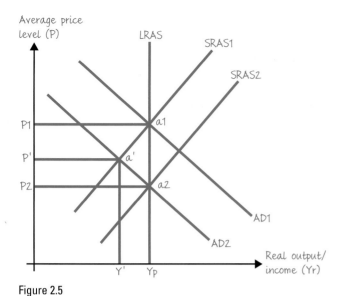

Figure 2.5

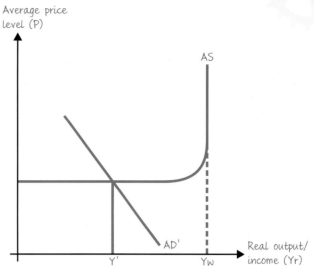

Figure 2.6

In the long run, money wages will adjust and decrease to match the decrease in the average price level. The decrease in money wages increases the short run AS shifting the curve to the right to SRAS2. The real wage rate will therefore decrease providing the incentive to firms to increase production so that potential (full employment) output is restored. The economy will again find itself in long run equilibrium at point a2 with a lower average price level P2 and real GDP at its potential level.

A recessionary (deflationary) gap cannot persist in the long run within the monetarist or new classical model.

Example 8

Explain, using appropriate diagrams, how an economy can get stuck below the full employment level of output within the Keynesian model.

Assume that AD is at AD' as illustrated in Figure 2.6. The economy is operating below its maximum or 'wall' level of output, Yw. Money wages and prices are 'sticky' downwards within the Keynesian world so there is no automatic mechanism present to induce firms to increase output and remove the recessionary (deflationary) gap, which is equal to the line segment (or Y'Yw). The decrease in AD has forced firms to adjust only output.

For the Keynesian model, the driving force in an economy is effective demand which we call AD. If AD is insufficient to generate full employment, then the economy is stuck at an equilibrium level of output such as Y'. It follows from this perspective that there is a role for the government as it may influence AD directly through changes in the level of government spending G or, indirectly, through the manipulation of taxes (which could influence consumption and investment expenditures).

Note that in the diagram above, if AD increases and shifts to the right (as a result, say, of government intervention) then it is not necessary for the average price level to increase. The reason is that within this extreme version of the Keynesian model (with a horizontal AS segment), an equilibrium along the flat segment implies depression-like conditions in the economy with extremely high unemployment and under-utilized capacity. Output can expand without any increase in wages or other resource prices, and so without firms raising their prices. This is true up to the point where 'bottlenecks' appear, in which case both real output and the average price level will be rising. The closer to Yw the economy is operating, the greater the effect of a further increase of AD on the average price level.

Note that in this extreme version of the Keynesian model, the more contemporary idea of potential output, where prices and wages are flexible and some normal or natural unemployment exists, is not accommodated.

Example 9

Determine whether the following statements are true or false. Explain your answers.

1 Within the monetarist or new classical perspective long run equilibrium will always be restored.

True. The assumed flexibility of money (nominal) wages guarantees that output returns to its potential level.

2 Within the Keynesian (extreme) model an increase in AD will always increase prices.

False. The existence of very significant levels of unemployment when an economy is in a deep recession (depression) implies that an increase in real output can be achieved without prices rising if, for some reason, AD starts to increase.

3 The Keynesian model assumes that money wages may increase but they are 'sticky' downwards.

True. This is also known as the 'ratchet effect'. It is this downwards 'stickiness' in money wages that prevents automatic restoration of full employment.

4 The key distinction between the short run and the long run is time: if the time period is greater than one year we are in the long run.

False. The contemporary distinction between the short run and the long run in macro rests on whether money (nominal) wages are or are not flexible. If they are flexible and they can match any change in the average price level then we are in the long run.

5 The (extreme) Keynesian concept of full employment differs from the monetarist or new classical idea of potential output where the LRAS is vertical and where some unemployment persists.

True. The Keynesian model made no distinction between the short run and the long run. Within the Keynesian model the idea of full employment can be thought of as a 'wall', or a 'maximum' level of output. The concept of a 'natural' rate of unemployment was introduced much later (in 1968) by Milton Friedman. It was originally defined as the equilibrium rate of unemployment, i.e. the one that would prevail when money wages adjusted and equilibrium was restored in the labour market.

To accommodate the more contemporary idea that some unemployment will always be present (normal or natural unemployment) one can include the potential level of output to the left of the maximum level of output in the rising section of the Keynesian AS curve.

Example 10

Rewrite the following statements and fill in the blanks by using the terms provided below. Some terms may be used more than once or not at all.

AD	three
left	wages
maximum	attract
bottlenecks	scarce
normal (or natural)	average price level

The Keynesian AS curve consists of (1) _____ distinct regions. In region 1 it is flat which indicates that increases in (2) _____ will not lead to increases in the average price level. In region 2, as AD increases real output will also increase, but (3) _____ in production will create pressure for prices to also rise. Labour will become more (4) _____ so firms will be forced to bid up (5) _____. Only in this way will firms be able to (6) _____ workers to produce more and thus satisfy the increased AD. At some point the economy's (7) _____ output will be reached; defined as the output level where no unemployment exists so that any further increase in AD can only increase the (8) _____. One may indicate the level of potential output somewhere to the (9) _____ of the maximum (or 'wall') output to acknowledge the existence of some (10) _____ unemployment.

(1) three, (2) AD, (3) bottlenecks, (4) scarce, (5) wages, (6) attract, (7) maximum, (8) average price level, (9) left, (10) normal (or natural)

The Keynesian multiplier

- Marginal in economics means change. So, marginal propensity to consume is the change in consumption (because of a change in income), or

  $MPC = \dfrac{\Delta C}{\Delta Y}$

- Marginal propensity to save is the change in savings (because of a change in income), or

  $MPS = \dfrac{\Delta S}{\Delta Y}$

- Marginal rate of tax is the change in taxes (because of a change in income), or

  $MRT = \dfrac{\Delta T}{\Delta Y}$, etc.

- Withdrawals (or leakages) in the circular flow include savings (S), taxes (T) and spending on imports (M).

- Injections include government expenditures (G), investment spending (I) and exports (X).

There are three equations to use in calculations involving the multiplier.

- $\Delta Y = k\Delta J$, where k is the multiplier and J represents injections in the circular flow which include X, I and G (export revenues, investment spending by firms and government expenditures).

- $k = \dfrac{1}{(1 - MPC_d)}$, where MPC_d

  is the marginal propensity to consume domestic goods and is the change in consumption induced by a change in income, or

  $MPCd = \dfrac{\Delta C}{\Delta Y}$.

- Or $k = \dfrac{1}{MPW}$ as $(1 - MPC_d)$

  $= MPW = (MPS + MPM + MRT)$,

  where MPW is the marginal propensity to withdraw which is the sum of the marginal withdrawals.

Tip

Always start in all calculations with what you know; write it down and proceed step by step.

Example 11

Why could the concept of the Keynesian multiplier be significant?

There are three reasons of potential significance relating to the source of each of the three injections.

- Private sector investment spending (I): if private investment is volatile then national income (Y) will be volatile as the multiplier could magnify any changes in private investment. In this way, changes in private investment magnified through the operation of the multiplier could be responsible for the business cycle.

- Export revenues (X): a recession abroad will force foreigners to cut down spending on domestic goods and services. The resulting decrease in export revenues (X) may lead to a magnified decrease in national income (Y) because of the multiplier. This may explain the international transmission of the business cycle.

- Government expenditures (G): an increase in government spending (G) may lead to a magnified increase in national income because of the multiplier. This is of great importance because it means that the government can influence national income by changing its level of government expenditures. It suggests that the government could close a recessionary gap by increasing its spending by only a fraction of the gap, as the multiplier will magnify this increase in G sufficiently to restore potential output. In addition, the government could influence the level of national income through manipulating taxes (T), a withdrawal from the circular flow of income. By lowering taxes (T), a withdrawal, national income could increase by a multiple through the operation of the multiplier.

Example 12

Determine whether the following statements are true or false. Explain your answers.

1 The multiplier is larger the smaller the propensity to consume domestic goods.

False. The multiplier is $k = \dfrac{1}{1 - MPC_d}$ so if MPC_d decreases, then $(1 - MPC_d)$ increases, and the fraction $\dfrac{1}{1 - MPC_d}$ decreases. It makes sense since the less is spent on domestic goods, the less remains inside the circular flow.

2 The multiplier effect is exaggerated as the additional rounds of extra spending are conducted using the same money. Money has not increased.

False. Using the example of dollars as the currency, we should not focus on the dollar bills circulating but on the economic activity created. If the government spends $100 on me to build a birdhouse for a school and I then spend $80 from my $100 extra income on you to give me a haircut, then the same dollar bills may have been used but national output has increased by one birdhouse plus one haircut.

3 An increase in government spending may have a minimal effect on national income if individuals realize that the extra government spending now means higher future taxes.

True. If individuals are sufficiently forward looking (strictly speaking, a number of additional assumptions are also needed) then they may increase their savings now (a leakage) to be able to meet the higher taxes that will be needed in the future to pay off the current increase in government spending.

Example 13

In an economy the government is planning to spend an extra $200 billion. What will national income be equal to if the marginal propensity to withdraw is 0.59 and current equilibrium income is $1.2 trillion?

The multiplier k is given by the equation $k = \dfrac{1}{MPW}$.

Substituting into this equation the value of MPW yields a multiplier equal to 1.7.

It follows that since $\Delta Y = k\Delta J$ or, in this case, $\Delta Y = k\Delta G$, then $\Delta Y = 0.7 \times 200 = \$14$ billion.

National income will increase by $140 billion. Thus the new equilibrium national income will be the initial one (i.e. $1.2 trillion) plus $140 billion: $1.34 trillion.

Example 14

Assume that in an economy MPM = 0.1, MPS = 0.2 and taxes are given by the equation T = 0.2Y. If the equilibrium level of national income is originally at $85 billion and exports shrink by $4 billion, calculate the new level of equilibrium income.

Since taxes are a fixed proportion of income (i.e. the average tax rate $\dfrac{T}{Y}$ is constant and equal to 0.2), it follows that the marginal tax rate (MRT) is also constant and equal to 0.2. Thus the MPW (the sum of the marginal withdrawals) is $(0.1 + 0.2 + 0.2) = 0.5$.

The multiplier k is then equal to $\dfrac{1}{0.5} = 2$.

Since $\Delta Y = k\Delta X$, it follows that $\Delta Y = 2 \times (-4) = -\$8$ billion.

The new level of national income is $8.0 billion less, or $85 - \$8 = \$77$ billion.

Exercise 6

Calculate the value of the multiplier if:

1 income has increased by $120 billion following an increase in private sector investment by $50 billion.
2 income decreases by $20 billion when the government cuts its spending from $62.5 billion to $54.5 billion.
3 the marginal propensity to withdraw is 0.45.
4 the marginal propensity to consume in a closed economy without government intervention is 0.85.

Exercise 7

Rewrite the following statements and fill in the blanks by using the terms provided below. Some terms may be used more than once or not at all.

temporary	short run AS
inflationary	equilibrium
full employment	money or nominal
vertical	

Within the monetarist or new classical perspective, the long run AS is
(1) _____ at the potential output level and any deviation of
(2) _____ output from the potential (full employment) level will only be
(3) _____ and a result of fixed (4) _____ wages in the short
run. When money wages change, the (5) _____ shifts and helps the
economy return to its long run (6) _____ equilibrium.
Recessionary and (7) _____ gaps cannot persist into the long run within
this framework.

Exercise 8

Calculate the size of the necessary increase in government spending:

1 to close an $850 million recessionary gap if the marginal propensity to import is 0.19, $20 is taken away as taxes from every extra $100 earned and the marginal propensity to save is 0.11.
2 to increase income from $1.56 trillion to $1.66 trillion given an estimated value for the multiplier of 3.2.
3 if income is 1.6 % below the full employment level estimated at $680 billion, the multiplier is estimated at 2.8 and the goal is to reach full employment.

Exercise 9

Calculate the change in national income:

1 in a closed economy if injections increase by $12 billion, the marginal propensity to save is 0.25 and government taxes income at a flat rate of 15 %.
2 if export revenues increase by $6 billion in an economy where MPM = 0.12, taxes are 14 % of income and the savings rate is 24 %.
3 if the multiplier is estimated at 1.7 and the government initiates an increase of $350 billion.

Exercise 10

Assume a closed economy. Calculate the size of the marginal propensity to consume if an increase by the government of expenditures by $122 billion was responsible for national income increasing from $0.860 billion to $1.104 trillion.

Low unemployment

Remember

- Low unemployment (or a high level of employment) is one of the macroeconomic policy goals as unemployment is a costly phenomenon for the economy as well as for individuals and society.

Example 1

Determine whether the following statements are true or false. Explain your answers.

1 To deal with cyclical unemployment, demand-side policies are typically employed.

   True. Since cyclical unemployment is a result of insufficient AD (and is also known as demand deficient or Keynesian unemployment) it is expected that policy makers will try to increase AD to lower cyclical unemployment. Later, it will be seen that these demand-side policies include fiscal policy, whereby the government tries to increase AD by increasing its expenditures G or by decreasing taxes T, and also monetary policy, whereby (typically) the central bank tries to increase AD by lowering interest rates r or by pumping more money into the economy.

2 There is not much that can be done for the seasonally unemployed.

   True. Construction workers in the winter in areas where temperatures drop to sub-zero levels (such as in New England in the USA) are regularly unemployed for several weeks and collect unemployment benefits. Some are highly skilled workers so it makes no sense for them to seek alternative employment as clerks at a food store. That is why monthly unemployment statistics are 'seasonally adjusted' which just means that the effect of seasonal unemployment is isolated from the data. For seasonally unemployed unskilled workers, unemployment may decrease if better and faster information about job availabilities is open to them.

3 Structural unemployment will decrease if the government increases its expenditures.

   False. Structural unemployment may decrease only through:

   – interventionist supply-side measures (such as providing retraining, assisting relocation of individuals to areas with job vacancies they can fill or providing tax breaks to firms willing to move to areas with high regional unemployment)

   – market-oriented supply-side policies (SSPs) that aim to make the labour market more flexible (such as lowering the level of unemployment benefits, making it easier for firms to dismiss workers so that they become more willing to hire workers when the business outlook is good instead of trying to rely only on their existing labour force, or abolishing minimum wage laws and collective bargaining processes).

Example 2

Rewrite the following statements and fill in the blanks by using the terms provided below.

labour costs	collective
searching	fire
natural	stopped
discouraged	tax
permanent	hire
structural	employed
decrease	technological
rigidity	moving
increases	accept
skills	mismatch
unemployment benefits	security
retraining	part-time

An individual is considered unemployed if he or she is actively (1) _____ for a job but cannot find one. It follows that (2) _____ workers who have been unemployed for so long that they have (3) _____ looking for a job are not included in official unemployment statistics. In addition, (4) _____ workers are also excluded from official statistics as they are gainfully (5) _____.

As a result of unemployment, government spending (6) _____ because most governments pay (7) _____ to eligible unemployed individuals. At the same time, high unemployment will, ceteris paribus, lead to lower (8) _____ revenues for the government as the unemployed have lost their wage income and tend to spend less.

High unemployment benefits may (9) _____ the probability that an unemployed worker will (10) _____ a job offer. Job (11) _____ and labour protection laws may also be responsible for increased level of unemployment as firms hesitate in an upturn to (12) _____ new workers fearing that it will be difficult to (13) _____ them if things turn sour for the firm. (14) _____bargaining adds to labour-market (15) _____ as wages cannot differ and change to clear labour markets. These factors tend to increase (16) _____ unemployment and consequently (17) _____ unemployment.

Perhaps more importantly, structural unemployment is a result of a (18) _____ between the (19) _____ the unemployed possess and the skills in demand in the labour market. Some jobs may have disappeared because of (20) _____ advancements while other jobs may have disappeared because of firms (21) _____ elsewhere in the country or abroad in search of lower (22) _____. These (23) _____ decreases in the demand for certain skills imply that only through (24) _____ of these workers will they be able to find work again.

(1) searching, (2) discouraged, (3) stopped, (4) part-time, (5) employed, (6) increases, (7) unemployment benefits, (8) tax, (9) decrease, (10) accept, (11) security, (12) hire, (13) dismiss, (14) collective, (15) rigidity, (16) structural, (17) natural, (18) mismatch, (19) skills, (20) technological, (21) moving, (22) labour costs, (23) permanent, (24) retraining

Example 3

The following data refer to Lalaland in 2010.

Population	2,251,503
Population aged 15–64 years	1,627,071
Labour force	1,192,000
Unemployment rate	5.5%

Calculate the number of unemployed in Lalaland.

The unemployment rate is the number of the unemployed as a proportion of the labour force. The statistics provided above about the size of the general population of individuals between 15 and 64 years old is irrelevant to this problem.

Solving the unemployment rate equation

$$\text{Unemployment rate} = \frac{\text{number of unemployed}}{\text{labour force}}$$

for the number of unemployed we get:

Number of unemployed
$= 1,192,000 \times 0.055$
$= 65,560$ individuals unemployed

Remember that to express a percentage as a decimal you move the decimal point two positions to the left, so that $5.5\% = 0.055$.

Example 4

The labour force of the Armania Republic in 2011 was 2.95 million, of which 182,900 individuals were without a job but actively searching for one. Calculate the rate of unemployment in Armania for 2011.

This is again a matter of substituting the numbers. Care should be taken in that the labour force is given in millions: you have to move the decimal six positions to the right so it becomes 2,950,000 individuals.

The equation used to compute the rate of unemployment is:

$$\text{Unemployment rate} = \frac{\text{number of unemployed}}{\text{labour force}}$$

Substituting yields:

$$\text{Unemployment rate} = \frac{182,900}{2,950,000}$$

$$= 0.062$$
$$= 6.2\%$$

Example 5

Unemployment in Fairyland in 2010 was at 5.2 % with a labour force of 62.44 million. Calculate the number of unemployed.

Remember to express the unemployment rate as a decimal: 5.2% = 0.052 (moving the decimal two positions to the left).

Applying the equation

Unemployment rate = $\frac{\text{number of unemployed}}{\text{labour force}}$ yields:

$0.052 = \frac{x}{62.44}$

$x = 0.052 \times 62.44 = 3.24688$ million

(3.25 million or 3,246,880 individuals)

Exercise 1

Determine whether the following statements are true or false. Explain your answers. Use a diagram to illustrate if possible.

1 Policy makers aim at lowering unemployment to as close to 0 % as possible.
2 Structural unemployment tends to be of a short-term nature.
3 Some frictional unemployment is unavoidable.
4 Official unemployment statistics tend to both overestimate and underestimate true unemployment.
5 If unemployment decreases then the production possibilities curve of a country will shift outwards.
6 The LRAS curve of an economy will shift to the right if cyclical unemployment decreases.
7 The LRAS curve of an economy will shift to the right if structural and frictional unemployment decreases.

Exercise 2

Rewrite the following statements and fill in the blanks by using the terms provided below. Some words may be used more than once or not at all.

money	taxes	interest rates
deficient	frictional	seasonal
short	information	increases
durable	sticky	labour
recession	confidence	consumption
higher	cyclical	government spending
aggregate demand	investment expenditures	

Unemployment that is a result of people moving between jobs is referred to as (1) _____. This type of unemployment is of a (2) _____ term basis and can decrease if labour market participants had faster access to better labour-market related (3) _____. On the other hand, unemployment because of the weather, for example among construction workers during very cold winters, is known as (4) _____

unemployment and typically not much can be done about it. Unemployment resulting from insufficient (5) _____ is known as demand (6) _____ or (7) _____ unemployment. This type of unemployment (8) _____ in a (9) _____ as real GDP then is decreasing. Demand for (10)_____ by firms decreases but because (11) _____ wages are (12) _____ downwards, excess supply of labour results, i.e. unemployment. The deeper the recession the (13) _____ this type of unemployment will be. Governments try to prop up aggregate demand to lower cyclical unemployment. Policy makers may increase (14) _____ or lower (15) _____. Central banks also decrease (16) _____ to induce higher (17) _____ expenditures by households on (18) _____ goods such as cars or appliances and higher (19) _____ expenditures by firms on capital goods. There is no guarantee that these policies will work if consumer and business (20) _____ levels are very low.

Exercise 3

Using an appropriate diagram explain structural unemployment and evaluate policies that may be adopted to lower it.

Exercise 4

Explain the different types of unemployment and policies that may be employed to reduce each. What difficulties arise in addressing the problem of unemployment?

Exercise 5

Maintaining unemployment at a low level is considered an important macroeconomic objective. Why? Is it possible to drive the unemployment rate to zero?

Exercise 6

Discuss the possible consequences of unemployment (economic, personal and social).

Low and stable rate of inflation

Remember

- Low inflation is a macroeconomic goal because inflation is costly as it:
  - redistributes income haphazardly
  - increases uncertainty lowering investment and therefore growth
  - erodes the competitiveness of exports
  - distorts the signalling power of relative price changes increasing allocative inefficiency.
- Inflation exists when prices are rising.
- Disinflation exists when prices continue to rise but at a slower rate (for example if the inflation rate decreased from 4.6 % to 3.6 % and prices continued to increase but by 3.6 % instead of by 4.6 %).
- Deflation is when prices on average are decreasing (for example there is a negative inflation rate).

- Inflation is considered 'demand pull' if it is a result of AD rising too fast, and 'cost push' if it is a result of increased production costs across the board.
- No matter what the cause of inflation, the first line of attacking it is for policy makers to increase interest rates to choke off AD (which is known as tight monetary policy) as well as to lower government expenditures and raise taxes (known as contractionary fiscal policy). SSPs that aim to increase AS are also employed but have a more long-term horizon.
- The consumer price index (CPI) is used to track the cost of a fixed basket of goods bought by the typical consumer in some base period (year). Inflation in year t is the percentage increase in the CPI, i.e. in the cost of buying this basket compared with year $(t-1)$.

Remember

- To calculate the CPI:
  - determine the basket of goods (i.e. the quantity of each good consumed)
  - calculate the cost of buying this basket each year
  - divide the cost of buying the basket in year t by the cost of buying the same basket in the base year and multiply by 100.

- To calculate the inflation rate of year t, calculate the percentage change in the CPI between year t and year $(t-1)$.

Example 6

Match each term or concept with the appropriate definition or explanation.

1 Demand pull inflation
2 Underlying (core) inflation
3 Stagflation
4 Disinflation
5 Phillips curve (short run)
6 Deflation
7 Structural and frictional unemployment
8 Consumer price index
9 Phillips curve (long run)
10 Inflation
11 Natural rate of unemployment

a The natural rate of unemployment consists mostly of these types of unemployment

b Suggests that an inverse relationship between inflation and unemployment exists

c Inflation that is mostly a result of AD increasing

d The unemployment that persists in the long run when prices and wages are flexible, the economy is producing at its potential output level and the labour market is in equilibrium

e A sustained increase in the average price level

f Suggests that there is no inverse relationship between unemployment and inflation

g When the average price level continues to rise but at a slower rate; the inflation rate remains positive but a becomes a smaller number

h The coexistence of rising inflation and stagnating output; when both inflation and unemployment are rising

      i a weighted index of the prices of the goods and services that the typical consumer purchases where the weights are fixed and reflect the spending on each good expressed as a proportion of total spending

      j When the average price level decreases; negative inflation

      k Inflation after excluding food and energy prices

(1, c), (2, k), (3, h), (4, g), (5, b), (6, j), (7, a), (8, i), (9, f), (10, e), (11, d)

Example 7

Determine whether the following statements are true or false. Explain your answers.

1 Core inflation focuses only on price changes of the basic goods consumers buy.

> False. Core (also referred to as underlying inflation) is based on a CPI that typically excludes food and energy even though both are very basic to consumers. The reason for excluding food and energy is that prices of both are volatile in the short run. When food and energy are removed we strip away these short run movements and thus get a better picture of the long run inflation rate faced by households.

2 Cost-push inflation is very costly as not only are prices rising but output may be declining.

> True. You can visualize this by either looking at an AD/AS diagram with AS shifting left or (HL only) through a short run Phillips curve diagram where the Phillips curve shifts outwards.

3 By reducing inflation and achieving price stability, lower unemployment may be achieved in the long run (ceteris paribus).

> True. Inflation, especially high and volatile inflation, increases uncertainty for businesses and higher uncertainty dampens investment spending. If low and stable inflation is achieved then one can in general expect higher investment rates and thus higher growth which is associated with more job creation.

4 Inflation and unemployment are inversely related. **HL**

> False. For the statement to be considered true it has to be qualified by adding 'in the short run'. In the short run there is a trade-off between the two variables (illustrated by the short run Phillips curve) but this trade-off disappears in the long run if prices and wages are flexible as the real wage will adjust to its equilibrium level and the economy will return to its potential (full employment) level of output

> (the vertical long run Phillips curve at the natural rate of unemployment).

5 Since deflation refers to decreasing prices it follows that deflation is desirable.

> False. Deflation is a greater evil than inflation as the experience of Japan has clearly illustrated. Deflation is typically a result of chronically weak and decreasing AD. Consumers postpone purchases and firms are forced to further reduce prices creating a vicious circle; real debt (money debt divided by the average price level) of households and firms increases, lowering their ability and willingness to borrow and spend; banks accumulate bad loans which weakens their position; the lower spending in the economy increases unemployment; lastly, monetary policy cannot be used to lower interest rates as nominal interest rates cannot become negative.

Example 8

Explain the meaning of Friedman's phrase 'Inflation is the one form of taxation that can be imposed without legislation.'

> One of the costs of inflation is that it redistributes income. This phrase refers to a redistribution of income from taxpayers to the government as a result of taxpayers' incomes moving up the tax brackets. Assume that Chandler's money income (say, his salary) increased by 10% while prices also increased by 10%. In real terms, i.e. in terms of purchasing power (what Chandler can buy with his money income) nothing has changed: his real income is constant. But if this increase in nominal income pushes him into a higher income tax bracket (with a higher marginal tax rate – see later) then his tax obligation to the government will have risen faster than his income and than prices. Effectively his real tax obligation will have increased as more purchasing power is transferred away from Chandler to the government. The government increased its revenues without having to introduce new or higher taxes.

HL

Example 9

The following table has the prices in euros of three goods in an economy.

Year	Price of good X	Price of good Y	Price of good Z
2010	€8.00	€0.60	€2.00
2011	€8.40	€0.64	€2.05
2012	€8.60	€0.75	€2.25

We assume that the basket of the typical consumer contains 10 units of good X, 20 units of good Y and 30 units of good Z.

1 Construct a weighted price index for all three years assuming that 2010 is the base year.

2 Calculate the inflation rate for 2011 and 2012.

First, calculate how much it would cost the typical consumer to purchase the same basket each year. The price of each product in each year is multiplied by the quantity purchased in the base year (2010).

Year	$\sum_1^3 P_i q_2 = P_1 q_1 + P_2 q_2 + P_3 q_3$	Cost of basket
2010	(€8.00 × 10) + (€0.60 × 20) + (€2.00 × 30) = €80.00 + €12.00 + €60.00	€152.50
2011	(€8.40 × 10) + (€0.64 × 20) + (€2.05 × 30) = €84.00 + €12.80 + €61.50	€158.30
2012	(€8.60 × 10) + (€0.75 × 20) + (€2.25 × 30) = €86.00 + €15.00 + €67.50	€168.50

To construct a weighted price index for any year t you need to divide the cost of the basket in year t by the cost of the basket in the base period (2010) and multiply by 100.

Year	Formula: $\dfrac{\text{cost of basket in year } t}{\text{cost of basket in base year 2010}} \times 100$	Price index
2010 (base year)	$\dfrac{152.50}{152.50} \times 100$	100
2011	$\dfrac{158.30}{152.50} \times 100$	103.80
2012	$\dfrac{168.50}{152.50} \times 100$	110.49

The inflation rate of a year is defined as the percentage change in the average price level (expressed as a price index like the CPI).

So: inflation rate of period $t = \%\Delta(CPI)$

$$= \frac{\text{index}(t) - \text{index}(t-1)}{\text{index}(t-1)} \times 100$$

Year	Inflation rate
2010	—
2011	$\dfrac{(103.80 - 100.00)}{100.00} \times 100 = 3.80\%$
2012	$\dfrac{(110.49 - 103.80)}{103.80} \times 100 = 6.45\%$

Example 10

1 Construct a weighted price index for 2009, 2010 and 2011 using the information provided below about prices, and assuming that the typical basket includes one book, two MP3 downloads and three burgers. Consider that 2009 is the base year.

2 Calculate the annual inflation rate for this economy.

Year	Price of a book	Price of an MP3 download	Price of a burger
2009	$30	$0.99	$2.50
2010	$35	$0.90	$2.60
2011	$42	$0.75	$2.80

First, calculate how much it would cost the typical consumer to purchase the same basket each year. The price of each product in each year is multiplied by the quantity purchased in the base year (2009).

Year	$\sum_1^3 P_i q_i = P_1 q_1 + P_2 q_2 + P_3 q_3$	Cost of basket
2009	($30 × 1) + ($0.99 × 2) + ($2.50 × 3)	39.48
2010	($35 × 1) + ($0.90 × 2) + ($2.60 × 3)	44.60
2011	($42 × 1) + ($0.75 × 2) + ($2.80 × 3)	51.90

To construct a weighted price index for any year t you need to divide the cost of the basket in year t by the cost of the basket in the base period (2009) and multiply by 100.

Year	Formula: $\dfrac{\text{cost of basket in year } t}{\text{cost of basket in base year (2009)}} \times 100$	Price index
2009	$\dfrac{39.48}{39.48} \times 100$	100
2010	$\dfrac{44.60}{39.48} \times 100$	112.97
2011	$\dfrac{51.90}{39.48} \times 100$	131.46

The inflation rate of a year is defined as the percentage change in the average price level (expressed as a price index like the CPI).

So: inflation rate of period $t = \%\Delta(\text{CPI})$

$= \dfrac{\text{index}(t) - \text{index}(t - 1)}{\text{index}(t - 1)}$

Year	Inflation rate
2010	–
2011	$\dfrac{(112.97 - 100.00)}{100.00} \times 100 = 12.97\%$, or 13%
2012	$\dfrac{(131.46 - 112.97)}{112.97} \times 100 = 16.37\%$, or 16.4%

Exercise 7

Determine whether the following statements are true or false. Explain your answers. Use a diagram to illustrate if possible.

1 Inflation can be decreased if the central bank lowers interest rates.
2 Unexpected inflation benefits borrowers.
3 Inflationary expectations may be responsible for increased inflationary pressures.
4 An increase in AD carries a higher risk of inflation the greater the recessionary gap.
5 The CPI is a better predictor of future inflation than the PPI.

6 The value of money is proportional to the price level.
7 The export sector of an economy may help it exit a period of deflation.
HL 8 An adverse supply shock may give rise to a rightward shift to the short run Phillips curve.
HL 9 A short run trade off between unemployment and inflation exists only because of money illusion.
HL 10 For policy makers, the cost of disinflating an economy depends on how credible they are.

Exercise 8

Discuss the possible costs of inflation. Since sustained increases in the average price level are undesirable it follows that a sustainable decrease in prices should be more than welcome. Do you agree?

Exercise 9

Evaluate the use of government policies to deal with different types of inflation.

HL
Exercise 10

1 Construct a weighted price index for 2009, 2010 and 2011 using the information provided about prices, assuming that the typical basket includes five books, 12 MP3 downloads and 20 burgers, and that 2009 is the base year.
2 Calculate the rate of inflation in 2010 and in 2011.

Year	Price of a book	Price of an MP3 download	Price of a burger
2009	$6.50	$0.99	$2.50
2010	$6.60	$1.05	$2.55
2011	$6.40	$1.00	$2.40

Economic growth

Remember

- Economic growth can be illustrated either by a shift outwards of the production possibility frontier (PPF) itself, a rightwards shift of the LRAS or a movement from some point inside to another point closer to the PPF. Which diagram is appropriate to use depends on why the economy has grown.

- Better use of existing resources and/or lower unemployment means movement inside the PPF.

- More or better resources and/or better technology means a shift of the PPF or of the LRAS.

- Growth has many benefits, and this may explain why it is considered the single most important macroeconomic goal, but it may entail serious costs.

Tip

A common error is to shift the PPF outwards if you are told that unemployment has decreased. There is no shift of the curve as there is no increase in the size of the labour force. Total output has increased as the economy moves closer to its frontier.

Example 11

Rewrite the following statements and fill in the blanks by using the terms provided below. Some terms may be used more than once or not at all.

unemployment	productivity
potential	grown
output	efficiency
physical	rightward
shifting	human
education	labour force
skills and experience	technological
LRAS	same
natural capital	greater

Economic growth can be achieved by better use of existing resources: if in production there are (1) _____ gains then the (2) _____ amount of resources will be able to produce (3) _____ levels of total output. Also, with the size of the (4) _____ the same, a decrease in (5) _____ will increase total output. In both cases the economy will have (6) _____.

Investment in (7) _____ capital, defined as the (8) _____ embodied in the labour force, can accelerate growth because they lead to higher labour (9) _____ defined as (10) _____ per worker. Investments in (11) _____ such as reforestation and soil improvement will also permit higher growth. Finally, growth can be achieved by investments in (12) _____ capital and through (13) _____ advancements. Growth that expands the productive capacity of an economy can be illustrated either by (14) _____ outwards the production possibilities curve or by a (15) _____ shift of the economy's (16) _____ curve as (17) _____ output will have increased.

(1) efficiency, (2) same, (3) greater, (4) labour force, (5) unemployment, (6) grown, (7) human, (8) education, skills and experience, (9) productivity, (10) output, (11) natural capital, (12) physical, (13) technological, (14) shifting, (15) rightward, (16) LRAS, (17) potential

Example 12

Is producing on the PPF the same as producing the potential level of real output? Can the PPF be considered the same as the LRAS curve of an economy?

Absolutely not. The production possibilities model is a technological relationship. It shows the maximum levels of output that can be produced by an economy given resources and technology, nothing more. It has nothing to do with prices and wages. On the other hand, potential output is defined as that level of output that can be produced in an economy in the long run when prices and wages are flexible and unemployment is at its normal or natural level. So at the level of potential output there is always some unemployment. This is not the case within the production possibilities curve model.

Nevertheless, there is a conceptual equivalence which permits us, with caution and awareness of the building blocks of each model, to use either to show economic growth. Remember that we can illustrate economic growth by shifting to the right the vertical LRAS curve. Also, the factors that shift the PPF outwards will also shift the LRAS to the right.

HL **Example 13**

The data below refer to Dottyland. GDP figures are in billion dollars. Calculate the annual growth rates that Dottyland achieved. When was Dottyland in a recession?

Year	Nominal GDP	GDP deflator
2007	86.22	96
2008	91.39	100
2009	94.32	102.5
2010	95.26	104
2011	98.12	105

To calculate the growth rate of a country we use real GDP, so we have to first calculate real GDP from the data. Real GDP can be calculated by dividing nominal (or money GDP, or GDP at current prices) with the GDP deflator for the year and multiplying the result by 100.

Year	Nominal GDP	GDP deflator	Real GDP
2007	86.22	96	89.81
2008	91.39	100	91.39
2009	94.32	102.5	92.02
2010	95.26	104	91.60
2011	98.12	105	93.45

The growth rate g of a year is the percentage change of real GDP with respect to the previous year. Denoting the growth rate in year t as g_t and real GDP of year t as y_t:

$$g_t = \frac{(y_t - y_{(t-1)})}{y_t}, \text{ so:}$$

Year	Nominal GDP	GDP deflator	Real GDP	Growth rate
2007	86.22	96	89.81	–
2008	91.39	100	91.39	1.76
2009	94.32	102.5	92.02	0.69
2010	95.26	104	91.60	–0.46
2011	98.12	105	93.45	2.02

Remember that a recession implies a decrease in real GDP (for at least six months) or, equivalently, that the country registers a negative growth rate. Dottyland was therefore in recession in 2010 because real GDP decreased from $92.02 billion to $91.60 billion and it registered a negative growth rate (– 0.46 %).

Exercise 11

Rewrite the following statements and fill in the blanks by using the terms provided below. Some terms may be used more than once or not at all.

unemployment	degradation
sustainable	exports
inflation	distribution of income
imports	worsening
natural resources	GNP
appropriate	capital intensive
GDP	

Economic growth is desirable but it is not necessary that it is devoid of problems or costs. Economic growth may be accompanied by environmental (1) _____ and it may be a result of the depletion of (2) _____. In such a case it is not (3) _____. If the process of growth makes the rich richer and the poor poorer, in other words if it worsens the (4) _____, it is also not sustainable.

It may also lead to higher (5) _____ if it is a result of AD rising faster than AS. It is not even necessary that it lowers (6) _____ as it may not be based on (7) _____ technology, defined as a technology that employs the country's abundant factor. For example, it may be a result of more (8) _____ production processes in a country where labour is the abundant factor. In such a case it will lead to a (9) _____ income distribution, especially if the increased profits remain in the country. If they do not, then most probably (10) _____ will be higher than (11) _____.

Lastly, a growing economy will probably absorb more (12) _____. If growth was not a result of higher (13) _____ then the current account deficit which exists when the value of imports of goods and services is bigger than export revenues may also widen.

HL **Exercise 12**

The data below refer to The Republic of Oz. GDP figures are in billion dollars. Calculate the annual growth rates that Oz achieved. Did economic activity in Oz decrease in 2010?

Year	Nominal GDP	GDP deflator
2007	345.12	94.8
2008	363.88	98.4
2009	393.51	100.0
2010	420.39	103.4
2011	431.50	105.6

Equity in the distribution of income

Remember

- Equitable means fair and not equal.

- Endowments are not equal for all at the starting line, so market forces may fuel income inequality.

- The Gini coefficient ranges from 0 to 1. Countries with highly unequal income distributions have a Gini coefficient around 0.60, whereas countries with more equal income distributions have a Gini coefficient around 0.25.

- In a Lorenz curve diagram, the further away from the diagonal, the more unequal income distribution is.

- Actual income inequality ratios in the world of the highest to the lowest decile (10%) range are over 40 to roughly 5: the top 10% earn 5 to 40 times more than the bottom 10% of the population.

- Policies to redistribute income and promote equity are not considered to necessarily lower efficiency and hamper growth. On the contrary, a more equitable income distribution may increase efficiency and accelerate growth.

- Taxes can be in principle an effective tool to promote equity but they can harm incentives, decrease efficiency and lower growth.

Tip

'Quintile' means fifth or 20% and 'decile' means tenth or 10%.

Example 14

Explain the meaning of the terms 'marginal tax rate' and 'average tax rate'. How can these terms help define progressive, proportional and regressive taxes?

Remember that the word 'marginal' in economics always means extra. Thus, the marginal tax rate (MTR) is the extra tax paid on extra income or the change in taxes paid over the change in income. It is the tax paid on the last dollar earned.

(1) Marginal tax rate (MTR) $= \dfrac{\Delta T}{\Delta Y}$

The average tax rate (ATR) is defined as the ratio of the tax paid over income (or, more generally, the tax base which is a term used to refer to whatever is being taxed).

(2) Average tax rate (ATR) $= \dfrac{\text{tax paid}}{\text{income (or tax base)}}$

A tax is a progressive tax if higher-income individuals pay proportionately more. The key word here is 'proportionately'. If you have double my income you pay more than double taxes: you do not only pay more, you pay proportionately more.

So, in equation (2) opposite, as the denominator increases, the numerator increases faster. A tax is thus a progressive tax if the ATR increases as income or, more generally, the tax base increases.

A tax is a proportional tax if higher income individuals pay proportionately the same. The key word here is again 'proportionately'. If you have double my income you will pay double the taxes: you do pay more, but you pay proportionately the same. So, in equation (2) opposite, as the denominator increases, the numerator increases as fast. A tax is thus a proportional tax if the ATR remains constant as income or, more generally, the tax base increases.

Lastly, a tax is a regressive tax if higher-income individuals pay proportionately less. Once again, the key word is 'proportionately'. If you have double my income you will pay more tax than I will but less than double, so you pay proportionately less. In equation (2) opposite, as the denominator increases, the numerator increases, but not as fast. A tax is thus a regressive tax if the ATR decreases as income or, more generally, the tax base increases.

HL ## Relationships between marginal and average variables

Remember the general relationships relating to marginal and average variables. They of course hold here in the case of MTR and ATR.

If MTR > ATR then ATR increases
If MTR < ATR then ATR decreases
If MTR = ATR then ATR stays the same

So, we can classify taxes into progressive, regressive and proportional by examining the relationship between MTR and ATR.

If MTR > ATR then the tax is progressive
If MTR < ATR then the tax is regressive
If MTR = ATR then the tax is proportional

Figure 2.7 shows how the relationship between the amount of tax paid as income (or the tax base) increases, the slope of the function at any point on it, such as point A, is thus the MTR.

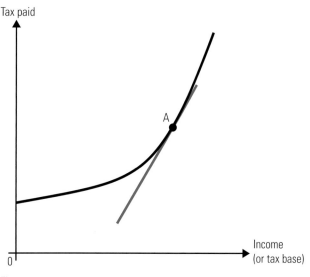

Figure 2.7

In Figure 2.8 the average tax rate is the slope of the 'ray' 0A: this slope is equal to Y1A over Y10 which is the ratio of the tax paid (as Y1A = 0T1) over income. The tax illustrated on these diagrams is a progressive tax because MTR is greater than ATR as the slope of the function at point A exceeds (is steeper) than the slope of the 'ray' 0A.

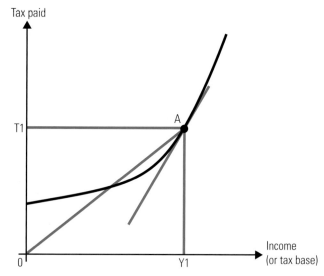

Figure 2.8

Example 15

The following table contains information about the income tax system in a country.

Income bracket	Tax rate
0–$10,000	0%
$10,001–$20,000	15%
$20,001–$35,000	25%
$35,001 +	40%

Assume three individuals, Deborshi, Marcin and Joey, have annual income levels and expenditures on goods and services as presented below.

	Annual income level	Annual spending on goods and services
Deborshi	$14,500	$13,000
Marcin	$29,000	$24,000
Joey	$43,500	$35,000

1 Calculate the income tax that each individual has to pay.

Set up a table with extra columns to write the tax for which each individual is liable in each income tax bracket. The common error is for candidates to look at the total income, determine the tax bracket that level of income belongs to and then apply the tax rate for that income bracket on the whole income level. The tax rate of each tax bracket is an MTR. Take Joey, for example. His income is $43,500 per annum. His **first** $10,000 is taxed with 0% rate so his tax liability is zero dollars. The next $10,000 he earned is subject to a 15% tax rate so he owes $1,500 (i.e. 0.15 × 10,000). His next (extra)

$15,000 is now subject to a 25% rate so he owes $3,750 (i.e. 0.25 × 15,000). He then has earned another $8,500 taxed at the top 40% rate so he owes $3,400 (i.e. 0.40 × 8,500).

Income bracket	Tax rate	Deborshi (Y = $14,500)	Marcin (Y = $29,000)	Joey (Y = $43,500)
0–$10,000	0%	$0.00	$0.00	$0.00
$10,001– $20,000	15%	$675.00	$1,500.00	$1,500.00
$20,001– $35,000	25%	–	$2,250.00	$3,750.00
$35,001 +	40%	–	–	$3,400.00
		Tax to pay: $675.00	Tax to pay: $3,750.00	Tax to pay: $8,650.00

2   Determine the ATR of each individual and compare it to his MTR.

The ATR is defined as

$$\frac{tax\ paid}{income\ (or\ tax\ base)} \times 100.$$

Substituting the numbers we arrive at the following:

Taxpayer	ATR	MTR (rate on the last dollar earned)	So:
Deborshi	4.66%	15%	MTR > ATR
Marcin	12.93%	25%	MTR > ATR
Joey	19.89%	40%	MTR > ATR

3   Provide two ways of explaining that the income tax system in this country is progressive.

A tax is a progressive tax if the ATR rises. The second column in the table above shows that the ATR is rising, which means that higher-income individuals pay proportionately more. The third column compares the MTR with the ATR and reveals that the marginal rate is higher than the average rate (as expected).

4   Assume that the amount paid by each individual on goods and services does not include taxes. Calculate the amount of indirect tax each will pay if it equals 20% of their spending on goods and services.

Since 20% of their spending on goods and services will represent indirect taxes we need to multiply each individual's spending by 0.20.

	Annual spending on goods and services	Indirect tax bill
Deborshi	$13,000	0.20 × 13,000 = $2,600
Marcin	$24,000	0.20 × 24,000 = $4,800
Joey	$35,000	0.20 × 35,000 = $7,000

Note that if the amount spent on goods and services included the indirect tax then the process is a bit more complicated. Let P_{gross} represent the gross price of a good (including the tax), P_{net} the net of tax price and t the tax rate. The following holds:

$$P_{gross} = (P_{net} + tP_{net}) = (1 + t)P_{net}$$

$$P_{net} = \frac{P_{gross}}{(1 + t)}$$

Subtracting the net of tax price from the (gross) price paid will give us the amount of the tax paid. For example, if I buy a jacket for $246 and this includes 23% VAT, then the net price for the jacket is: $\frac{$246}{1.23} = 200, and the indirect tax paid to the store is $246 − $200 = $46.

In the case of Deborshi in our example, if the amount he paid in goods and services ($13,000) included 20% indirect tax, then the amount he spent on goods and services was:

$$\frac{$13,000}{1.20} = $10,833.33$$

It follows that the indirect tax he was burdened with was:

$13,000 − $10,833.33 = $2,166.67

You must **read very carefully the wording** of the problem you are asked to solve.

5   Express the amount of indirect tax paid by each individual as a proportion of his income.

	Income level (1)	Amount spent on indirect taxes (2)	Proportion of income representing indirect taxes paid $\left(\frac{2}{1}\right)$
Deborshi	$14,500	$2,600	17.93%
Marcin	$29,000	$4,800	16.55%
Joey	$43,500	$7,000	16.09%

Exercise 13

Match each term or concept with the appropriate definition or explanation.

1 Progressive tax
2 Relative poverty
3 Average tax rate (ATR)
4 Equity
5 Proportional tax
6 Income redistribution policies
7 Direct taxes
8 Inequality ratio

a Taxes that are paid directly to the government by the entity being taxed, such as taxes on income, property, wealth or profits

b The ratio of the tax paid over the tax base (where the tax base is what is being taxed, for example it can be income or expenditures)

c Fairness

d A tax where the ATR remains constant as the tax base increases (so that ATR = MTR)

e The ratio of income (or consumption) shares of the richest (top) fifth to the poorest (bottom) fifth of the population

f Increases when income inequality ratios increase

g A tax where the average tax rate increases as the tax base increases (so that MTR > ATR)

h Policies that aim at redistributing income to achieve greater levels of equity which include transfer payments (for example pensions, unemployment benefits and child care support), subsidized or direct provision of basic merit goods and services, a progressive tax system, etc.

Exercise 14

Explain three causes and three consequences of rising poverty.

Exercise 15

Evaluate policies that may be adopted to promote greater equity in the distribution of income.

HL ## Exercise 16

The following table contains information about the income tax system in a country.

Income bracket	Tax rate
0 – €5,000	0 %
€5,001 – €15,000	5 %
€15001 – €30,000	15 %
€30,001 – €50,000	30 %
€50,000 +	40 %

Assume three individuals, Sara, Rebekah and Sanjeet, have annual income levels and expenditures on goods and services as presented opposite.

	Annual income level	Annual spending on goods and services
Sara	€16,000	€15,000
Rebekah	€32,000	€30,000
Sanjeet	€48,000	€40,000

1 Calculate the income tax that each individual has to pay.
2 Determine the ATR of each and compare it with her MTR.
3 Provide two ways of explaining that the income tax system in this country is progressive.
4 Assume that the amount paid by each individual on goods and services does not include taxes. Calculate the amount of indirect tax each will pay if it equals 20 % of her spending on goods and services.
5 Express the amount of indirect tax paid by each as a proportion of her income.

Remember

- A government collects revenues mostly from direct and indirect taxes but also from the sale of goods and services. Proceeds from privatizations are also included. Its expenditures are divided into current (for example public sector wages, goods for current use), capital (for example spending on a bridge, capital goods) and transfer payments (for example unemployment benefits, all social welfare-related payments that do not reflect contribution to current production).

- If G > T then we have a budget deficit.

- If T > G then we have a budget surplus.

- If G = T then we have a balanced budget.

- Budget decisions can foster or hinder long-term growth.

- Automatic stabilizers refer to income-induced changes in the budget that tend to stabilize the business cycle. An economy entering recession will witness an automatic increase in unemployment benefits disbursed and a decrease in taxes collected that makes the downturn milder, while in an overheating economy a progressive tax system means that tax collection rises faster, thus somewhat cooling down the rate at which AD is rising.

- The time lags characterizing fiscal (and monetary) policy are:
  - recognition, detection lag
  - administrative or decision lag
  - impact, execution or implementation lag.

  These may be responsible for destabilizing instead of stabilizing economic activity.

Example 1

Determine whether the following statements are true or false. Explain your answers. Use a diagram to illustrate if possible.

1 Fiscal policy can destabilize instead of stabilizing economic activity.

   True. The reason is that fiscal policy is characterized by long time lags so there is always the chance that the expansionary impact of, say, a stimulus plan (i.e. of deficit spending) may materialize after recovery is underway on its own (say because of stronger export demand). In such a case the upswing of the business cycle may be too steep, meaning that growth may prove inflationary.

2 Within the monetarist or new classical perspective, expansionary fiscal policy cannot increase the level of potential output.

   True. In the short run the economy may produce a level of real output above its potential as a result of money wages being fixed in the short run and the average price level rising. When money wages adjust and catch up with the price level increase then the short run AS will decrease and shift to the left until the economy returns to Yp but with an even higher price level.

3 Within the Keynesian perspective, the effect of deficit spending depends on the shape of AS.

   True. To the extent that the economy is operating far below its potential level of output, the AS curve (note that within the Keynesian perspective there is really no reason to specify SRAS) will be (relatively) flat so the effect of the increase in AD will be mostly on real output and employment and much less on the average price level. If, though, the economy was close to its capacity level of output then the impact on the increase in AD would prove mostly inflationary. So, the size of the deflationary (recessionary) gap matters a lot.

4 The expansionary bias that often characterizes fiscal policy refers to its effectiveness during recessions.

   False. The term 'expansionary bias' of fiscal policy refers to the aversion many politicians have to increasing taxes and lowering government expenditures as such a contractionary policy mix is thought to lower their re-election chances.

5 **Deficit spending shifts the cost of expansionary fiscal policy onto future generations.**

True. Deficit spending implies government borrowing now and repayment of the principal and interest in the future. So it is the future generation that pays the bill. On the other hand, if the spending represented the construction of an airport then it will also be future generations enjoying the benefits derived from the present expenditures so they should bear some of the costs.

6 **If there is a high marginal propensity to import and to save then deficit spending will be less effective.**

True. One of the main arguments against using expansionary fiscal policy is that the increase in output will not really be worth the risks involved. The size of the multiplier does decrease the greater the leakages from the circular flow. These withdrawals include spending on imports and saving. If a country has a high marginal propensity to import (meaning that spending on foreign goods and services are a big proportion out of each extra dollar of income earned) any multiplier effect will be weakened. If households have a high marginal propensity to save (meaning that they tend to save a big proportion out of each extra dollar of income earned) or if they increase their marginal propensity to save, foreseeing additional future taxes resulting from the increased government spending now, then again the size of the multiplier will decrease.

7 **A country in recession with a wide social welfare system requires a smaller stimulus package than a country in recession where a smaller proportion of the population has unemployment insurance and other benefits.**

True. Unemployment benefits are an automatic stabilizer (and so are taxes). If an economy enters a recession which means that real income is falling (from, say, the potential level Yp in the diagram opposite to Y1, creating a recessionary gap) and is equipped with unemployment insurance for most of its labour force then, as people are made redundant, their incomes will not drop as unemployment benefits will start automatically.

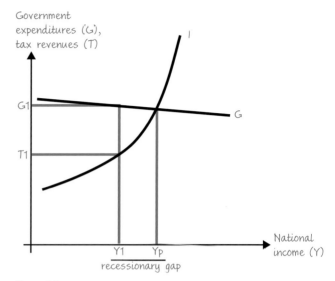

Figure 2.9

Private spending will therefore not fall as fast so a smaller stimulus package may be needed. In the diagram, even though a balanced budget was assumed at the level of potential output, a (cyclical) budget deficit was created. The bigger the increase in social insurance payments that start as a result of people losing their jobs and seeing their incomes dwindle, the smaller the necessary increase in government spending needed (ceteris paribus). Interestingly, this was the argument Europeans voiced to US suggestions that European governments adopt a bigger stimulus package to deal with the recession that started in 2007–08.

Exercise 1

Examine reasons for which governments should control their expenditures.

Exercise 2

Explain the routes through which reflationary fiscal policy is expected to affect economic activity and unemployment. What factors may limit its effectiveness?

Exercise 3

Explain why budget decisions may foster or hinder long-term economic growth.

Exercise 4

Explain how AD will be affected if income tax rates decrease.

2.5 Monetary policy

Tip

Demand for money often confuses students. To understand the concept, remember that you are given the choice of holding money (which **does not** earn interest) and bonds (that do earn interest). In this set-up, why would one ever demand money? The most important reason is to be able to finance transactions. So, if interest rates are higher the opportunity cost of holding money (instead of bonds) increases and the demand for money decreases giving rise to a negatively sloped money demand curve.

Tip

Always keep in mind that there could be a big difference between how, based on a model, we expect economic variables to behave and how they actually do behave. In your essays, opt to use the word 'may' or the expression 'is expected to': for example, 'if interest rates decrease then consumer expenditures **are expected to** increase'. Such a choice of words will automatically give you more opportunity to discuss or evaluate the issue.

Example 1

Match each term or concept with the appropriate definition or explanation.

1 Interest rate
2 Central bank
3 Demand for money
4 Easy monetary policy
5 Inflation targeting

a A practice adopted by some central banks which announce an explicit target rate of inflation gearing monetary policy towards achieving it

b The price paid by borrowers for using money or earned by lenders for lending money for a period of time expressed as a percentage

c An institution which oversees the operation of commercial banks and which is responsible for monetary and exchange rate policy

d The desire to hold money, a non-interest bearing asset, instead of other forms of wealth (such as bonds)

e A demand-side policy aiming to increase total spending on domestic goods by lowering interest rates (or increasing the money supply)

(1, b), (2, c), (3, d), (4, e), (5, a)

Example 2

Explain how easy monetary policy is expected to close a recessionary (deflationary) gap. Why is the shape of the AS curve important?

Assume that the central bank decides to adopt easier monetary policy. It will increase the money supply (by buying bonds in the open market) thus decreasing interest rates.

Lower interest rates are expected to increase consumption expenditures. This increase can be the result of saving becoming less attractive; if households save less they will tend to spend more as:

■ borrowing from commercial banks to finance the purchase of consumer durables such as cars will become cheaper

■ monthly payments of households with adjustable mortgage loans will decrease in size leaving more income available to spend.

Lower interest rates are expected to increase investment expenditures. This can be the result of borrowing becoming cheaper for firms so that more investment projects are considered profitable.

Also, lower interest rates will lower the value of the exchange rate (it will depreciate; this is explained later) rendering exports more competitive and imports less attractive. Net exports, another component of AD, will tend to increase.

If C and I and NX increase following a decrease in interest rates, then AD will shift to the right closing the recessionary gap of the economy. The shape (slope) of the AS curve determines the size of any resulting inflationary effect.

Example 3

Explain and show with a diagram how equilibrium interest rates are determined.

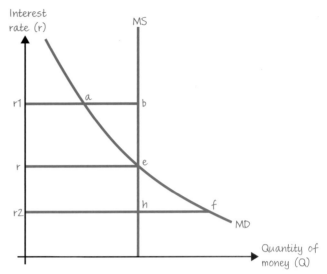

Figure 2.10

Within this simplified framework the money supply is assumed to be fully determined by the central bank. It is assumed to be independent of the interest rate and that explains why it is drawn as a vertical in the diagram above.

Money demand is inversely related to the interest rate. The interest rate represents the opportunity cost of holding money, so at higher interest rates individuals will wish to hold less money and more bonds, and vice versa.

At the interest rate r1 there is excess money supply which will push down the interest rate. As it decreases people will wish to hold more money so the excess supply of money decreases until equilibrium is achieved at interest rate r, where the quantity of money demanded equals the quantity of money supplied.

At interest rate r2 there is excess demand for money which will exert pressure on the interest rate to rise until equilibrium is restored.

Exercise 1

Match each term or concept with the appropriate definition or explanation.

1 Bond
2 Money supply
3 Exchange rate
4 Commercial banks
5 Tight monetary policy

a Profit-maximizing firms which attract deposits and make loans

b A demand-side policy aiming to decrease total spending on domestic goods by increasing interest rates (or decreasing the money supply)

c The quantity of money circulating in an economy which comprises not only coins and notes but also current account (sight) deposits

d Interest earning securities (assets) issued by governments (but also by firms)

e The price of a currency expressed in terms of another currency

Exercise 2

Determine whether the following statements are true or false. Explain your answers. Use a diagram to illustrate if possible.

1 In a recession, the effect of appropriate monetary policy may be dampened if business and consumer confidence is low.
2 Easy monetary policy may prove totally ineffective.
3 Monetary policy is easily reversible whereas fiscal policy is not.
4 Counter-cyclical monetary policy involves lowering interest rates in the upswing of the business cycle and raising interest rates in the downswing.

Exercise 3

Evaluate the effectiveness of monetary policy.

Exercise 4

Rewrite the following statements and fill in the blanks by using the terms provided below. Some terms may be used more than once or not at all.

inflation rate	guarantee
smaller	interest rates
decrease	bank panics
growth and employment	large
ambiguous	moral hazard
low cost	

If monetary policy significantly affects auto sales and the housing market then, for any desired change in AD, the necessary change in interest rates will be (1) _____.

The effect on real GDP of an increase in the money supply and a decrease in consumer confidence is (2) _____ even though interest rates will (3) _____.

If a central bank decides to control the money supply, it loses control over (4) _____. It cannot simultaneously control both. Also, if it decides to target the (5) _____ it limits its ability to affect overall (6) _____.

A flat AS will permit expansionary monetary policy to achieve (7) _____ gains in output and employment at a (8) _____ of inflation.

Many governments (9) _____ deposits to avoid (10) _____ but this creates a (11) _____ problem as it increases the incentive of banks to take risks. On a similar vein, the 'too big to fail' policy creates a similar incentive for (12) _____ banks.

133

- The supply side refers to the production side of an economy, so supply-side policies (SSPs) aim to increase (and shift to the right) the LRAS curve.

- SSPs can be either interventionist (meaning that the government is in charge of implementation) or market based (meaning that the role of markets is increased and that of the government is decreased).

- Investment spending by governments on infrastructure, on human capital and on research and development (R&D) affect AD in the short run while shifting the LRAS to the right.

- Industrial policy may also affect AD in the short run (even though the effect of tax breaks or subsidies aimed at a handful of firms may not significantly affect AD). If industrial policy is successful and targeted in key industries and sectors then LRAS may also be positively affected.

- Market-based SSPs aim at increasing competition in product markets through:
  - deregulation, privatization and trade liberalization
  - rendering labour markets more flexible (mainly by weakening labour unions, lowering job security and unemployment benefits and decreasing or abolishing the minimum wage)
  - improving incentives to work and to invest (mainly through tax cuts).

  Evaluating their effectiveness is more difficult as there have been spectacular successes as well as failures involved in their implementation.

Example 1

Determine whether the following statements are true or false. Explain your answers.

1 If the demand-side effect of a tax cut is greater than its supply-side effect then an increase in output and a decrease in prices is expected.

   False. AD will shift to the right as a tax cut will increase disposable income and thus consumption. Assuming that the tax cut improves incentives to work and to invest then the LRAS will also increase and thus shift to the right. But if the effect on AD is greater then both output and the average price level will rise.

2 Privatization aims at increasing economic efficiency.

   True. The central idea is that privately owned firms have a greater incentive to cut costs as their goal is to maximize profits. Of course, privatizations have also been a source of government revenue.

3 SSPs may worsen income distribution.

   True. Certain SSPs related to the labour market negatively affect labour income, especially of employed unionized workers, while certain tax cuts have increased the income of the well-off. This explains why market-based SSPs have met with opposition in many countries.

4 Increased spending on education and health will necessarily improve the stock of human capital of a country and thus lead to an increase in potential output and a shift right of the LRAS.

   False. The key word in the statement above is 'necessarily'. Public expenditures on health and/or on education in many countries have been notoriously inefficient. It is the quality of education and of health that is available to the people of a country and not just the quantity that matters. Conversely, there may be so much waste in a health care system that decreasing expenditures related to health care may not adversely affect health services but may even improve them.

5 Tax cuts increase potential output and shift LRAS to the right.

False. It all depends on the design, the size and the targets of a tax-cutting policy. Deceasing tax rates only for the highest income earners may not transform to an increase in domestic investment spending if most of the tax savings finance imported luxury goods and services or are invested abroad. A well-designed tax cut in many cases can have a positive impact on the incentive to work and to invest but we should not generalize.

6 Privatizations of monopolies may prove counter-productive.

True. A state-owned monopoly can, in principle at least, be prevented from abusing its monopoly power and if it is profitable these profits are collected by the state and may be used to finance public and merit goods. If the firm is privatized, then any profits are captured by the new owners while there is no guarantee that efficiency gains will follow.

7 A major advantage of SSPs over demand-side policies is that the former do not imply a trade-off between unemployment and inflation.

True. Unless the AS curve is flat, any increase in AD will also translate to some increase in the average price level, i.e. output may increase and unemployment decrease but at the cost of some inflationary pressures. In contrast, a successful SSP will increase potential output at any given rate of inflation.

Example 2

Rewrite the following statements and fill in the blanks by using the terms provided below. Some terms may be used more than once or not at all.

dismissal	minimum wage
wages	high
upturn	hire
insurance contributions	unemployment benefits
poverty	collective bargaining
costs	job offer
labour unions	flexible
outsiders	safety
productivity	insiders
market	balance

(1) _____ based SSPs often include labour market reforms. The goal of these reforms is to make the labour market more (2) _____, i.e. better able to adapt to changing market conditions.

Decreasing the power of (3) _____ is important as unions often keep (4) _____ higher than equilibrium to the benefit of (5) _____ (employed union members) and the detriment of (6) _____ (individuals searching for a job who are not able to find one because the wage rate is too (7) _____).

Lowering (8) _____ is also often on the agenda as more unemployed individuals would be willing to accept a (9) _____ if their alternative was not as attractive, while doing away with the (10) _____ will make hiring more attractive.

Making the (11) _____ of workers easier for firms is an additional supply-side measure as this would induce firms to (12) _____ more people instead of trying to rely on their existing labour force in the (13) _____ of the cycle.

Since wage costs for a firm include not only wages paid but also (14) _____ they make towards health and pension plans of their employees, decreasing the latter costs may also induce firms to hire more.

Lastly, since (15) _____ processes are seen as impediments to the ability of the labour markets to clear, market-based SSPs may also propose eliminating these altogether. In this way, wages will move up and down more freely and thus bring demand for labour into (16) _____ with supply of labour in each market.

Many critics claim that the adverse side effects are too significant to ignore. Here are some examples: labour unions that could be negatively affected by market-based SSPs serve to protect workers' (17) _____ in the factory; lower wages and work benefits decrease morale and thus (18) _____ leading to increased instead of decreased average production (19) _____ for firms; for the unemployed, low unemployment benefits may push many who have no other source of income or an extended family into (20) _____.

(1) market, (2) flexible, (3) labour unions, (4) wages, (5) insiders, (6) outsiders, (7) high, (8) unemployment benefits, (9) job offer, (10) minimum wage, (11) dismissal, (12) hire, (13) upturn, (14) insurance contributions, (15) collective bargaining, (16) balance, (17) safety, (18) productivity, (19) costs, (20) poverty

Exercise 1

Determine whether the following statements are true or false. Explain your answers. Use a diagram to illustrate if possible.

1 A government should only finance general R&D programmes and not product-specific research. (Hint: the idea of market failure is important here.)

2 Trade liberalization decreases any monopoly power in an industry.

3 The underlying logic behind industrial policy is that governments need to ensure that certain strategic industries, for example steel, aircraft and high technology industries, are large enough.

4 SSPs aim at stabilizing the economy.

5 The effect of privatization and deregulation on unemployment is ambiguous.

Exercise 2

Evaluate the effectiveness of SSPs.

Exercise 3

Rewrite the following statements and fill in the blanks by using the terms provided below. Some terms may be used more than once or not at all.

imports	subsidies
opposite	industrial policies
income distribution	minimum wage
opportunity cost	disposable income
normal	work
leisure	income inequality
budget deficit	misallocation
AD	tax breaks
incentive	

It is not certain that a cut in income tax rates will increase the (1) _____ to work. There are two effects which run in (2) _____ directions. On the one hand, a lower tax rate will increase the (3) _____ of leisure as the individual will sacrifice more by not choosing to (4) _____ more, but on the other hand the resulting increase in (5) ____ _____ may increase the demand for (6) _____ as it is considered a (7) _____ 'good'.

Criticisms of supply-side inspired tax cuts include that their effect may prove greater on (8) _____ proving inflationary; that they may widen a (9) _____; that they could worsen (10) _____; and that they may end up increasing (11) _____ of luxuries.

One of the major criticisms of (12) _____ is that governments are pretty bad in picking winners i.e. industries that have high potential and are thus worthwhile to nurture with (13) _____, subsidized loans or even direct (14) _____.

Lowering the (15) _____ may decrease production costs for firms and induce them to hire more people but the resulting reduction in income for the unskilled may increase (16)_____. Of course this must be weighed against the possibility that others without a job may at least be able to find one.

Concerning interventionist SSPs, a major argument against reliance on such polices is that they lead to (17) _____ of scarce resources and to waste.

3.1 International trade

Free trade

■ Trade does not refer only to the exchange of consumer goods but also, and very importantly, to raw materials and intermediate goods that firms use in their production processes.

Example 1

Determine whether the following statements are true or false. Explain your answers. Use a diagram to illustrate if possible.

1 To decrease domestic monopoly power a government could embrace free trade.

True. Liberalizing trade is a most effective policy option for governments wishing to diminish monopoly power in domestic markets. Opening up competition from abroad forces domestic firms to become more efficient. To survive they must cut costs and waste and reduce prices.

2 Social surplus increases with free trade but not all parties are better off.

True. Free trade increases consumer surplus but domestic, import-competing producers are worse off. The gains to consumers are enough to compensate producers fully so social surplus increases. The diagram below illustrates the point.

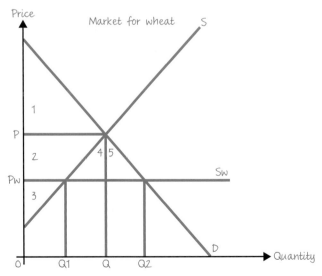

Figure 3.1

If the doors are 'locked' and there is no trade (the 'autarky case', when a country is economically self-sufficient and when 'prohibitive barriers' exist) then the equilibrium price will be P and the equilibrium quantity will be Q. Consumer surplus (the area above the price paid and below the demand curve for the units consumed) is equal to area (1) while producer surplus (the area above the supply and below the price earned for the units produced) is equal to area (2,3). Social surplus is area (1,2,3).

If the doors 'open' (in other words, if there is free trade) and the price of the good in the world market is at Pw then this price will also prevail in the domestic market (see the tip above). At this price, Pw, only the most efficient domestic firms will be able to offer Q1 units, while at that price consumers will buy Q2 units. The difference between the quantity that consumers buy (Q2) and what domestic producers offer (Q1) is made up of imports (units Q1Q2). Consumer surplus is now area (1,2,4,5) and producer surplus is area (3).

Area (2) was transferred from domestic producers to consumers but there has been a net gain in social surplus of area (4,5) as a result of free trade.

3 The efficiency benefits of free trade are fully realized when geographical and occupational mobility within the country characterizes the labour force.

True. The basic idea is that free trade will permit a country to focus and specialize in a subset of goods. For this to happen, resources (especially labour) must be able to move away from the production of goods that the country will start to import towards the production of goods that the country will start to export. Liberalizing trade requires re-allocation of resources. Re-allocation of labour will not be easy if workers lack the necessary skills or are geographically immobile.

HL

Remember

In absolute advantage what matters is whether the country can produce the good with fewer inputs; in comparative advantage what matters is whether the country can produce the good with fewer units of another good sacrificed.

Tip

When calculating opportunity costs of the production of a good for a country it is convenient to adopt a compact notation. You could adopt something like this:

'OC(X)/Kenya = ' which stands for 'the opportunity cost of producing good X in Kenya is ...'.

Tip

The slope of the production possibility frontier (PPF) is the opportunity cost of producing the good on the horizontal axis. Assuming that the horizontal axis measures units of good X while the vertical axis measures units of good Y, then the slope of the PPF is $\frac{\Delta Y}{\Delta X}$ and this is the opportunity cost of producing good X. A minus sign mirrors the idea of sacrifice. The inverse of the slope, i.e $\frac{\Delta X}{\Delta Y}$, is the opportunity cost of producing the good on the vertical.

Example 2

The data below refers to two countries, Melonia and Beefland, and the combinations of beef and melon output each can achieve if one unit of labour is employed.

	Melons (units of)	Beef (units of)
Melonia	600	0
	0	300
Beefland	800	0
	0	100

Draw their PPF curves and determine which country will specialize in and export beef, and why.

Step 1: Focus on one country and construct its PPF.

Let us focus initially on Melonia: if we measure beef on the horizontal and melons on the vertical then its linear PPF will look like the diagram opposite. (Note: If graph paper is provided you must measure to find the horizontal and vertical intercepts with precision.)

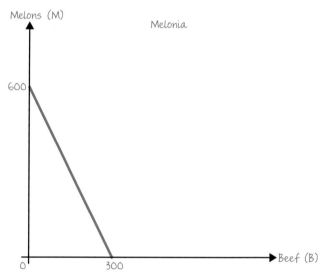

Figure 3.2

Make sure you write the quantities that can be produced of each good on each axis. Here, if Melonia produces 0 units of beef it can, at the most, produce 600 units of melons, whereas if it produces 0 melons it can produce, at the most, 300 units of beef.

Step 2: Focus on the other country now and construct its PPF (on the same diagram).

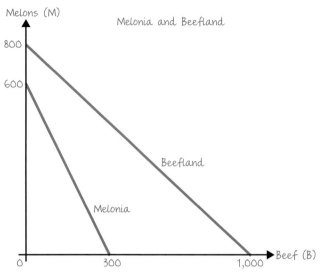

Figure 3.3

Here, if Beefland produces 0 units of beef it can produce, at the most, 800 units of melons, and if it produces 0 units of melons it can produce, at the most, 1,000 units of beef.

Step 3: Find the opportunity cost of producing beef for each country. Remember that for the good on the horizontal axis you just need to determine the slope of the PPF, so:

$$OC(B)/Melonia = \frac{-600}{300} = -2 \text{ units}$$
of melons

Melonia needs to sacrifice 2 melons to produce a unit of beef:

$$OC(B)/Beefland = \frac{-800}{1000} = -\frac{8}{10} \text{ units}$$
of melons

Beefland only needs to sacrifice less than a unit of melons ($\frac{8}{10}$ of a unit) to produce a unit of beef.

It follows that since Beefland can produce beef by sacrificing only $\frac{8}{10}$ of a unit of melons whereas Melonia needs to sacrifice 2 units of melons, Beefland has a lower opportunity cost in beef production and should thus specialize in and export beef. Conversely, Melonia should specialize in and export melons.

Exercise 1

Rewrite the following statements and fill in the blanks by using the terms provided below. Some terms may be used more than once or not at all.

economies of scale	capital
intermediate	role of the government
less efficient	technology
producers	shut down
adjustment	unemployed
inputs	lower
domestic markets	transfer and diffusion
raw	retrained

The lower prices resulting from free trade benefits domestic (1)_____ using imported (2)_____ materials and (3)_____ products in their production process. Not only will their production costs be (4)_____ but also they will be able to find (5)_____ with the exact specifications required which could improve the quality of their own product. Since (6)_____ goods embody (7)_____, free trade is a vehicle for the (8)_____ of technology which also spurs growth. Firms located in smaller countries with small (9)_____ will also benefit from (10)_____ as free trade will permit these firms to sell their product outside their small country. Of course some (11)_____ firms will suffer and be forced to (12)_____. Some workers will lose their jobs and become (13)_____. To the extent that these workers can be (14)_____ and become available for other businesses this development is efficient. It also points to the (15)_____ when trade is liberalized: (16)_____ costs for dislocated members of society must be mitigated and shared by all.

Exercise 2

Describe the objectives and functions of the World Trade Organization (WTO).

Exercise 3

The data below refer to two countries, Alpha and Beta, and the combinations of corn and wheat each can produce if one unit of labour is employed.

	Wheat	Corn
Country Alpha	0	1,800
	3,600	0
Country Beta	0	4,500
	6,000	0

Draw their PPF curves. Determine which country will import corn, and why.

Restrictions of free trade: trade protection

Remember

- Trade protection implies a shift away from more efficient foreign producers to less efficient domestic producers. This leads to misallocation of resources.

- Consumers in general lose. The exception is in the case of production subsidies where the import price remains unchanged, the volume of consumption remains unchanged and there is no decrease in consumer surplus.

- Domestic producers of the protected good as well as labour employed in the protected industry are always better off (but see tip opposite).

- In the case of a tariff, the government earns revenue (but see tip opposite) and it may earn revenues in the case of a quota if it auctions off the licenses to the highest bidders.

- Trade protection hurts exporting countries and this is important as it may lead to retaliation.

 Tip

When analyzing (discussing, evaluating) the effects of a trade protection policy, avoid restricting yourself to the term 'consumers'. Use instead the word 'buyers' in your analysis as it will help remind you that protected products very often refer to raw materials or intermediate goods that are used as inputs by other firms. If this is the case then production costs of these firms will be higher and thus their prices will be higher. They will become less competitive, losing sales and market share both domestically and perhaps abroad (if they are exporting firms) to foreign competitors. Government will collect lower revenues on lower sales and profits and employment levels may very well decrease or not increase. Therefore, the government may witness a decrease in revenues even if a tariff was imposed, while the net effect on employment could be negative even if jobs are maintained in the protected industry. Finally, a current account deficit (a trade deficit more specifically) may worsen despite the reduced import expenditures on the protected product.

Example 3

Match each description with the appropriate area or line segment on the diagram.

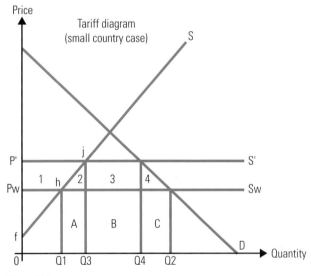

Figure 3.4

1 Volume of imports under free trade

2 Tariff revenues

3 Volume of imports following tariff

4 Decrease in consumer surplus as a result of the tariff

5 Value of imports after tariff is imposed (and export revenues collected by foreign producers after tariff is imposed)

a Area(1 + 2 + 3 + 4)

b Area(A + B + C)

c Line segment (fhSw)

d Area(2) and area(4)

e Line segment (Q1Q2)

f Line segment (PwP')

6 Increase in producer surplus as a result of the tariff

7 Supply of the good under free trade

8 Welfare loss as a result of the tariff

9 Production inefficiency as a result of the tariff

10 Supply of the good after the tariff is imposed

11 Consumption inefficiency as a result of the tariff

12 Value of imports under free trade (and export revenues foreign producers collect under free trade)

13 Size of the tariff imposed

14 Consumer spending on the good after the tariff is imposed

g Area(B) and area(3)

h Area(B)

i Area(2)

j Line segment (Q3Q4)

k Area(3)

l Line segment (fjS')

m Area(1)

n Area(4)

(1, e), (2, k), (3, j), (4, a), (5, h), (6, m), (7, c),
(8, d), (9, i), (10, l), (11, n), (12, b), (13, f), (14, g)

Example 4

Assume that the EU decides to protect its frozen strawberries market from cheaper Chinese frozen strawberries by imposing a tariff. What would you consider if you were to evaluate such a decision?

To go about questions like this one, first you need to brainstorm and jot down whatever your theoretical background offers you. The easiest way is to sketch a tariff diagram. You should realize that the clear 'winners' of such a policy choice include domestic (EU) producers of frozen strawberries as well as the labour employed in this industry. The clear losers of such a policy decision are consumers of frozen strawberries as they will face a higher price and consumption levels will drop.

It is here that you have to be careful. Very many products that are traded are not final consumer goods. A huge bulk represents either raw materials or intermediate products that are used as inputs by other firms. So if the consumers of frozen strawberries are not you or me but firms using frozen strawberries as an input (for example yoghurt or ice-cream producers) then their production costs and prices will be higher. They will lose domestic market share and perhaps lose export markets. Employment may drop, so any employment gains in the protected market may be wiped out. The net employment effect may be negative.

Concerning protected employment positions, we must consider the number of employees involved. Will many workers or just a few be affected? Most importantly, are they highly specialized workers who will be unable to find employment elsewhere and will require extensive retraining, or are they unskilled or semi-skilled workers who can easily be channelled to other production activities?

Even if the protected good is a consumer good the fact remains that real incomes (purchasing power) will be diminished as a result of the higher price for imports. This will mean that consumers will be forced to decrease demand across the board and employment and tax revenues will fall, imperceptibly perhaps in each separate market but significantly if you total the effects across all markets.

With respect to tariff revenues: yes, the government will collect that little rectangle in the diagram but because of the possible negative repercussions it may end up losing more revenues, making the net effect on its income negative.

Of course you need to bring in the issue of efficiency. Tariffs (and quotas or VERs) result in both production and consumption inefficiency. Protected firms have less of an incentive to cut costs and/or innovate so the long run adverse effects may be very serious for the economy.

Lastly, any trade protection move invites retaliation and the risk of trade frictions and a trade war. Such developments are extremely costly for all parties involved.

HL

Example 5

Assume that a quota is imposed on imports of good X. Answer the following questions using the information in the diagram below.

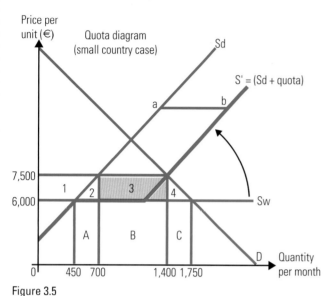

Figure 3.5

1 What is the size of the quota imposed?

The quota imposed is the volume of imports permitted into the country. Since at the new price (€7,500) domestic production is 700 units per month and domestic consumption is 1,400 units per month, their difference is the volume of imports, i.e. the size of the quota imposed: 1,400 units − 700 units = 700 units per month.

2 Calculate the value of imports (i.e. import expenditures on the good or export revenues of the foreign firms) under free trade.

Before the quota was imposed the price in the domestic market was €6,000 and equal to the world price of the product. At that price domestic firms offered 450 units per month while consumers demanded 1,750 units per month. The difference was the monthly volume of imports: 1,750 − 450 = 1,300 units imported per month. The size of import expenditures is the product of the price paid per unit multiplied by the number of units imported, or 6,000 × 1,300 = €7.8 million per month. This is area (A+B+C).

3 Calculate the revenues earned by domestic producers under free trade.

Multiplying the price per units (€6,000) by the volume of their sales (450 units) we can calculate the revenues earned by domestic firms: 6,000 × 450 = €2.7 million.

4 Calculate consumer expenditures on the good under free trade.

Multiply price paid per unit by the number of units consumed, or 6,000 × 1,750 = €10.5 million.

5 Calculate the change in the volume of imports as a result of the quota.

To find the decrease in the volume of imports subtract the quota from the original volume of imports: 1,300 − 700 = 600 fewer imported units per month.

6 Calculate import expenditures after the quota was imposed and the change that occurred as a result of the quota.

Be careful here: the quota (i.e. the restriction of the quantity imported) led to a higher price for consumers to pay in the domestic market. The difference between the original (per-quota) price and the new (post-quota) price is typically earned by foreign exporters but may be earned by domestic importers or even the government.
Assuming that foreign exporters earn the resulting difference in price, *the new import expenditures are equal to 7,500 × 700 = €5.25 million. This is area (B+3). Given that the initial value of imports was earlier calculated to be equal to €7.8 million, the difference is €2.55 million.*

If the difference in price was pocketed by domestic entities (firms or the government) then the price per unit earned by foreign exporters did not change but remained at €6,000 per unit, so the new import expenditures would be 6,000 × 700 = €4.2 million. This is area (B). In this case, import spending as a result of the quota decreased by more. Specifically, it decreased by €3.6 million (= 7.8 − 4.2).

7 How much did consumers spend on the good after the quota was imposed?

For all units purchased (1,400 per month) consumers paid €7,500 per unit, so they spent 7,500 × 1400 = €10.5 million.

8 What can you infer about the price elasticity of demand (PED) for the good given the price change in the market?

Since consumer expenditures remained the same (at €10.5 million) it follows that demand must be unitary elastic (PED = 1). To double-check:

$$PED = \frac{\%\Delta Q}{\%\Delta P} = \frac{(1,400 - 1,750)/1,400}{(7,500 - 6,000)/6,000} = -1$$

9 Calculate the size of the quota rents. Who earns these rents?

Quota rents represent 'money up for grabs' that resulted only because of the artificial restriction of the quantity of the good in the domestic market. It is equal to shaded area (3) in the diagram above, or

1,500 × 700 = 10.5 million
(€10.5 million per month).

Who collects this money depends on who receives the limited import licenses. The domestic government could auction off these licenses in which case the domestic government earns the quota rents. But the licenses could be allocated to domestic importing firms, foreign exporters or the government of the foreign exporters.

10 Calculate the resulting decrease in the consumer surplus.

Consumer surplus will have decreased by area (1 + 2 + 3 + 4) which is a trapezium (trapezoid).

The area of a trapezium is $\frac{B + b}{2} \times h$,

so $\frac{(1,750 + 1,400)}{2} \times 1,500$

= €2,362,500 (per month).

11 Calculate the resulting increase in the producer surplus.

This is area (1): $\frac{(700 + 450)}{2} \times 1,500$

= €862,500 (per month).

12 What is the resulting production inefficiency equal to?

This is area (2), the area of a right-angled

triangle: $\frac{(b \times h)}{2} = \frac{250 \times 1,500}{2}$

= €375,000 (per month).

13 Calculate the resulting consumption inefficiency.

This is area (4), another right-angled triangle:

$\frac{350 \times 1,500}{2}$ = €262,500 (per month).

Example 6

Assume that a subsidy is granted to the producers of good X. Answer the following questions using the information in the diagram below.

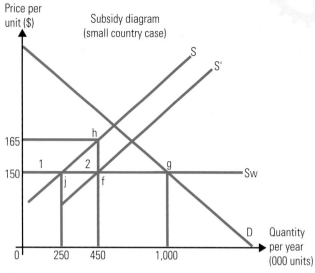

Figure 3.6

1 What is the size of the subsidy granted (on a per unit basis)?

The subsidy is the vertical distance (hf) between the two domestic supply curves, or $165 – $150 = $15 per unit.

2 Calculate the annual value of imports (i.e. import expenditures on the good or export revenues of the foreign firms) under free trade.

At the world price $150, domestic consumption was 1 million units per year of which 250,000 were domestically produced. It follows that 750,000 units were imported at an annual basis (or 1,000,000 – 250,000). Import expenditures were thus $112.5 million, the product of price per unit multiplied by the number of units imported.

3 Calculate the annual revenues earned by domestic producers under free trade.

Domestic producers were selling 250,000 units annually at a unit price of $150 and so earning revenues of $37.5 million.

4 Calculate annual consumer expenditures on the good under free trade.

Consumers paid $150 per unit and consumed 1 million units annually, spending $150 million.

5 Calculate the annual change in the volume of imports as a result of the subsidy.

After the subsidy was granted, domestic producers (facing lower costs) were willing to offer 450,000 units annually at $150 per unit. Consumption remained at 1 million units (as the price remained at $150) so imports decreased to 550,000 units (1,000,000 – 450,000) or by 200,000 units (750,000 – 550,000).

6   Calculate annual import expenditures after the subsidy was granted and the change that occurred as a result of the subsidy.

The post-subsidy expenditures on imports were $82.5 million. Since the pre-subsidy expenditures were calculated above at $112.5 million, it follows that annual spending on imports decreased by $30.0 million ($112,500,000 − $82,500,000).

7   How much did consumers spend annually on the good after the subsidy was granted?

Since neither the price paid by consumers nor their volume of consumption changed, it follows that their annual expenditures on the good remained the same (at $150 million).

8   Calculate the annual total revenues domestic firms collected after the subsidy was granted.

Producers earned $165 per unit produced after the subsidy. Multiplying this by the number of units sold at this price (450,000 units) gives us their annual revenues: $74.25 million.

9   Calculate the annual cost of the subsidy to the government.

The government will spend $15 per unit multiplied by the 450,000 units produced, i.e. $6.75 million annually.

10 Calculate the change in the consumer surplus.

Consumer surplus will not have changed as neither the price paid by consumers per unit of the good nor the amount they consume has changed.

11 Calculate the resulting increase in the producer surplus.

Producer surplus has increased by area (1). The area of this trapezoid is
$$\frac{250,000 + 450,000}{2} \times 15$$
= $5.25 million (which is the annual producer surplus).

12 What is the resulting production inefficiency equal to?

Production inefficiency is equal to area (2), or
$$\frac{200,000 \times 15}{2} = \$3 \text{ million (annually)}$$

13 Calculate the resulting consumption inefficiency.

Since there has been no change in consumption as a result of the subsidy, there is no consumption inefficiency in the market.

Exercise 4

Discuss the logic and validity of economic arguments used in favour of trade protection.

HL   **Exercise 5**

Assume that a tariff is imposed on good X. Answer the following questions using the information in the diagram below.

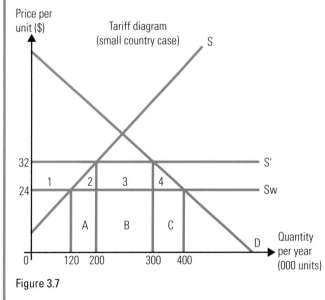

Figure 3.7

1   What is the size of the tariff imposed?

2   Calculate the pre-tariff volume of imports.

3   Calculate the value of imports (i.e import expenditures on the good or export revenues of the foreign firms) under free trade.

4   Calculate the revenues earned by domestic producers under free trade.

5   Calculate consumer expenditures on the good under free trade.

6   Calculate the post-tariff volume of imports and their change.

7   Calculate import expenditures after the tariff was imposed and the change that occurred as a result of the tariff.

8   How much did consumers spend on the good after the tariff was imposed?

9   The money spent by consumers after the tariff was imposed was collected by foreign exporters, domestic producers and the government. Calculate how much each group collected.

10 What is the resulting production inefficiency equal to?

11 Calculate the resulting decrease in the consumer surplus.

Exercise 6

Assume that Mexico imposes a quota on the imports of good X. Answer the following questions using the information in the diagram below.

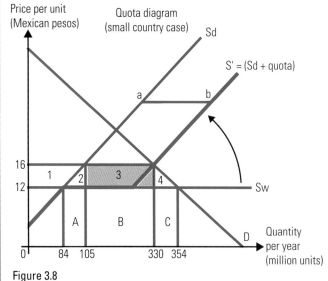

Figure 3.8

1 What is the size of the quota imposed?

2 Calculate the value of imports (i.e. import expenditures on the good or export revenues of the foreign firms) under free trade.

3 Calculate the revenues earned by domestic producers under free trade.

4 Calculate consumer expenditures on the good under free trade.

5 Calculate the change in the volume of imports as a result of the quota.

6 Calculate import expenditures after the quota was imposed and the change that occurred as a result of the quota.

7 How much did consumers spend on the good after the quota was imposed?

8 Calculate the size of the quota rents. Who earns these rents?

9 Calculate the resulting decrease in the consumer surplus.

10 What is the resulting production inefficiency equal to?

11 Calculate the resulting consumption inefficiency.

3.2 Exchange rates

Freely floating, fixed and managed exchange rates

Remember

- The exchange rate is simply a price: the price of a currency, for example the price for one euro, or one Australian dollar or one Danish krone. It must be expressed in terms of some other currency. For example, the price of one euro on 22 December 2010 was 1.33 Canadian dollars or 109.9 Japanese yen. The price of the Australian dollar on the same date was 45.09 Indian rupees or 3.13 Malaysian ringgit; the price of the Danish krone that day was 0.177 Canadian dollars or 1.06 Norwegian krone, etc.

- The exchange rate of a currency in a floating exchange rate system is determined by the interaction of the demand for and the supply of the currency: thus any factor that changes the demand and/or the supply will tend to change the exchange rate.

- A currency is demanded and bought in the foreign exchange market in order to buy a country's exports, its bonds and stocks, to invest directly in the country or just in the hope of selling the currency later at a higher price. Similarly, a currency is supplied and sold in the foreign exchange market to buy imports from other countries, to buy bonds and stocks in other countries, to invest directly in other countries or just to buy other currencies in the hope that their price will rise.

  It follows that any change in the above or in any factor affecting the above will in turn affect the exchange rate. Such changes include changes in relative inflation rates, relative interest rates, relative growth rates and in expectations.

- Changes in the exchange rate may affect the current account balance, inflation, employment, growth prospects, income distribution, etc.

Tip

- Students often make mistakes when labelling the axes in a foreign exchange diagram. Start by using very descriptive labels, and when you feel comfortable perhaps switch to more compact labels.

- Assume that you are interested in illustrating the Brazilian real (BRL). On the vertical axis write 'price of Brazilian real (BRL)' and below this write 'expressed in dollars: $/BRL'. Make sure you understand that the vertical axis here depicts US dollars (as the dollar is the currency in which you chose to express the price of BRL). Since on the vertical you have the price of BRL, go to the horizontal and write 'quantity of BRL per period' or simply 'BRL/period'. The demand curve should read 'D for BRL' and the supply curve should read 'S of BRL'.

Tip

- Excess demand in the foreign exchange market will tend to increase the value of a currency while excess supply will tend to lower it.

- If the price of a currency increases it is referred to as an appreciation (in a floating system) or a revaluation (in a fixed system).

- If the price of a currency decreases it is referred to as a depreciation (in a floating system) or a devaluation (in a fixed system).

Example 1

Match each term or concept with the appropriate definition or explanation.

1 Exchange rate	c	The price of a currency expressed in terms of another currency
2 Depreciation	g	A decrease in the price of a currency in a floating exchange rate system
3 Revaluation	e	An increase in the price of a currency in a fixed exchange rate system
4 Floating exchange rate system	b	A system where exchange rates are determined only by market forces without any intervention by governments of central banks
5 Managed exchange rate system	f	A system of exchange rate determination in which central banks intervene periodically when the currency moves in the wrong direction or too fast
6 Fixed exchange rate system	h	A system where the exchange rate is determined (fixed) by central banks which are thus required to intervene to maintain it
7 Appreciation	a	An increase in the price of a currency in a floating exchange rate system
8 Devaluation	d	A decrease in the price of a currency in a fixed exchange rate system

(1, c), (2, g), (3, e), (4, b), (5, f), (6, h), (7, a), (8, d)

Example 2

Determine whether the following statements are true or false. Explain your answers.

1   A weaker currency will result in higher inflation due to dearer imports.

True. A decrease in the value of a currency implies a higher domestic price for imports. The average price level thus automatically increases. Production costs of domestic firms may also increase if they import raw materials and intermediate goods.

2   An undervalued Chinese renminbi (yuan) implies lower inflationary pressures for the USA.

True. If the Chinese yuan renminbi is undervalued with respect to the US dollar then Chinese products imported into the USA are cheaper, decreasing any inflationary pressures in the US economy.

3   Revaluation and appreciation both mean an increase in the value of a currency but the former is used in a flexible (floating) exchange rate system whereas the latter is reserved for a fixed system.

False. The first part of the statement is correct (both imply a stronger currency) but appreciation is reserved for use in a floating system and revaluation is used in a fixed system.

4   In a fixed exchange rate system there is less uncertainty but the government is deprived of monetary policy.

True. Less uncertainty for importers and exporters of goods and services as well as for investors is one of the most important advantages of a fixed system. On the other hand, policymakers cannot employ monetary policy as any change in interest rates will immediately affect the exchange rate.

5   In a floating exchange rate system trade imbalances tend to be corrected automatically, assuming proper elasticities.

True. A current account deficit will tend to weaken a currency which in turn will make exports more competitive and imports less attractive and (elasticities permitting) this will correct the imbalance (and vice versa).

6   A growing economy will absorb more imports, leading to a depreciating currency.

False. A growing economy will absorb more imports and this will create pressure for the currency to weaken, but it may also attract more investments from abroad which will counter the tendency for the currency to depreciate. In addition, growth may be export driven in which case the widening surplus will create pressure for the currency to appreciate.

7   If higher interest rates attract hot monies into a country then the country with the highest interest rate will attract all hot monies.

False. If interest rates increase in country A then its bonds as well as deposits in its currency will become more attractive to foreign financial investors. They expect a higher return on their investments. Their actual return, though, also depends on what the currency is worth. In order to purchase these bonds or to make these deposits they first need to buy the currency so the increased demand for it will exert pressure for it to appreciate.

8   If currency A appreciates by 100 % against currency B, it follows that currency B depreciated by 100 % against currency A.

False. If it was true then currency B would become worthless. Let 1 unit of currency A be worth initially 100 units of currency B. If 1 unit of currency A becomes worth 200 units of B then currency A has appreciated by 100%. What about currency B? Initially, 100 units of currency B were worth 1 unit of currency A but now, 100 units of currency B are worth only 50 units of currency A so currency B depreciated by 50% against A.

Example 3

Rewrite the following statements and fill in the blanks by using the terms provided below. Some terms may be used more than once or not at all.

investments	inflation
floating	relative
more attractive	portfolio
differentials	absorption
supply	devalue
intervention	demand
growth	less competitive
increase	appreciate
buying	fixed
depreciate	strengthen
foreign goods and services	central bank

In a (1)_____ exchange rate system the exchange rate is determined only by market forces without any (2)_____ by governments or central banks. An (3)_____ in the demand for a country's exports will tend to increase the price of the currency while an increased appetite for (4)_____ will tend to weaken it. Changes in (5)_____ interest rates also affect the exchange rate. For example, if the UK adopts a tighter monetary policy then (6)_____ for the pound sterling will increase as foreigners will want to increase their holdings of UK bonds and/or to increase their pound deposits. As a result the currency will (7)_____. Inflation rate (8)_____ are another factor affecting the value of a currency. Higher domestic (9)_____ weakens a currency as exports become pricier and (10)_____ decreasing export demand (and so the demand for the currency) while imports become (11)_____ so (12)_____ of the currency increases. The effect is for the currency to (13)_____. The effect of higher economic (14)_____ is ambiguous as, on the one hand, the resulting higher import (15)_____ rates tend to weaken the currency, but, on the other hand, a strong economy attracts (16)_____ from abroad, both (17)_____ and foreign direct investment.

In a (18)_____ exchange rate system, the government or the (19)_____ must continuously intervene in the foreign exchange market to neutralize any market-induced change in demand or supply of the currency. If there is excess supply of the currency and thus pressure to (20)_____, then the intervention takes the form of (21)_____ the currency using foreign exchange reserves.

(1) floating, (2) intervention, (3) increase,
(4) foreign goods and services, (5) relative,
(6) demand, (7) strengthen, (8) differentials,
(9) inflation, (10) less competitive,
(11) more attractive, (12) supply, (13) depreciate,
(14) growth, (15) absorption, (16) investments,
(17) portfolio, (18) fixed, (19) central bank,
(20) devalue, (21) buying

Example 4

Explain why demand for a currency, say the Brazilian real (BRL), may increase in the foreign exchange market.

An increase in the demand for the BRL may be a result of an increased foreign appetite for Brazilian goods and services (Brazilian exports). It may also be the result of an increased appetite for Brazilian assets (bonds, deposits, stocks, firms, etc.) by foreign investors (capital inflows into Brazil). Or, the Brazilian government may start buying its own currency by selling foreign currencies, say, to stabilize it. Lastly, speculators may want to buy the BRL if they expect it to strengthen in the future and would like to take advantage of this.

Example 5

Explain two reasons why an increased foreign appetite for Brazilian physical or financial assets may arise.

First, an increase in Brazilian interest rates will increase foreign appetite for Brazilian bonds and deposits in the BRL as the return on such fixed income assets will be greater. The same effect would be expected if US interest rates decreased as what matters are changes in 'relative interest rates' or changes in 'interest rate differentials'. The decreased US interest rates would force investors to switch to other assets. Brazilian interest rates will have relatively increased, attracting funds into the country.

Also, capital will flow into Brazil if the prospects look good for the Brazilian economy. Higher expected profitability for Brazilian firms will attract both investments in Brazilian shares (stocks) and foreign direct investment.

Example 6

Fill in the labels in the following diagram aiming to illustrate the price of Australian dollars (AUD) expressed in terms of the euro (EUR).

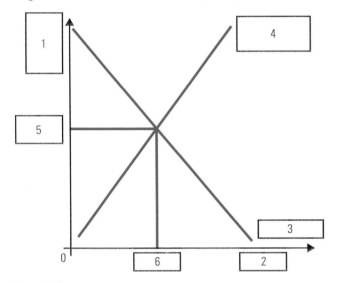

Figure 3.9

1 Price of AUD expressed in terms of EUR (i.e. EUR/AUD). (Note: this is a source of many errors. Remember that whatever is in the denominator is also on the horizontal axis.)

2 AUD traded per period (quantity of AUD).

3 Demand for AUD (exports of AU; inflows of financial capital).

4 Supply for AU (imports of AU; outflows of financial capital).

5 e (er or EUR/AUD).

6 Quantity of AUD traded.

Note: there are many abbreviations you can use. Follow your teacher's advice but make sure the ones you use are explicit enough, at least until you become comfortable using such diagrams.

Example 7

Assume that the currency of a country sharply depreciates. Make a list of the possible consequences on the economy.

- A weaker currency means that the foreign price of exports decreases. Exports, in other words, become more competitive abroad.

- A weaker currency means that the domestic price of imports increases. Imports become less attractive.

- **HL** What happens to the current account balance (the trade balance, also known as the balance of trade: BOT) depends on the PED for exports and the PED for imports. If the sum of the two elasticities exceeds one (the Marshall–Lerner condition, discussed later) then the current account will improve (whether measured in the domestic or foreign currency). In the long run a current account deficit will tend to improve.

- Net exports (NX = X − M), a component of aggregate demand (AD), will tend to increase, assuming proper elasticities.

- The increase in AD will tend to increase real output (growth) but also the price level.

- The extent to which real output and the price level increase depends on the shape of the aggregate supply (AS) curve. An economy in recession will benefit in terms of increased output and employment (think of the shape of the AS curve; think of the size of the recessionary gap). An economy operating close to capacity will suffer from higher inflation.

- Cost of living automatically increases since the basket of goods and services purchased by the typical consumer also includes imports. If this leads to demands for higher wages then an inflationary spiral may start. Also, if domestic firms import raw materials and intermediate goods then domestic production costs increase, leading to cost-push inflationary pressures.

- Exporting firms as well as import-competing firms have less of an incentive to strive for efficiency as the depreciation renders both more competitive.

- Any benefits to the exporting sector may dissipate if inflationary pressures are not contained.

- **HL** The terms of trade (discussed later) of the country worsen as imports become relatively pricier. The volume of imports attainable by a unit of exports decreases. Its command over foreign goods is eroded.

> **Remember**
>
> - If the exchange rate of currency α in terms of currency β is e, then the exchange rate of currency β in terms of α will be the inverse, or $1/e$. For example, if €1.00 = \$1.3148 then \$1.00 = €(1/1.3148) or €0.7606.

HL Calculating the equilibrium exchange rate and quantity

You may be given a linear demand and a linear supply for a currency and asked to calculate the equilibrium exchange rate e and the volume Q of the currency traded.

The procedure is identical to the one described in microeconomics when determining the equilibrium price and quantity of a good.

The equilibrium condition is:

Qd = Qs

So there are three equations and three unknowns:

(1) Qd = a – be

(2) Qs = c + de

(3) Qd = Qs

Solve whichever way you find most convenient. You could substitute (1) and (2) for Qd and Qs in the equilibrium condition (3) and solve for e. Once you find the equilibrium exchange rate e, substitute it into either (1) or (2) to determine the equilibrium volume traded.

Example 8

In the table below the price of the Australian dollar (AUD) is given in terms of a number of world currencies as of 22 December 2010. Calculate the exchange rate of each of these currencies expressed in terms of the AUD.

Abbreviation	Currency unit	Units per AUD
CLP	Chilean peso	468.7801
DKK	Danish krone	5.6620
EUR	Euro	0.7602
HKD	Hong Kong dollar	7.7729
INR	Indian rupee	45.0787
KES	Kenyan shilling	80.5208
MYR	Malaysian ringgit	3.1314

Abbreviation	Currency unit	Units per AUD
NZD	New Zealand dollar	1.3427
RUB	Russian ruble	30.6745
SGD	Singapore dollar	1.3081
SEK	Swedish krona	6.8066
CHF	Swiss franc	0.952
GBP	UK pound sterling	0.6468
USD	US dollar	0.9996

Since the exchange rate of currency α in terms of currency β is e, then the exchange rate of currency β in terms of α will be the inverse, or $1/e$. So we just need to find the inverse of each number above:

Price of:	in AUD
Chilean pesos	0.0021
Danish krone	0.1766
Euro	1.3154
Hong Kong dollar	0.1287
India rupee	0.0222
Kenyan shilling	0.0124
Malaysian ringgit	0.3193
New Zealand dollar	0.7448
Russian ruble	0.0326
Singapore dollar	0.7645
Swedish krona	0.1469
Swiss franc	1.0504
UK pound sterling	1.5461
US dollar	1.0004

HL

Example 9

The following equations describe the demand for and supply of Australian dollars (AUD), where e is the price of the Australian dollar expressed in euros (EUR), Qd is the quantity of Australian dollars demanded and Qs is the quantity of Australian dollars supplied per week (in millions).

$Qd = 497.6 - 4e$; $Qs = 366.7 + 7e$

1 Determine the exchange rate of the Australian dollar in euros (EUR/AUD).

Since the equilibrium condition is Qd = Qs, you could substitute into the demand and supply equations provided:
Qd = 497.6 − 4e = Qs = 366.7 = 7e

Solving for e:
497.6 − 366.7 = 7e + 4e
130.9 = 11e
e = 11.9

2 Determine the volume of Australian dollars traded per week.

Substitute the price of the AUD in EUR into either the demand or the supply equation: into the demand equation, Qd = 497.6 − (4 × 11.9) = 450 million per week. Double-checking:
Qs = 3667 + (7 × 119) = 45 million per week.

Example 10

The following equations describe the daily demand for and supply of euros (EUR) in December 2010, where e is the price of the euro expressed in US dollars (USD), Qd is the quantity of euros demanded per day and Qs is the quantity of euros supplied per day (in billions).

$Qd = 352.92 - 6e$; $Qs = 338.4 + 5e$

1 Determine the exchange rate of the euro in US dollars (USD/EUR).

Since the equilibrium condition is Qd = Qs, you could substitute it in the demand and supply equations provided:
352.92 − 6e = 338.4 + 5e

Solving for e:
352.92 − 338.4 = 5e + 6e
14.52 = 11e
e = 1.32

2 Determine the volume of euros traded per day.

Substituting the price of the euro in USD into either the demand or the supply equation: into the demand equation, Qd = 352.92 − (6 x 1.32) = 345 billion euros per day.
Double-checking:
Qs = 338.4 + (5 x 1.32)
= 345 billion euros per day.

Example 11

The following table presents the price of the Swiss franc (CHF) in terms of five different currencies at three different points in time: on 27 December 2000, 2005 and 2010. Determine the percentage by which the Swiss franc appreciated or depreciated with respect to each of these currencies between 2000 and 2005 as well as between 2005 and 2010.

	Units per Swiss franc (CHF)		
	27 Dec 2000	27 Dec 2005	27 Dec 2010
Australian dollar	1.099	1.048	1.038
Euro	0.659	0.642	0.793
Japanese yen	70.009	89.088	86.342
UK pound sterling	0.413	0.440	0.676
US dollar	0.614	0.761	1.043

It makes sense to split the table into two so that it is easier to follow the changes.

	Change in CHF value between 27 Dec 2000 and 27 Dec 2005			
	27 Dec 2000	27 Dec 2005	% change	CHF:
Australian dollar	1.099	1.149	4.64%	appreciated by 4.64%
Euro	0.659	0.642	−2.58%	depreciated by 2.58%
Japanese yen	70.009	89.086	27.25%	appreciated by 27.25%
UK pound sterling	0.413	0.440	6.54%	appreciated by 6.54%
US dollar	0.614	0.761	23.94%	appreciated by 23.94%

Change in CHF value between 27 Dec 2005 and 27 Dec 2010				
	27 Dec 2005	27 Dec 2010	% change	CHF:
Australian dollar	1.048	1.038	−0.95%	depreciated by 0.95%
Euro	0.642	0.793	23.52%	appreciated by 23.52%
Japanese yen	89.001	86.342	−3.08%	depreciated by 3.08%
UK pound sterling	0.440	0.676	53.64%	appreciated by 53.64%
US dollar	0.761	1.043	37.06%	appreciated by 37.06%

Exercise 1

Determine whether the following statements are true or false. Explain your answers. Use a diagram to illustrate if possible.

1 Higher inflation, ceteris paribus, will create pressure for the exchange rate to decrease in value.

2 Easy monetary policy in the USA will, ceteris paribus, create pressure on the Brazilian currency to appreciate in value.

3 Whenever there is excess demand for a currency in the foreign exchange market there will be a tendency for its value to increase.

4 If in a fixed exchange rate system there is pressure for the currency to weaken, the central bank will defend it by selling it and/or by lowering interest rates to induce financial capital inflows.

5 A benefit of an appreciating currency is that it may force domestic firms (both exporters and import-competing firms) to become more efficient.

Exercise 2

Assume a sharply appreciating currency. Make a list of the possible consequences on the economy.

Exercise 3

Rewrite the following statements and fill in the blanks by using the terms provided below. Some terms may be used more than once or not at all.

periodic	attractiveness	certainty
flexible	opportunity cost	price
monetary	devaluation	unemployment
competitiveness	fiscal	decreases
interest	depreciating	widening
reserves	deficits	
inflation	managed	

The term (1)_____ is reserved to describe a decrease in the price of a currency in a fixed exchange rate system. A weakening currency in a floating (also, referred to as a (2)_____ system) is known as a (3)_____ currency.

A major advantage of a fixed regime is the increased (4)_____ in conducting trade-related business and cross-border investments. Firms and investors alike do not have to worry about movements in the exchange rate which would change the relative (5)_____ of exports and imports as well as the (6)_____ of both portfolio and foreign direct investments. In addition, governments are forced to keep (7)_____ under control as otherwise export (8)_____ would be eroded and (9)_____ trade deficits are not compatible with fixed exchange rates.

On the other hand, a major drawback is that policymakers are deprived of (10)_____ policy. They can not lower (11)_____ rates to boost economic activity as this would lead to devaluation. Also, trade (12)_____ have to be corrected by adopting contractionary (13)_____ policy so that national income (14)_____ and imports decrease. This implies higher (15)_____. Lastly, the central bank must maintain sizable foreign exchange (16)_____ at a high (17)_____ to be able to intervene in the foreign exchange market and maintain the parity.

(18)_____ exchange rates involve (19)_____ intervention by the authorities whenever exchange rates move too fast or in the wrong direction.

Exercise 4

The following equations describe the daily demand for and supply of UK pounds sterling (GBP) in December 2010, where e is the price of the pound expressed in US dollars, Qd is the quantity of pounds demanded per day and Qs is the quantity of pounds supplied per day (in billions).

$Qd = 701.24 - 18e$

$Qs = 618.64 + 4e$

1 Determine the exchange rate of the UK pound sterling in US dollars (USD/GBP).

2 Determine the volume of euros traded per day.

Exercise 5

The following equations describe the monthly demand for and supply of Chilean pesos (CLP) in December 2010, where e is the price of the Chilean peso expressed in Colombian pesos (COP), Qd is the quantity of Chilean pesos demanded per day and Qs is the quantity of Chilean pesos supplied per month (in millions).

$Qd = 919.76 - 16e$

$Qs = 837.56 + 4e$

1 Determine the exchange rate of the Chilean peso expressed in Colombian pesos (COL/CLP).

2 Determine the volume of Chilean pesos traded per month.

Exercise 6

A leading IB economics textbook was priced by an online retailer at USD33.59. The table below provides the price of the US dollar in different currencies. Calculate the price of this textbook in each of these currencies.

Abbreviation	Currency unit	Units per USD
CLP	Chilean peso	469.950
DKK	Danish krone	5.667
EUR	Euro	0.760
HKD	Hong Kong dollar	7.780
INR	Indian rupee	45.213
KES	Kenyan shilling	80.649
MYR	Malaysian ringgit	3.097
NZD	New Zealand dollar	1.335
RUB	Russian ruble	30.456
SGD	Singapore dollar	1.298
SEK	Swedish krona	6.832
CHF	Swiss franc	0.958
GBP	UK pound sterling	0.648

Exercise 7

The following table presents the price of the UK pound sterling (GBP) in terms of 12 different currencies at two different points in time: on 29 December 2005 and 2010. Determine whether each of these currencies strengthened or weakened with respect to the pound between 2005 and 2010 and by what percentage. For example, did the Australian dollar appreciate or depreciate against the pound? By what percentage? (Answer: the Australian dollar appreciated by 55.4 % or, equivalently, the pound depreciated by 35.65 %.)

Currency and abbreviation	Units per GBP	
	29 Dec 2005	29 Dec 2010
Australian dollar AUD	2.359	1.518
Canadian dollar CAD	2.011	1.536
China yuan renminbi CNY	13.932	10.188
Euro EUR	1.457	1.171
Japanese yen JPY	203.499	126.374
New Zealand dollar	2.530	2.019
Norway krone NOK	11.686	9.151
Singapore dollar SGD	2.874	1.993
Swiss franc CHF	2.269	1.465
US dollar USD	1.726	1.539
Mexico peso MXN	18.469	19.011
South Korea won KRW	1,747.790	1,759.992

3.3 Balance of payments

The structure of the balance of payments, current account deficits, current account surpluses

Remember

- The balance of payments (BOP) is just a record of all transactions of a country with the rest of the world over a period of time (typically a year).

- It is broken down into the current account, the capital account and the financial account (which includes changes in reserves). The sum of these three accounts by construction balances as the sum total of outflows of currency from the country must either have been earned or borrowed or foreign reserves must have been run down.

- If currency flows into the country then the transaction is recorded with a plus sign and it is a credit item; if currency flows out of the country then the transaction is recorded with a minus sign and it is a debit item.

- The current account and the financial account are interdependent through net income: for example, the purchase by an investor resident in country A of German bonds and stocks is registered as a debit item in the financial account of country A (as currency flows out of A) but the interest payments and dividends collected in the future will be registered as credit items (inflows of currency) in the net income (from investments) section of country A's current account.

- The capital account is small and of minor importance so just be aware that it includes credit and debit entries for 'non-produced, non-financial assets and unilateral capital transfers' between residents and non-residents.

- Any change in any component of the BOP will tend to affect the exchange rate. It follows that given the capital and financial account balance, if a country records a current account deficit then more of its currency is offered by it to buy imports than is demanded by its trading partners to buy its exports. This will put pressure on its currency to weaken, and vice versa.

- Since $M = f(Y^+_d, er)$ and $M = f(Y^+_f, er)$ where Yd is domestic income, Yf is foreign income and er is the exchange rate, it follows that to correct a current account deficit either domestic income has to grow slower than foreign income (or decrease) or the exchange rate has to depreciate or devalue so that import prices increase, making domestic goods relatively cheaper. Expenditure-reducing policies aim to achieve the former whereas expenditure-switching policies aim to achieve the latter.

- Assuming that devaluation or sharp depreciation is chosen within an expenditure-switching framework to correct a current account deficit, its success depends upon the PED for exports and for imports. More specifically, for the deficit to narrow: $(PED_x + PED_M) > 1$. This is the Marshall-Lerner condition which is not satisfied immediately as elasticities are low in the short run (due to lack of information, habits and contracts) giving rise to the J-curve effect.

Example 1

Match each term or concept with the appropriate definition or explanation.

1. Debt forgiveness
2. Balance of payments (BOP)
3. Financial account
4. Natural resources; contracts, leases, and licenses; marketing assets; goodwill
5. Debit item

a. Examples of capital transfers that are included in the capital account
b. This account includes entries for non-produced, non-financial assets as well as unilateral capital transfers
c. Examples of marketing assets
d. Exists when the sum of net exports of goods and services plus net income from investments plus net transfers is negative
e. The voluntary cancellation of all or part of a debt obligation

6 Brand names, trademarks, logos, domain names and the sale of franchises

7 Credit item

8 Current account deficit

9 Trade balance

10 Debt forgiveness and investment grants

11 Current account

12 Investment grants

13 Capital account

14 Direct investment

15 Transfer

f A record of all transactions of a country with the rest of the world over a period of time

g Capital transfers made by governments or international organizations to finance the costs of specific investment projects such as large construction projects

h Includes direct investment, portfolio investment, other investment and reserve assets

i Investment associated with a resident in one country having control or a significant degree of influence on the management of an enterprise that is resident in another economy

j Examples of non-produced, non-financial assets

k Transactions leading to an outflow of foreign exchange

l Transactions leading to an inflow of foreign exchange

m Includes net exports of goods and services, net income from investments and net current transfers

n A transaction that does not involve an exchange

o Exports of goods less imports of goods

(1, e), (2, f), (3, h), (4, j), (5, k), (6, c), (7, l), (8, d), (9, o), (10, a), (11, m), (12, g), (13, b), (14, i), (15, n)

Example 2

Determine whether the following statements are true or false. Explain your answers.

1 Receipts from the export of goods and services are registered with a minus sign as they represent an outflow of domestic output.

False. Exports lead to an inflow of currency. They are thus a credit item and are recorded with a plus sign.

2 In 2010, a UK resident bought $1.2 million worth of US stocks which earned her $120,000 in investment income (dividends) in 2011. These were recorded in the US BOP as credit and debit entries in 2010 and 2011 respectively in the US current account.

False. Portfolio investment (the buying and selling of stocks and bonds) is recorded in the financial account. Income earned or paid in the future is recorded in the current account. So, in 2010 the transaction represented a credit item ($1.2 million) for the US financial account while in 2011 the $120,000 earned was recorded as a debit in the US current account.

3 The proceeds from the sale of a Turkish bank to Italian investors is recorded as a credit item in the Turkish financial account and it represents foreign direct investment into Turkey.

True. Foreign direct investment is a component of the financial account. Since currency flowed into the Turkish economy it was a credit item in the Turkish BOP.

4 A rise in foreign exchange reserves will result after a central bank's intervention to offset currency weakness.

False. If the value (the price) of the currency is decreasing then the central bank has to enter the foreign exchange market and start buying it using (i.e. running down) its foreign exchange reserves. A fall in foreign exchange reserves will follow.

5 The BOP is constructed in such a way that it always balances.

True. Any outflow of currency must either have been earned or borrowed or foreign reserves must have been run down. This means that the sum of the current account, the capital account and the financial account, including changes in official reserves as well as official borrowing or lending, will be equal to zero.

6 A widening current account deficit creates pressure on the value of a currency to rise.

False. A widening current account deficit means that import spending (supply of the currency) rises relatively to export earnings (demand for the currency) or that excess supply of the currency will result, pushing the price of the currency down.

7 Ceteris paribus, an increase in exports will increase the demand for the currency in foreign exchange markets and the resulting excess demand for it may lead to an appreciation.

True. For foreigners to buy the goods and services of a country (i.e. its exports) they must first buy its currency in the foreign exchange market. The demand for a currency therefore reflects the value of exports of a country (assuming away capital and financial account transactions) so a rise in exports implies an increase in demand for the currency and thus an increase in its value (appreciation).

HL 8 A devaluation or sharp depreciation will correct a current account deficit only if demand for exports is price elastic.

False. The Marshall–Lerner condition states that it suffices that the sum of PED for exports and PED for imports is greater than unity. So PED for exports could be only 0.6 (inelastic) but if PED for imports is greater than 0.4 then a devaluation or sharp depreciation will narrow a current account deficit.

9 The J-curve effect refers to the typical behavior of the balance on goods and services following a sharp depreciation of the currency.

True. As a result of the Marshall–Lerner condition not being satisfied in the short run, a devaluation or sharp depreciation will initially widen a deficit and only later narrow it. Tracing this on the current account through time gives rise to the letter 'J'.

10 Expenditure-switching policies in the face of fundamental current account deficits attempt to make imports pricier and exports cheaper.

True. A government will try to switch spending away from imports towards domestic products by making them pricier, either through a devaluation or sharp depreciation or by imposing trade protection barriers. At the same time exports will become cheaper in foreign markets if the exchange rate weakens.

Example 3

Determine the account in which each of the following transactions is recorded for the country in bold as well as whether it is recorded as a credit item or debit item.

1 A **Dutch** multinational builds a new factory in China.

2 A **South African** supermarket imports wine from Chile.

3 A **Swiss** pharmaceutical corporation pays the salary of an executive working in Turkey.

4 **Greek** parents pay for their daughter to study at a UK university.

5 The brand name Goody's is sold to Burger King, a US fast food company, from its current **Greek** owner.

6 A Mexican migrant worker in the **US** sends part of her salary back home to Mexico.

7 A **Malaysian** insurance company buys US stocks and US bonds.

8 A **Swedish** multinational corporation buys insurance from a Cypriot insurance broker.

9 **Emirates Airlines (Dubai)** buys jet fuel at the El Venizelos airport of Athens, Greece.

10 An **Australian** mining company sells mineral rights to a German company.

11 A **Russian** entrepreneur buys shares of a US company that entitles him to 50 % of the voting power in the company.

1	A Dutch multinational builds a new factory in **China**.	financial account (direct investment)	credit item
2	A South African supermarket imports wine from **Chile**.	current account (visible export)	credit item
3	A Swiss pharmaceutical corporation pays the salary of an executive working in **Turkey**.	current account (income)	credit item
4	**Greek** parents pay for their daughter to study at a UK university.	current account (current transfer)	debit item
5	The brand name Goody's is sold to Burger King, a US fast food company, from its current Greek owner.	capital account (non-produced, non-financial)	debit item
6	A Mexican migrant worker in the US sends part of her salary back home to **Mexico**.	current account (current transfer)	credit item
7	A **Malaysian** insurance company buys US stocks and US bonds.	financial account (portfolio investment)	debit item
8	A Swedish multinational corporation buys insurance from a Cypriot insurance broker.	current account (services)	debit item
9	Emirates Airlines (**Dubai**) buys jet fuel at the El Venizelos airport of Athens, Greece.	current account (visible import)	debit item
10	An **Australian** mining company sells mineral rights to a German company.	capital account (non-produced, non-financial	credit item
11	A **Russian** entrepreneur buys shares of a US company that entitles him to 50% of the voting power in the company.	financial account (direct investment)	debit item

Example 4

Given the data below from Australia's 2008–09 BOP, calculate the entries X1, X2, X3, X4, X5, X6 and X7.

BOP items	AU$ (millions)
A. Current account	X4
Receipts	
Goods	231,564
Services	52,877
Income	42,824
Current transfers	6,657
Payments	
Goods	220,649
Services	56,170
Income	88,231
Current transfers	7,652
Balances	
Goods and services	X1
Income	X2
Current transfers	X3
B. Capital account	−611
C. Financial account	X5
Net direct investment abroad	17,665

BOP items	AU$ (millions)
Net portfolio investment	49,220
Net other investments	−14,505
Reserve assets	−11,896
Total capital and financial accounts	X6
Balancing item (net errors and omissions or statistical discrepancy)	X7

The entries X1 to X3 are the balances of the subcategories of the current account.
To calculate X1, the balance on goods and services, find export revenues from goods and services, 231,564 + 52,877 = 284,441
Find import expenditures on goods and services: 220,649 + 56,170 = −276,819

The balance on goods and services is calculated if we subtract the expenditures on imports from export revenues: 284,441 − 276,819 = 7,622 (X1)

To calculate net income subtract the income payments made from income receipts:

$42,824 - 88,231 = -45,407$ (X2)

To calculate net current transfers subtract the payments made from receipts:

$6,657 - 7,652 = -995$ (X3)

The balance on the current account is the sum of all three sub-balances:

X4 = X1 + X2 + X3 or

X4 = $7,622 + (-45,407) + (-995)$

$= -38,780$ (X4)

To calculate X5, the balance on the financial account, we need to add net direct investment abroad + net portfolio investment + net other investments + reserve assets:

$17,665 + 49,220 + (-14,505) + (-11,896)$

$= 40,484$ (X5)

To calculate X6, total capital and financial accounts, we need to add the financial account balance to the capital account balance:

$(-611) + 40,484 = 39,873$

The sum of the current, capital and financial accounts should be equal to zero. If it is not then there are measurement errors, referred to as 'errors and omissions'. The balancing item is the result of the sum of the three accounts with the opposite sign. Summing the three accounts:

$(-38,780) + (-611) + 40,484 = 1,903$

So, the balancing item must be this sum with the opposite sign, or $-1,903$ (X7).

Exercise 1

Determine whether the following statements are true or false. Explain your answers. Use a diagram to illustrate if possible.

1   A fall in foreign exchange reserves will result after a central bank's intervention to offset currency weakness.

2   Financing a current account deficit may force a country to run down its foreign exchange reserves, to increase interest rates or to borrow from abroad.

3   A persistent and large current account deficit decreases a country's ability to pursue domestic objectives such as higher growth and lower unemployment.

4   The money spent on hotels by foreigners visiting London at Christmas represent an import of tourism for the UK.

5   When a London-based mutual fund buys shares on the Shanghai stock exchange in 2010, then a debit is recorded in China's financial account (portfolio investment) in 2010.

6   The interest earned in 2011 by a Brazilian investor from the purchase of US government bonds in 2009 are recorded as a credit item for Brazil in its current account.

HL   7   A devaluation or sharp depreciation will correct a current account deficit if the sum of the PED for exports and the PED for imports exceeds unity.

HL   8   The trade balance of a surplus country will trace a J-curve following an appreciation of its currency.

HL   9   Expenditure-reducing policies attempt to slow down growth in order to curb demand for imports.

Exercise 2

Rewrite the following statements and in the blanks by using the terms provided below. Some terms may be used more than once.

selling	supply	surplus
demand	competitive	unemployment
domestic	habits	cheaper
J-curve effect	imports	growth
unity	export driven	downward
widening	reducing	appreciate
manage	interest rates	undervalued
inflation	rising	price elasticities
deficit	informational	narrow
contracts	foreign exchange	worsens
Marshall-Lerner	inflows	short run

A (1)_____ current account (2)_____ puts pressure on the currency to depreciate or to devalue. Why? Because if the value of imports is (3)_____ faster than the value of exports, then (4)_____ of the currency is increasing faster than (5)_____ for the currency in the (6)_____ market. The resulting excess supply of the currency exerts (7)_____ pressure on its price. Conversely, rising export revenues resulting from (8)_____ growth will create a current account (9)_____ and pressure on the currency to (10)_____. Often, countries in such a situation (11)_____ their currency by (12)_____ it in foreign exchange markets to keep it (13)_____ and so maintain their exports (14)_____ at the risk, though, of inducing (15)_____ at home.

Financing a deficit may force (16)_____ up in order to induce capital (17)_____. This, though, stifles (18)_____ and may increase (19)_____. To correct a persistent deficit the policymakers may opt for either expenditure-switching or expenditure- (20)_____ policies. Expenditure-switching policies aim at switching spending away from (21)_____ towards (22)_____ output by making imports pricier. Devaluation or sharp depreciation may do the trick with exports also becoming (23)_____ in foreign markets. The effect depends on (24)_____ of demand for exports and imports. It can be shown that for a deficit to (25)_____ it suffices that the sum of the price elasticities of demand for exports and imports exceeds (26)_____. This is known as the (27)_____ condition. Since elasticities in general tend to be low in the (28)_____, the condition is not immediately satisfied giving rise to the (29)_____. The current account deficit initially (30)_____ and only later, typically after 12 to 18 months, does it start to improve. Reasons for which price elasticities of demand for imports are low in the short run include (31)_____ constraints, as buyers do not immediately become aware of the new prices, (32)_____ (as buyers are used to specific products or sources of supply) and, more importantly, (33)_____ as importing and exporting companies have often signed long-term contracts with suppliers.

Exercise 3

Match each term or concept with the appropriate definition or explanation.

1 Visible or merchandise trade balance
2 Official reserves
3 Current transfers
4 Portfolio investment
5 Balance of trade in goods and services
6 Current account balance
7 Balancing item

a The sum of net exports of goods and services plus net income from investments (including employees' compensation) plus net current transfers

b Defined as cross-border buying and selling of debt (bonds) or equity (stocks) and securities

c Net exports of goods (of physical merchandise)

d Errors and omissions

e Include foreign workers' remittances, pension payments to workers living abroad, payments of foreign aid, etc.

f Net exports of goods and services

g Include foreign currencies, gold and special drawing rights that are available to the monetary authorities for meeting balance of payments financing needs as well as for intervention in foreign exchange markets to affect the exchange rate

HL

Exercise 4

Given the data below from Australia's 2009–10 BOP, calculate the entries X1, X2, X3, X4, X5, X6 and X7.

Balance of payments items	AU$ (millions)
A. Current account	X4
Receipts	
Goods	201,463
Services	52,751
Income	35,718
Current transfers	6,219
Payments	
Goods	204,490
Services	53,499
Income	84,295
Current transfers	7,939
Balances	
Goods and services	X1
Income	X2
Current transfers	X3
B. Capital account	−289
C. Financial account	X5
Net direct investment abroad	17,456
Net portfolio investment	66,423
Net other investments	−35,331
Reserve assets	5,928
Total capital and financial accounts	X6
Balancing item (net errors and omissions or statistical discrepancy)	X7

Exercise 5

Explain the policies that may be employed to correct a persistent current account deficit.

Exercise 6

What are the relative advantages and disadvantages of adopting expenditure-reducing versus expenditure-switching policies to correct a persistent current account deficit?

Exercise 7

Explain whether a current account surplus is a cause of concern.

Remember

- There are several degrees of economic integration, ranging from simple preferential agreements of a limited scope to economic and monetary unions.

- The most significant issue surrounding the proliferation of regional preferential agreements relate to whether the role of the WTO as a vehicle of multilateral trade liberalization is undermined.

- Whether a trading block enhances welfare depends on the relative size of trade creation and trade diversion, as well as on the size and importance of the resulting dynamic (long-term) effects.

Example 1

Match each term or concept with the appropriate definition or explanation.

1 Customs union	a Refers to the increased trade following the establishment of a regional trading bloc where production shifts away from higher-cost domestic producers to lower-cost imports from other members
HL 2 Trade creation	
3 Economic (and monetary) union	b Results when countries eliminate tariff and other barriers of trade between them and, in addition, adopt a common external tariff on imports from non-members
4 Economic integration	c The weakest form of economic integration where tariff reductions are only offered to some product categories from certain countries; the term may also refer to all forms of regional trading blocs
5 Common market	
6 Free trade area	d When countries have achieved free trade in goods and services (having also adopted a common external tariff), free movement in labour and capital and, in addition, agreed to coordinate certain economic policies (particularly macroeconomic and regulatory policy), even adopting a common currency
HL 7 Trade diversion	
8 Preferential trade agreement	e Results when members of a customs union integrate further by agreeing, in addition, to permit free movement of labour and capital

f A process aimed at decreasing or eliminating trade as well as other economic barriers between countries to facilitate trade and, more generally, economic activity

g When, following the establishment of a regional trading bloc, trade shifts away from a more efficient non-member towards an artificially cheaper member

h Results when a group of countries agree to eliminate tariff (and other) barriers between themselves, but with each maintaining its own external tariff on non-members

(1, b), (2, a), (3, d),(4, f), (5, e), (6, h), (7, g), (8, c)

Example 2

Rewrite the following statements and fill in the blanks by using the terms provided below. Some terms may be used more than once or not at all.

factors of production	capital and labour	trade negotiations
WTO	multilaterally	customs union
153 member	group	competition
common currency	bargaining	common market
technology	free trade area	long-term
some product	barrier	language
economic union	efficiency	prices
common external tariff	preferential trading agreement	macroeconomic and regulatory

Economic integration can be achieved (1)_____ or regionally. The multilateral approach is through multilateral (2)_____ that the WTO conducts in which the (3)_____ countries participate. Trade liberalization through the regional approach involves a (4)_____ of countries that agree to lower tariff and other barriers to trade between them. The degree of integration ranges from signing a (5)_____ where tariff reductions are offered only on (6)_____ groups all the way to forming an (7)_____ where members not only agree to the free movement of goods, services and (8)_____ but also coordinate certain (9)_____ policies and may even adopt a (10)_____.

In a (11)_____ members agree to lower or eliminate tariffs and other trade barriers but each maintains its own trade policy towards non-members, whereas if members form a (12)_____ then members adopt a (13)_____ and, more generally, a common trade policy towards non-members.

Pursuing further integration implies forming a (14)_____. In a common market there is also free movement of factors of production. (15)_____ move freely within the member countries. Concerning labour this means that workers can choose to work in any member country they wish but (16)_____ may emerge as the biggest and most difficult (17)_____ to overcome.

Trading blocks result in dynamic effects of a (18)_____ nature. Dynamic advantages are closely related to the benefits of freer trade. For example, (19)_____ will be enhanced with all the resulting benefits such as lower (20_____ and greater (21)_____ in the allocation of resources, investment may increase due to the enlarged markets, (22)_____ will be diffused faster and growth may accelerate. Member countries may also enjoy greater (23)_____ and political power. On the other hand, preferential trading associations are considered by many as 'stumbling blocks' instead of 'building blocks' towards a liberalized multilateral trade system, as the role of the (24)_____ is undermined.

(1) multilaterally, (2) trade negotiations, (3) 153 member, (4) group,
(5) preferential trading agreement, (6) some product, (7) economic union,

(8) factors of production, (9) macroeconomic and regulatory,
(10) common currency, (11) free trade area, (12) customs union,
(13) common external tariff, (14) common market, (15) capital and labour,
(16) language, (17) barrier, (18) long-term, (19) competition, (20) prices,
(21) efficiency, (22) technology, (23) bargaining, (24) WTO

Example 3

List possible advantages and disadvantages of a monetary union for member economies.

Advantages include:

- lower transaction costs as currency conversions are not necessary
- greater price transparency, facilitating comparisons of prices of goods, services and resources with competition increasing and prices falling
- elimination of exchange rate risk and the resulting associated uncertainty costs
- possible greater influence in negotiations.

Most advantages are of a microeconomic nature.

Disadvantages include:

- members being deprived of an independent monetary policy
- members being deprived of an independent exchange rate policy
- limited room for pursuing independent fiscal policy
- loss of economic sovereignty
- difficulty in coordinating monetary policy in the face of asynchronous business cycles.

Most disadvantages are of a macroeconomic nature.

Exercise 1

Rewrite the following statements and fill in the blanks by using the terms provided below. Some terms may be used more than once or not at all.

positive	trade creation	member
trading bloc	outweighed	trade
non-member	trade diversion	

Whether a (1)_____ increases welfare must be determined on a case-by-case basis. On the one hand (2)_____ increases welfare, but on the other hand trade diversion may decrease welfare. Even if (3)_____ flows increase between members the (4)_____ effect of trade creation, due to more trade with members, may be (5)_____ by the potentially negative effect of (6)_____ resulting from the substitution of (7)_____ country products for cheaper (8)_____ products.

Exercise 2

Trade creation and trade diversion are known as the static effects resulting from customs unions. Regional economic integration may also be evaluated along other dimensions. Discuss two possible benefits and two possible costs of regional integration.

3.5 Terms of trade

HL The meaning of terms of trade

Remember

- To calculate terms of trade (TOT): $\text{TOT} = \dfrac{P_x}{P_m} \times 100$, where P_x is the average price of exports and P_m is the average price of imports (both expressed as index numbers).

- The TOT show the volume of imports attainable by a unit of exports. The ratio P_x/P_m can increase (decrease) in many ways which are all captured by saying that the TOT will increase (decrease) if average export prices rise (fall) **relatively** to average import prices.

  If the TOT increase we refer to it as an improvement or a favourable movement in the following specific sense: that now the country **can attain** a grater volume of imports by a unit of exports (that the same volume of imports **is attainable** by a smaller volume of exports); whether this is 'good' or 'bad' for the trade balance is a different issue.

- The TOT can change as a result of:
  - short-term changes in demand conditions for tradables (where cyclical variations are often responsible)
  - short-term changes in the supply conditions for tradables (say, because of a crop failure)
  - changes in exchange rates
  - changes in relative inflation rates
  - long-term changes in the pattern of demand (where varying income elasticities are the driving force)
  - long-term changes in the pattern of supply (where technological or productivity changes are the driving force).

Tip

An easy way to remember the meaning of the TOT is by thinking of a country exporting one good, say coffee, at $2,000 per ton and importing TV sets at $500 each. Its terms of trade are 2000/500 or 4. What does this '4' signify? It is the volume (i.e. the number) of TV sets the country can import if it exports one ton of coffee. If the TOT increases to become equal to 5 then it is reasonable to refer to it as an improvement, as now five TV sets can be imported by exporting one ton of coffee. The TOT can increase to 5 if the price of coffee climbs to $2,500, if the price of TV sets drops to $400, if both prices rise but coffee prices rise faster (say, by 50% to $3,000 per ton) than TV set prices (say by 20% or $600 each), etc.

Remember

- Consequences of changes in the TOT can best be understood within the following simplified framework.
  - Long term changes in the TOT redistribute world income or output (the 'pie') against countries facing a decline. Since many developing countries significantly rely on the export of primary products and the import of manufactures it is this group that faces long-term deterioration in their TOT and thus a shrinking slice of world output.
  - Changes in the TOT also affect the trade balance of a country. The effect on the balance of trade (BOT) depends on the cause of the change in the TOT.

- If the TOT changed because of a change in the exchange rate or in supply conditions then price elasticities are important. If the TOT changed because of a change in demand conditions then elasticities are not relevant.

- TOT fluctuates in the short term only for countries where exports or imports are highly concentrated. Prices of manufactures and services do not fluctuate much in the short term (as oligopolies dominate these industries and prices are 'sticky') but prices of many primary products (commodities) are volatile. This means that mostly developing countries or, for example, oil exporters may face short-term volatility in their TOT.

Tip

> The following two tables present the effect of a change in the TOT on the BOT of a country where trade is concentrated in one or few commodities and world demand or supply conditions for this commodity (or commodities) change (think of oil, cereals or cotton textiles).

Commodity price increases because of an increase in demand or decrease in supply.

Cause	Country	Effect on TOT	Effect on BOT (X–M)
D↑ so P↑ and Q↑	Exporter	↑	↑
	Importer	↓	↓
S↓ so P↑ and Q↓	Exporter	↑	If ped(x) > 1: BOT↓
			If ped(x) < 1: BOT↑
	Importer	↓	If ped(m) > 1: BOT↑
			If ped(m) < 1: BOT↓

Note: If BOT↑ it means that a surplus widens or a deficit narrows, and vice versa.

Commodity price decreases because of a decrease in demand or increase in supply.

Cause	Country	Effect on TOT	Effect on BOT (X − M)
D↓ so P↓ and Q↓	Exporter	↑	↓
	Importer	↓	↑
S↑ so P↓ and Q↑	Exporter	↑	If ped(x) > 1: BOT↓
			If ped(x) < 1: BOT↓
	Importer	↓	If ped(m) > 1: BOT↓
			If ped(m) < 1: BOT↑

Note: If BOT↑ it means that a surplus widens or a deficit narrows, and vice versa.

Tip

> The following table presents the effect of a change in the TOT on the BOT of a country when the exchange rate appreciates or revalues (↑) or when it depreciates or devalues (↓).

Cause	Effect on and P_x and P_m	Effect on TOT	Effect on BOT (X − M)
er↓	P_x↓	↓	If ped(x) + ped(m) > 1: BOT↑
	P_m↑		If ped(x) + ped(m) < 1: BOT↓
er↑	P_x↑	↑	If ped(x) + ped(m) < 1: BOT↑
	P_m↑		If ped(x) + ped(m) > 1: BOT↓

Note: If BOT↑ it means that a surplus widens or a deficit narrows, and vice versa.

Example 1

Determine whether the following statements are true or false. Explain your answers.

1 The terms of trade improve following a depreciation of a country's currency

False. Depreciation increases the domestic price of imports (and lowers the foreign price of exports). As a result the TOT deteriorate (there is unfavourable movement).

2 A favourable movement (i.e. an improvement in the TOT) may not result if both the average price of imports and the average price of exports increase through time.

*False. The TOT may indeed improve as it is the **relative** price of exports and imports that determines the direction of change in the TOT. So, if both the average price of exports and of imports increase, but the average price of exports increases faster, then the TOT will improve.*

3 Deteriorating TOT resulting from a depreciation of a currency will improve (narrow) a trade deficit if the Marshall-Lerner condition holds.

True. Depreciation decreases the foreign price of exports, increases the domestic price of imports and worsens the TOT. The effect this development will have on the BOT does depend on the PED of exports and imports as expressed in the Marshall–Lerner condition, namely that the sum of the absolute values of the PED for exports and the PED for imports must exceed unity.

4 Increased prices for commodities due to rising world demand will improve a commodity-exporting country's TOT only if demand for its exports is price inelastic.

False. Elasticities are irrelevant in this case as price and quantities change in the same direction. Assume a country with a high concentration of its exports in commodities. Now assume a boom in the world economy so that demand for commodities (which are inputs in manufacturing processes) increases. Since the exporter will face higher prices and higher volumes (quantities) of exports its export revenues will unambiguously increase.

Example 2

Country A is a major coffee exporter with coffee the **sole** source of its export revenues. Assume that it **only** imports 'machinery'. The table below presents data on the average annual world price of coffee (P_{coffee}), the average annual price of a unit of 'machinery' (P_{mach}) and its annual coffee export revenues.

Year	P^x_{coffee} (US$/ton)	P^x_{coffee} (index)	$P^M_{machinery}$ ($/unit)	$P^M_{machinery}$ (index)	X revenues (US$ billions)	Index of export revenues	Volume of coffee exports (tons)
2006	1,821		24,560		1.03		
2007	1,756		24,890		1.01		
2008	1,653		25,500		0.98		
2009	1,624		26,358		0.97		
2010	1,589		26,598		0.96		
2011	1,440		27,452		0.95		

1 Using the year 2007 as the base year, convert export and import prices facing country A into index numbers.

To convert export prices into index numbers using 2007 as the base year we divide the export price(s) in each year by the export price prevailing in 2007 (the base year) and multiply by 100. The same holds for import prices.

Year	P^x_{coffee} (US$/ton)	P^x_{coffee} (index)	$P^M_{machinery}$ (US$/unit)	$P^M_{machinery}$ (index)
2006	1,821	$\frac{1,821}{1,756} \times 100 = 103.7$	24,560	$\frac{24,560}{24,890} \times 100 = 98.67$
2007	1,756	$\frac{1,756}{1,756} \times 100 = 100.0$	24,890	$\frac{24,560}{24,890} \times 100 = 100.00$
2008	1,653	$\frac{1,653}{1,756} \times 100 = 94.13$	25,500	$\frac{24,560}{24,890} \times 100 = 102.45$
2009	1,624	$\frac{1,624}{1,756} \times 100 = 92.48$	26,358	$\frac{26,358}{24,890} \times 100 = 105.90$
2010	1,589	$\frac{1,589}{1,756} \times 100 = 90.49$	26,598	$\frac{26,598}{24,890} \times 100 = 106.86$
2011	1,440	$\frac{1,440}{1,756} \times 100 = 82.00$	27,452	$\frac{27,452}{24,890} \times 100 = 110.29$

2 Using the year 2007 as the base year, calculate the TOT of country A.

To calculate the TOT we first have to use the formula:

$TOT = \dfrac{P^x}{P^m} = 100$

Year	P^x_{coffe} (index)	$P^M_{machinery}$ (index)	$TOT = \dfrac{P^x}{P^m} = 100$
2006	$\dfrac{1{,}821}{1{,}756} \times 100 = 103.7$	$\dfrac{24{,}560}{24{,}890} \times 100 = 98.67$	$\dfrac{103.70}{98.67} \times 100 = 105.09$
2007	$\dfrac{1{,}756}{1{,}756} \times 100.00 = 100.00$	$\dfrac{24{,}890}{24{,}890} \times 100 = 100$	$\dfrac{100.00}{100.00} \times 100 = 100.00$
2008	$\dfrac{1{,}653}{1{,}756} \times 100 = 94.13$	$\dfrac{25{,}500}{24{,}890} \times 100 = 102.45$	$\dfrac{94.13}{102.45} \times 100 = 91.88$
2009	$\dfrac{1{,}624}{1{,}756} \times 100 = 92.48$	$\dfrac{26{,}358}{24{,}890} \times 100 = 105.90$	$\dfrac{92.48}{105.90} \times 100 = 87.33$
2010	$\dfrac{1{,}589}{1{,}756} \times 100 = 90.49$	$\dfrac{26{,}598}{24{,}890} \times 100 = 106.86$	$\dfrac{90.49}{106.86} \times 100 = 84.68$
2011	$\dfrac{1{,}440}{1{,}756} \times 100 = 82.00$	$\dfrac{27{,}452}{24{,}890} \times 100 = 110.29$	$\dfrac{82.00}{110.29} \times 100 = 74.35$

3 Interpret the change in country A's TOT between 2001 and 2011.

The TOT of country A have been continuously decreasing from 105.09 in 2006 down to 74.35 in 2011. This is referred to as deterioration or an unfavourable movement as it implies that each unit of exports of country A can buy fewer and fewer units of imports; or that to be able to buy the same volume of imports, a greater volume of exports is needed.

4 Convert export revenues (from coffee) into an index number (using 2007 as the base year).

To convert export revenues into an index number, divide the export revenues for each year by the export revenues of the base year 2007 and multiply by 100.

Year	X revenues (US\$ billions)	Index of export revenues
2006	1.03	$\dfrac{1.03}{1.01} \times 100 = 101.98$
2007	1.01	$\dfrac{1.01}{1.01} \times 100 = 100.00$
2008	0.98	$\dfrac{0.98}{1.01} \times 100 = 97.03$
2009	0.97	$\dfrac{0.97}{1.01} \times 100 = 96.04$
2010	0.96	$\dfrac{0.96}{1.01} \times 100 = 95.05$
2011	0.95	$\dfrac{0.95}{1.01} \times 100 = 94.06$

5 Calculate the volume of exports between 2006 and 2011 (in thousands of tons).

To calculate the volume of exports we need to divide the value of exports by the average price of exports. Here, coffee is the only source of export revenues so the division will be equal to how many thousands of tons country A exported.

Year	P^x_{coffee} (US$/ton)	X revenues (US$ billions)	Volume of coffee exports (thousands of tons)
2006	1,821	1.03	565,623
2007	1,756	1.01	575,171
2008	1,653	0.98	592,862
2009	1,624	0.97	597,291
2010	1,589	0.96	604,154
2011	1,440	0.95	659,722

6 From the information collected what can you infer about the PED for coffee?

Since revenues decreased while price decreased and quantity of tons of coffee purchased increased, it implies that demand must be price inelastic.

7 Calculate the PED for coffee between 2010 and 2011.

$$PED = \frac{\%\Delta Q}{\%\Delta P} = \frac{\frac{(659,722 - 604,154)}{604,154}}{\frac{1,440 - 1,589}{1,589}} = \frac{9.19}{-9.38} = -0.98$$

Exercise 1

Determine whether the following statements are true or false. Explain your answers. Use a diagram to illustrate if possible.

1 If the supply of oil in world markets decreases, then the change in the TOT and the BOT will be in the same direction if demand for the product is price inelastic, independently of whether the country is an exporter or an importer of oil.

2 Assume a country with a rising current account surplus. An appreciation of its currency will improve its TOT and automatically narrow its surplus as its exports will become pricier.

3 An increase or a decrease in the demand of a commodity will affect the TOT and the BOT of exporters and importers in the same direction.

4 A decrease in supply of a commodity will affect the TOT and the BOT of both an exporter and an importer in the same direction if demand for the commodity is price inelastic.

5 To determine the effect of a change in the TOT on the BOT, price elasticities are important if the change in the TOT is a result of exchange rate movements or of changes in the global supply of a commodity.

Exercise 2

Rewrite the following statements and fill in the blanks by using the terms provided below. Some terms may be used more than once or not at all.

inelastic	cause
balance of trade (BOT)	volume
supply	importers
same	increase
exceeds unity	deteriorate
goods	opposite
boom	worsen
services	elasticity of demand
absolute	exporters
improve	decrease
Marshall-Lerner	

Changes in the TOT affect the (1)_____. The BOT is defined as the difference between the value of exports and imports of (2)_____, but it is often interpreted to include trade in (3)_____ as well. Whether a movement in the TOT improves or worsens the BOT depends on the (4)_____ for which the TOT changed. Assume, for example, a commodity (5)_____ and an exporter of commodities. The TOT of this country will (6)_____ as there will be an (7)_____ in the average price of its exports. Its BOT will necessarily also improve as the (8)_____ of its commodity exports will also increase, ceteris paribus. On the other hand, the TOT of importers of commodities will (9)_____ and their BOT will (10)_____ assuming constant export earnings. Let's assume that OPEC decides to restrict output of oil. The decreased (11)_____ of oil increases the world price so the terms of trade of net oil (12)_____ improve while the TOT of net oil (13)_____ deteriorate. Since price and the volume of exports (and, imports) move in (14)_____ directions, price (15)_____ determines how trade balances will be affected. Since demand for oil is rather price (16)_____, we expect trade balances to move in the (17)_____ direction as the terms of trade.

An exchange rate depreciation will (18)_____ the TOT and the effect on the BOT depends on the (19)_____ condition. A trade deficit will narrow if the sum of the (20)_____ values of the price elasticities of demand for exports and for imports (21)_____.

Exercise 3

Cymmeria exports only good A and imports only good B. The table below presents data on the average annual world price of a unit of good A (P_A), the average annual price of a unit of good B (P_B) and Cymmeria's annual export revenues from good A between 2004 and 2009.

Year	P_A^X (US$/ unit)	P_A^X (as an index)	P_B^M (US$/unit)	P_B^M (as an index)	X revenues (US$ billions)	Index of export revenues	Volume of exports (units of A)
2004	18.00		120.50		2.13		
2005	21.00		121.20		2.82		
2006	22.00		121.80		3.24		
2007	22.50		122.30		3.58		
2008	24.60		122.90		3.98		
2009	25.10		123.20		4.32		

1   Using the year 2007 as the base year, convert export and import prices facing Cymmeria into index numbers.

2   Using the year 2007 as the base year, calculate the TOT of Cymmeria.

3   Interpret the change in Cymmeria's TOT between 2004 and 2009.

4   Convert Cymmeria's export revenues (from exports of good A) into an index number (using 2007 as the base year).

5   Calculate Cymmeria's volume of exports between 2004 and 2009.

6   Calculate the percentage change in the price of good A as well as the percentage change in the export revenues earned from good A between 2004 and 2009.

7   Provide two possible reasons why export revenues from good A increased while the price of good A also increased. Given the information available, which of the two reasons provided is refuted?

The nature of economic growth and economic development

Remember

- Development differs from growth.

- Growth is a one-dimensional and quantitative concept while development is a multidimensional and qualitative concept. Growth refers to increases in real GDP. Development refers to improved living standards.

- Living standards improve not only when the command over goods and services increases and poverty decreases, but also when the level of education and health of a population improves. Development also implies increased employment opportunities, decreased inequality, a better environment and empowerment of the people.

- Success does not always require fast growth and fast growth does not guarantee success: human development achievements have been realized in countries with modest gains in per capita income while in many countries growth did not translate into human development achievements.

Tip

- Working in groups often works wonders in the development section of your course as you may pool your resources, even across schools. There are many platforms you can use to create and share documents (available from Google, Microsoft, etc.). In addition, the following resources can be very useful in making the development experience even more interesting.

  - Create posters to share your work: www.glogster.com

  - Blog your work (many sites are available such as www.wordpress.org, www.blogger.com)

  - Investigate mapping at www.thebrain.com and at www.bubbl.us

  - Create and share non-linear presentations of your work at www.prezi.com

  - Very useful information on poverty in the developing world can be found at www.globalissues.org by clicking 'Poverty Facts and Stats'.

Tip

There are fantastic sites available to complement your work in development economics. The subject matter is continuously changing and the importance of using Internet resources in your course is huge. The resources found in the following sites are considered invaluable.

- Gapminder (Hans Rosling) at www.gapminder.org

- The World Bank Data at www.data.worldbank.org

- The human development reports by the UNDP at www.hdr.undp.org/en/reports

- UN Millennium Development Goals (MDGs) at www.un.org/millenniumgoals

- Food and Agriculture Organization at www.fao.org

- Global Issues at www.globalissues.org

- Development topics at the OECD: www.oecd.org (click 'Topics: development')

There are also a number of blogs that will help you appreciate what is going on in the world of development economics. Here are just a few (there are many others).

- William Easterly's Aid Watch at www.aidwatchers.com

- Dani Rodrik's weblog at www.rodrik.typepad.com

- Chris Blattman's blog at www.chrisblattman.com

There are also many development-related videos to watch online (and others on DVD). Here are a few sites where such videos can be watched.

- UNDP channel on youtube: www.youtube.com/undp

- International Fund for Agricultural Development (IFAD) videos: www.ifad.org/media/video/index.htm

- TED on development issues: www.ted.com/search?q=development&page=1

- Commanding Heights: The Battle for the World Economy (a bit dated but perhaps the best introduction to the idea of globalization, serving also as an introduction to macro) at: www.pbs.org/wgbh/commandingheights/hi/story/index.html

There are also many other development-related sites that have useful information for your work. Whether you go into the details depends on how interested you are, but they are worth looking at:

- Country reports at www.bertelsmann-transformation-index.de/en/bti/country-reports/ (Bertelsmann Stiftung and the Center for Applied Policy Research at Munich University)

- Country profiles at www.indexmundi.com

- 'Development Studies Internet Resources' at Wellesley College: www.wellesley.edu/Polisci/wj/DevelopmentLinks/index.htm

- The Abdul Latif Jameel Poverty Action Lab (J-AL) at MIT: www.povertyactionlab.org

- The Earth Institute at Columbia University: www.earth.columbia.edu/sections/view/9

- Statistical databases at The British Library for Development Studies: www.blds.ids.ac.uk/elibrary/db_stats.html

- The Development Research Institute at New York University: www.dri.fas.nyu.edu

- The Center for International Development at Harvard University: www.hks.harvard.edu/centers/cid

Example 1

Match each term or concept with the appropriate definition or explanation.

1 Physical capital
2 Poverty (absolute)
3 Appropriate technology
4 Economic growth
5 Human capital
6 Resource endowments
7 Natural capital
8 Institutions
9 Poverty (relative)
10 Economic development
11 Poverty cycle
12 Human development

a The education, training and skills embodied in the labour force of a country

b Measures the extent to which a household's income falls below the national average

c A multidimensional process involving improvements in the living standards of a population manifested in higher incomes, lower poverty, better education and health, lower inequality, increased employment opportunities, a better environment, etc.

d Produced means of production such as factories, machines and equipment

e Defined by the minimum income necessary to satisfy basic physical needs; the price of goods and services is expressed as international dollars, i.e. dollars that take into account differences in value across countries, known as purchasing power parities (PPP); the 2008 World Bank international poverty line is set $1.25 (PPP) per day

f The rules, norms, conventions and organizations within which economic activity is conducted

g Technology that relies mostly on the relatively abundant factor of production and is adaptable to local conditions of production

h When low income levels permit low savings leading to low investment and back again to low income

i Refers to increases in the real GDP or the per capita GDP of a country

j A process of 'enlarging people's choices'

k The natural resources ('land' in a broad sense) of an economy that may be improved upon or depleted

l Refers to the quantity and quality of resources a country has; may focus on the natural resources available in a country

(1, d), (2, e), (3, g), (4, i), (5, a), (6, l), (7, k), (8, f), (9, b), (10, c), (11, h), (12, j)

Example 2

Explain the most important sources of growth for less-developed countries.

Economic growth may be a result of the increased quantity of the factors of production available in the economy and improved quality of those factors, as well as better technology and an institutional framework more conducive to development. Factors of production include land (or natural capital), labour, capital and entrepreneurship. Technology may be considered as appropriate or inappropriate and institutions refer to the collection of laws, regulations and organizations within which all economic activity is.

Natural capital refers to the natural endowment of an economy: the minerals, metals and oil reserves, agricultural and non-agricultural land, forests, coastlines, lakes and rivers as well as the climate of the country. Abundance or an increase in natural capital may or may not induce growth (and, based on that, development). There are many countries rich in natural resources which have not achieved satisfactory growth rates (the 'curse of natural resources') and other poorly endowed countries which have grown spectacularly. It is very difficult to pinpoint the reasons for these diverging performances. Stating that the latter performed well because the lack of natural capital forced them to diversify into manufacturing and industrialize, whereas the former 'comfortably' relied on the production and export of the primary products they were blessed with, ignores both the role of history and the role of institutions. In any case, an increase or improvement in natural resources alone does not seem to be as important as increases in physical and human capital and improvements in the institutional framework of economies.

An increase in physical capital embodying appropriate technology may accelerate growth as it increases labour productivity, the volume of output per worker. More and better factories, machines and equipment allow output per worker to rise and so allow growth.

The role of the labour factor of production within this framework is also interesting. Given the high rates of unemployment and/or underemployment in many developing countries, it is not so obvious that an increase in the size of the labour force will lead to higher growth rates. The significant role of labour is better understood if the focus shifts to human capital. Human capital refers to the education, skills, training and experience embodied in the labour force. Better education and training and the acquisition of more skills and experience will lead to increased labour productivity, i.e. more output per worker, and so faster growth. Many countries that invested heavily in education witnessed accelerating growth rates, most notably in East Asia. On the other hand, the latest research finding by the UNDP that 'the relationship between economic growth and improvements in health and education is weak in low and medium HDI [Human Development Index] countries' is worth keeping in mind (see Human Development Report (HDR) 2010: *The Real Wealth of Nations: Pathways to Human Development* at www.hdr.undp.org/en/reports/global/hdr2010/chapters/en/).

Finally, the role of institutions as a source of growth and subsequently of development cannot be exaggerated. Institutions are considered by many as having played a pivotal role in shaping the growth and development trajectory of countries. The quality of institutions has been found to be a most significant determinant of income levels in the world. Good institutions can:

- create markets (for example, well-enforced property rights allow transactions such as borrowing to make investments)
- regulate markets properly (for example the regulatory institutions in financial services and telecommunications)
- stabilize markets (for example through central banks and fiscal rules)
- legitimize markets (for example institutions that provide protection and insurance and manage conflict) so that consensus is easier to achieve.

Good institutions provide the proper incentives and facilitate transactions by lowering transaction costs. Within a proper institutional framework, the fourth factor of production, entrepreneurship, will flourish whereas within a dysfunctional framework it will fail or become corrupt.

Example 3

Provide examples of specific countries for which growth has not come along with commensurate improvement in human development.

To answer all questions requesting examples, it is a good idea to check the human development reports at www.hdr.undp.org/en as well as the World Bank databank at www.data.worldbank.org

Since the central idea of human development is to 'create an enabling environment for people to live long, healthy and creative lives', one way to go about this exercise is to check for countries that rank highly in terms of per capita income achievement but lag significantly in terms of the two other dimensions of progress, namely education and health.

In HDR 2010 (p. 143) you will find Table 1 'Human Development Index and its components' (for a discussion of the HDI see the next section). Focusing on the column 'GNI per capita rank minus HDI rank' we find countries where the result is a negative number. This means that their achievements in education and/or health lag behind their achievements in per capita income level.

The set of countries where the difference is minus 35 or greater includes Qatar (– 36), South Africa (– 37), Botswana (– 38), Kuwait (– 42), Angola (– 47) and Equatorial Guinea (– 78).

More specifically, these are the facts about these countries.

- Qatar: in 2010 per capita GNI was $79,426 (one of the highest in the world) but mean years of schooling was only 7.3. Qatar is a major oil exporter.
- South Africa: in 2010 per capita income was $9,812 (an upper middle income country according to the World Bank classification of countries), mean years of schooling was 8.2 and life expectancy was only 52 years. South Africa is the world's largest producer of platinum, gold and chromium.
- Botswana: in 2010 per capita GNI was $13,204 (an upper middle income country according to the World Bank classification of countries), much higher than the average of the countries in the medium human development group to which it belongs, but mean years of schooling was 8.9 and life expectancy only 55.9 years. Botswana is home to the world's largest and richest diamond mine and is a major exporter of diamonds.
- Kuwait: in 2010 per capita GNI was $55,719 (one of the highest in the world), mean years of schooling was only 6.1. Kuwait is a major oil exporter.
- Angola: in 2010 per capita income was at $4,941 (a lower middle income country according to the World Bank classification of countries), much higher than the average of the countries in the low human development group to which it belongs, but mean years of schooling was 4.4 and life expectancy only 48.1 years. Angola is an oil and diamond exporter.
- Equatorial Guinea: in 2010 per capita GNI was 22,218 (a high income country according to the World Bank classification of countries), but mean years of schooling were 5.4 and life expectancy only 51.0 years. Equatorial Guinea is an oil exporter.

Still, this picture may not be fair because perhaps what matters more are the positive changes that may have taken place. For example, Botswana in the 2010 Report has been singled out as one of the top movers (the 14th) since 1990.

The relationship between growth in income and improvements in health and education levels has been found statistically very weak. This result is presented in the 2010 HDR (p. 47). Several interesting examples are provided: China has grown much faster than Tunisia over the past 30 years (8 % and 3 % respectively) but Tunisia has outperformed China in both fronts: a baby girl born in 1970 in Tunisia had a life expectancy of 55 years whereas in China this was 63 years; a baby girl born today in Tunisia can expect to live 76 years, a year longer than in China. On the other hand, in three countries with declining incomes (Iran, Togo and Venezuela) life expectancy has increased by an average of 14 years while enrolment in schooling has increased by 31 % since 1970.

Example 4

What are some common characteristics shared by developing countries? Provide examples that also illustrate the significant variations that exist between them and as well as within them.

Typically, the following are quoted as common characteristics of developing countries:

- low level of per capita income, extensive poverty and high income inequality
- high levels underemployment (defined as 'partial lack of employment, low employment income and underutilization of skills or low productivity')
- high dependence on agriculture and primary exports.

There are also many other characteristics that are shared in varying extents by many developing countries. For example, higher rates of population growth than those shared by advanced economies, younger populations, lower levels of education and health, poor infrastructure, civil unrest and higher levels of corruption.

To find data on any of these and other statistics, perhaps the best place to search is at www.data.worldbank.org/indicator as well as the data in any human development report found at www.hdr.undp.org/en/reports

For example, using www.data.worldbank.org/indicator, by clicking 'Employment in agriculture (% of total employment)' you can easily spot developing countries with a greater than 25 % share (such as Bangladesh with 48.1 % in 2005, Indonesia with 41.2 % in 2007 or the Philippines with 36.1 % also in 2007), as well as many other developing countries with a much lower proportion (such as South Africa with 8.8 % in 2007, Mauritius with 9.1 % in 2007 or Brazil with 19.3 % in the same year). You will also note that this percentage in the UK and the USA is around

1.5 %, in Norway and the Netherlands around 3 %, but in New Zealand it is around 7 %.

In the 'Education' section, if you click 'Literacy rate, adult total (% of people ages 15 and above)' you will find several developing countries with a rate of 45 % or lower (such as Burkina Faso with 29 % in 2007, then Chad in 2008 with 33 %, Ethiopia with 36 %, Guinea with 38 %, Sierra Leone with 40 %, Benin with 41 %, the Gambia with 45 %), others higher but below 75 % (such as

Bangladesh with 55 %, The Democratic Republic of Congo with 67 %, Madagascar with 71 %, Nepal with 58 %, Guatemala with 74 %) and then Cuba with 100 %, Zimbabwe with 91 % and Botswana with 83 %. The world average was 83 %.

If you visit the Food and Agriculture Organization at www.fao.org and search for statistics on 'Exports: Share on total agriculture/total merchandise (top 20 countries)' you can find the following statistics.

Rank	Country	%	HDI rank	Rank	Country	%	HDI rank
1	Guinea-Bissau	98.10 %	164	11	Djibouti	54.81 %	147
2	Rwanda	89.68 %	152	12	Vanuatu	53.95 %	–
3	Malawi	89.33 %	153	13	Kenya	53.37 %	128
4	Paraguay	89.28 %	96	14	Honduras	52.63 %	106
5	Ethiopia	84.38 %	157	15	Argentina	51.00 %	46
6	Burundi	81.57 %	166	16	Dominican Republic	49.33 %	88
7	Nicaragua	74.37 %	115	17	Samoa	48.46 %	–
8	Saint Vincent and the Grenadines	60.73 %	–	18	Belize	46.96 %	78
9	Uruguay	59.51 %	52	19	New Zealand	46.33 %	3
10	Burkina Faso	55.11 %	161	20	Côte d'Ivoire	**43.18 %**	146

Of the 17 countries ranked on the basis of the HDI in 2010, seven are classified in the low human development group (with HDI 2010 ranking of 128 and below), nine have an HDI ranking below 100 and only one was classified in the very high human development group, namely New Zealand which ranked third in 2010. All of these countries have a concentration of agricultural exports in excess of 43 %.

But the variation of any of these and other characteristics within countries is tremendous. The video *Debunking myths about the 'third world'* (which you can find at www.gapminder.org/videos or at www.ted.com/talks) is perhaps the best available visual presentation of these huge variations that exist in the world. Watch it and write notes.

Example 5

List the eight Millennium Development Goals (MDGs) and assess the current status of each using at least one indicator.

The eight MDGs are as follows.

1. Eradicate extreme poverty and hunger.

2. Achieve universal primary education.

3. Promote gender equality and empower women.

4. Reduce child mortality.

5. Improve maternal health.

6. Combat HIV/AIDS, malaria and other diseases.

7. Ensure environmental sustainability.

8. Develop a global partnership for development.

To monitor the current status of each of the above eight goals it is best to visit www.mdgmonitor.org where you can find detailed interactive maps and up-to-date country reports. Or visit www.un.org/millenniumgoals and click 'Reports' where you can find detailed reports as well as very good progress charts that are easy to digest.

You can also visit UNDP country sites (for Zimbabwe it is www.undp.org.zw or for Kenya it is www.ke.undp.org) where there are informative links on progress of the MDGs. For example, we can find out from the UNDP country site for Zimbabwe (see link above) the following relating to the status of MDG 1 (eradicate extreme poverty and hunger):

- In 2010 approximately 5.1 million inhabitants required food assistance.
- According to the 2003 PASS, 58 % of households in Zimbabwe consumed fewer than three meals per day.
- Acute malnutrition in children under 5 years was ranked 4.4 in 2010.
- The population living below the total consumption poverty line (TCPL) increased from 55 % in 1995 to 72 % in 2003.
- In 2003, 63 % of rural households and 53 % of urban households were living below TCPL.

- Feminization of poverty as depicted by higher prevalence of poverty among female-headed households was at 68 % TCPL in 2003.
- High levels of malnutrition in children under 5 years of age increased from 13 % in 1999 to 17 % in 2006.

Concerning Kenya and MDG 1, we can find out the following from the UNDP country site for Kenya (see link above):

- 'The country witnessed a decline in poverty from 56 % in 2000 to 45.9 % in 2006, attributable to improved governance and management of public resources and implementation of key reforms in various sectors of the economy. Poverty levels are still high (the country witnessed a 17 percentage point decline in poverty) and a lot of resources are required for basic social services against the capital expenditure. The problem of poverty has been coupled by high inequalities with the Gini coefficient of around 0.45.'

Exercise 1

- Most but not all developing countries are in the tropics.
- Many are resource rich but others are not.
- Their geography also varies considerably as some, for example, are landlocked but others are not.
- In the past 20 years many have suffered significant political instability, others have been relatively stable.
- In the past 20 years significant improvements in human development have been achieved by several countries with different political systems.

Using the resources on the Internet, try to find examples of developing countries in each of the above groups. Compare and contrast their progress on a variety of indicators since 1980. Work in groups and create posters using http://www.glogster.com as you can include pictures and videos that are relevant. You can work in groups using Google docs, or any other similar technology, and then post your reports on a blog that you create. Update the blog including more countries and more information on each as the course progresses.

Exercise 2

Provide examples of specific countries which have managed to achieve advances in people's wellbeing without registering high growth rates (hint: check the Internet links mentioned above).

Measurement methods

Remember

- The difference between GDP and GNI is that GNI excludes incomes earned domestically by foreign factors (which are paid abroad, e.g. the profits of multinational companies) but it includes incomes earned abroad by nationals of the country.

- The difference has become often significant as a result of globalization: multinationals may send their profits abroad while in many countries residents receive sizeable remittances from abroad.

- Per capita GNI or GDP is arrived at by simply dividing GNI or GDP of a country by mid-year total population of the country.

- Purchasing power parities (PPP) are referred to as 'international dollars', which have the same purchasing power over GDP as a US dollar in the USA. The idea is that cost of living may differ between countries substantially and market exchange rates do not necessarily adjust to capture these differences.

- For example, in January 2010, 1.00 USD = 6.6 yuan renminbi. If 660 yuan renminbi buy more goods and services in China than 100 US dollars in the US then converting China's market exchange rate would underestimate China's per capita income. In 2008, China's per capita GNI was $2,940 using market exchange rates while it climbed to $6,020 when calculated using PPP$.

- In 2010 the indicators used to measure progress in education and income in the calculation of the HDI were modified:
  - In the knowledge dimension, these measures were used: mean years of schooling of people aged 25 and older, and expected years of schooling that a child of school entrance age can expect to receive, if prevailing patterns of enrolment stay the same. (These measures were used instead of adult literacy and gross enrolment rate.)

  - GNI per capita (in PPP$) replaced GDP per capita.

- If the difference between GNI per capita rank and HDI rank (GNI per capita rank – HDI rank) is positive it means that the GNI per capita rank is a bigger **number** than the HDI rank. Roughly speaking, this means that the country ranks higher in the development achievement list than in the per capita income list: it is doing very well in terms of education and health considerations.

- If the difference between GNI per capita rank and HDI rank (GNI per capita rank – HDI rank) is negative it means that the GNI per capita rank is a smaller **number** than the HDI rank. Roughly speaking, this means that the country ranks higher up in the per capita income list than in the development achievement list: it is **not** doing very well in terms of education and health considerations.

- To find data on health and education related indicators, visit the World Bank at www.data.worldbank.org/indicator

- You can also find such data in the statistical tables at the end of each human development report. For example, in HDR 2010, Table 13 (pp. 192–196) presents education-related indicators, while Table 14 (pp. 197–201) presents health-related indicators. All reports can be downloaded from http://hdr.undp.org/en/reports

Example 1

Compare and contrast GNI per capita and GNI per capita in PPP$ for more and less developed countries. (Remember that GNI per capita has replaced GDP per capita in the indicators used to measure progress in education and income.)

The necessary data on per capita GNI and per capita GNI in PPP$ can be found in Table 1 of the World Bank Development Report 2010 (p. 378), available online (see above). The HDI country rankings can be found in the 2010 UNDP HDR. Seven countries were selected from the very high human development group and seven from the other categories.

In addition, for both sets of countries the ratio of per capita GNI in PPP$ to per capita GNI (in market exchange rates) is calculated: if the ratio is greater than 1 then prices in these countries are on average lower.

Very high human development					Low human development				
2010 HDI rank	Country	GNI per capita (2008)	PPP$ GNI per capita (2008)	$\dfrac{PPP\$ \, pcGNI}{pcGNI}$	2010 HDI rank	Country	GNI per capita (2008)	PPP$ GNI per capita (2008)	$\dfrac{PPP\$ \, pcGNI}{pcGNI}$
1	Norway	87,070	58,500	0.67	73	Brazil	7,350	10,070	1.37
3	New Zealand	27,940	25,090	0.90	83	Turkey	9,340	13,770	1.47
16	Finland	48,120	35,660	0.74	89	China	2,940	6,020	2.05
23	Italy	35,240	30,250	0.86	116	Guatemala	2,680	4,690	1.75
25	Austria	46,260	37,680	0.81	119	India	1,070	2,960	2.77
27	Singapore	34,760	47,940	1.38	143	Uganda	420	1,140	2.71
40	Portugal	20,560	22,080	1.07	161	Burkina Faso	480	1,160	2.42
Average per capita GNI of group		42,850		0.86	Average per capita GNI of group		3,469		1.64
Average per capita GNI in PPP$ of group		36,743			Average per capita GNI in PPP$ of group		5,687		

First, the per capita income levels in the former group are significantly higher. The average per capita income of the former group is 12.35 times the average per capita income of the latter group. When using per capita GNI figures in PPP$ there is still a huge difference but it shrinks to 6.5 times. All developing countries have a higher per capita GNI when expressed in PPP$. Prices are therefore on average lower. For example, in India, $1,070 buys as much as $2,960 in the USA. China's per capita income doubles when expressed in international dollars, i.e. PPP$ dollars that have the same purchasing power in China as they do in the USA. In China, per capita GNI doubles when measured in PPP$: prices are much lower in China than in the USA. On the other hand, Norway's per capita income shrinks by about a third from $87,070 to $58,500 when the price differences between the US and Norway are taken into consideration. The Norwegian currency is overvalued compared with its PPP value.

Example 2

Compare and contrast two health indicators for economically more-developed and economically less-developed countries.

There are many health indicators available to examine, for example:

- health expenditure (per capita)
- life expectancy at birth (years)
- infant mortality (per 1,000 live births)
- mortality of children under five (per 1,000)
- malnutrition prevalence: weight/height for age (% of children under 5)
- births attended by skilled health staff (% of total)
- maternal mortality ratio (per 100,000 live births)

- immunization, diphtheria and measles (% of children between 12–23 months)
- improved sanitation facilities (% of population with access)
- prevalence of HIV (% of population aged 15–49)
- physicians (per 10,000 people)
- hospital beds (per 10,000 people).

Life expectancy and infant mortality are two of the most commonly used and quoted statistics.

The following table presents life expectancy and infant mortality for a small set of countries in the 2010 very high human development group and in the low human development group.

Very high human development				Low human development			
2010 HDI rank	Country	Life expectancy	Infant mortality	2010 HDI rank	Country	Life expectancy	Infant mortality
2	Australia	81.9	4	135	Madagascar	61.2	41
4	USA	79.6	7	143	Uganda	54.1	79
9	Sweden	81.3	2	157	Ethiopia	56.1	67
25	Austria	80.4	3	165	Mozambique	48.4	96
40	Portugal	79.1	3	167	Burundi	51.4	101

In the two sets above there are very significant differences in both variables. But the two sets chosen are very disparate. Even though within the set of countries classified in the very high human development group in the 2010 HDR you will find countries where people have a life expectancy of 73.7 years (Estonia), or 75.1 (Slovakia) or 76.0 (Qatar), you will see that a few countries in the medium human development group achieve or approach these rates, such as Sri Lanka (74.4), Nicaragua (73.8) or China (73.5), and several developing countries with relatively low per capita GNI also achieve similar figures, such as Albania or Belize with 76.9.

Example 3

Compare and contrast two education indicators for economically more-developed and economically less-developed countries.

There are many education indicators available to examine, for example:

- literacy rate (% of people 15 and above)
- mean years of schooling (years)
- mean years of schooling of people above 25 (years)
- expected years of schooling (years)
- expenditure per student in primary, secondary and tertiary education (% of GDP, per capita)
- pupil–teacher ratio, primary
- ratio of girls to boys in primary and secondary education (%)
- school enrolment in primary, secondary and tertiary education (%)
- trained teachers in primary education (% of total teachers).

Mean years of schooling expected and school enrolment are two commonly used statistics and are used by the UNDP to measure achievements in education in the new HDI. The table on the next page presents averages for different groups of countries (based on HDR 2010, p. 146).

Some broad patterns are easily detected. Individuals in the very high human development group of countries have 2.75 times more years of schooling on average than the people in the low human development group, and 3.65 times those in the least developed group. But the promising point is that when looking at the expected years of schooling (the years of schooling that a child can expect to receive given current enrolment rates) the ratio decreases to 1.9.

Looking within HDI groups for all countries the biggest gains are expected to be realized (assuming current patterns continue) in the low human development group. The ratio of expected years of schooling to mean years of schooling is 2.0 for the low human development group and 2.16 for the least developed group. In fact, the expected years of schooling of the low human development group (8.2) is almost equal to the current mean years of schooling of the high human development group (8.3).

Make sure you always remember the very significant variations that exist within every group of countries and also the huge variations within individual countries (see the *Debunking myths about the 'third world'* video with the 'exploding' country bubbles at www.gapminder.org).

Group	Mean years of schooling	Expected years of schooling	Ratio of expected years of schooling to mean years of schooling
Developed			
OECD	11.4	15.9	1.39
Non-OECD	10.0	13.9	1.39
Developing			
Arab States	5.7	10.8	1.89
East Asia and the Pacific	7.2	11.5	1.60
Europe and Central Asia	9.2	13.6	1.48
Latin America and the Caribbean	7.9	13.7	1.73
South Asia	4.6	10.0	2.17
Sub-Saharan Africa	4.5	9.0	2.00
HDI groups			
Very high human development	11.3	15.9	1.41
High human development	8.3	13.8	1.66
Medium human development	6.3	11.0	1.75
Low human development	4.1	8.2	2.00
Least developed countries	3.7	8.0	2.16
World	7.4	12.3	1.66

Exercise 1

Find data on per capita GDP and per capita GNI for different countries. For countries where the differences are significant try to find the explanation. Make sure you include the Philippines, Mexico, Bangladesh, Albania and other countries or territories.

Table 16 in the 2010 HDR (pp. 206–210) has GDP per capita in PPP$ to use. You could also download the 2009 HDR.

Exercise 2

For a subset of the countries you may have already researched, try to find out the extent by which they are getting closer to achieving the MDGs. Beyond the MDG dedicated sites you could use Table 3 (pp. 382–383) in the 2010 WDR. If you enter the terms 'WDR 2010 selected indicators' into an Internet search engine you will find the table in pdf format.

Exercise 3

Compare and contrast HDI figures of:

1 high income OECD and non-OECD countries

2 very high, high, medium and low human development groups

3 groups in different geographical regions (the Arab states, East Asia and the Pacific, Europe and Central Asia, Latin America and the Caribbean, South Asia and Sub-Saharan Africa).

Within each group, find countries with divergent values from the average of the group it belongs in, in terms of:

a life expectancy

b mean years of schooling

c expected years of schooling

d per capita GNI in PPP$.

For example, New Zealand is number 3 in the HDI index even though its per capita GNI ranking is much lower.

Research the particulars for two (or more if you are working in groups) of these countries, trying to find out the reasons for the variations you have detected in the data. Once again, you could create 'posters' of your findings and post these on your IB development blog.

Domestic factors and economic development

Remember

- You are asked to examine how the following domestic factors contribute to economic development: health and education, the use of appropriate technology, access to credit and microcredit, the empowerment of women, income distribution.

- Improvements in health and education increase productivity and permit an individual to have more, better and higher-paid employment opportunities. Better education and better health are the foundations for living a longer and healthier life and both are considered as fundamental human rights per se.

- The type of technology employed determines whether any acceleration in growth rates achieved in a country will be translated into human development gains or not. Jobless growth is a type of growth to avoid and it results if the technology adopted is not based on the relatively abundant resource which, in the case of developing countries, is labour.

Remember

- Poverty reduction depends not only on income growth but also on how income is distributed. Poverty is reduced and development is achieved if there is growth accompanied by narrowing income inequality. At the same time, even in countries with an unequal income distribution, progress has been achieved if social expenditures were good (Chile, Mexico and Panama; HDR 2010, p. 55). Also, good social spending can improve income inequality.

- Continued and widening income inequalities hinders progress in human development as the very poor do not have access to education and health services, experiencing deprivations in many dimensions. The very poor also lack access to credit.

- Decreasing income inequality may permit consensus building among population groups. This in turn may facilitate adoption and implementation of necessary institutional and economic reforms. In addition, institutions which may have shaped to promote the interests of those in power may slowly change if greater income power is in the hands of the disadvantaged.

- Lower-income inequality may accelerate savings and so permit more investment and greater demand for locally produced goods and services which may increase income and further decrease inequality. But, income inequality within countries has been increasing: more countries have a higher Gini coefficient now than they did 30 years ago.

- Income distribution in the world has grown even more unequal as rich countries have grown much faster than poor ones in the past 40 years. Average income in 13 of the poorest countries of the world is lower than it was 40 years ago.

Remember

- Policies that aim to improve gender equity have been found to improve human development. There are numerous routes through which this can be accomplished.

  Women invest more than men in their children so policies empowering women will tend to improve the level of health and education of their children. An educated mother will ensure that her children are educated. She will also tend to have fewer and healthier children.

  Women's economic contributions are either not valued at all or grossly undervalued; empirical estimates value it at many trillions of dollars a year.

  'Human development if not engendered, is endangered.'

Remember

- Credit institutions are important in the development process as they give an incentive to people to save and allow them to borrow. Individuals can borrow to increase their human capital. They can borrow to set up or expand a business which may enable them to escape poverty, to meet adversities and to improve their living standards generally.

- Microcredit is directed at the very poor and is generally considered a powerful instrument for helping them deal with erratic income flows, allowing them to build assets and reducing their exposure to informal money lenders.

  In many less-developed countries, because of the lack of well-defined property rights, individuals typically cannot borrow, which deters capital formation and so growth. Using the Internet, research Hernando de Soto who emphasizes the importance of property rights and identifies lack of property rights as a major source of poverty.

  Microcredit targets individuals who do not qualify to borrow from regular banks.

  Microcredit has lately come under attack: '…most borrowers do not appear to be climbing out of poverty, and a sizable minority is getting trapped in a spiral of debt, according to studies and analysts' ('Microlenders, honored with nobel, are struggling', *New York Times*, 5 January 2011).

Example 1

Examine the graph titled 'Rural-urban differences intensify regional disparities in China' which you can find in the HDR 2006, p. 272.

1 What are the two types of inequalities evident from the figure?

Concerning China there are inequalities both between regions of the country (with Shanghai scoring significantly higher than the Gansu or Guizhou provinces) and within each region between urban and rural populations.

2 Provide two reasons why, in your opinion, urban populations score higher in the development front.

The industrial base (the factories) and everything else revolving around the export sector are located in or close to cities and, consequently, urban incomes are greater. The wage difference is what attracts millions of people from the farms to the factories. In addition, not only are there more schools and health care centres available but access to them is easier for the urban-based population (there are shorter distances and better roads and transportation, for example).

Exercise 1

Examine how income distribution has been affected in Mexico or Panama by public spending on services such as health care, and primary and secondary education. Find the extent of income inequality and poverty in one of these two countries and whether it has changed, as well as information on public policy on education.

Exercise 2

In Costa Rica, more than one quarter of public spending on health care targets the poorest fifth of the population (HDR 2010, p. 61).

Explain how this may affect human development in this country. Find and use data to support your arguments.

Exercise 3

Look at the HDR 2010, p. 59. Examine the three figures illustrating the relationship between inequality in health, education and income and HDI levels in 2010. Describe the pattern that emerges from all three. Which one of the three relationships exhibits the greatest dispersion? How would you interpret this? Can you think of any explanations?

Exercise 4

Examine the role of microcredit in the development process using information on the role of the Grameen Bank in Bangladesh. In late 2009, microcredit institutions in Bangladesh were heavily criticized. What are the arguments used against these credit institutions? Are there risks involved that may have to be addressed?

International trade and economic development

Remember

- Primary product prices have exhibited a downward long-term trend.

- A long-term decrease in agricultural primaries implies decreasing export revenues adversely affecting AD. National income and employment decreases. Balance of payment problems follow resulting in rising external debt problems. Rural populations suffer as incomes, investment and employment in the sector decreases and absolute poverty rises.

- Commodity booms do occur, though: since 2000 (with the exception of 2008–2009) the index of non-fuel primary commodity prices has been rising.

- Short-term price swings in agricultural primaries are typically a result of supply variations (for example due to weather or crop disease) coupled with low-price elasticities of demand.

- Price swings increase the degree of uncertainty and so hurt investments. When the prices rise (for example as a result of a bad crop elsewhere) the effects on the economy are very complex.

- Access to international markets is often limited or blocked. Many agricultural products are highly subsidized in the USA and Europe. As a result, not only are many developing countries unable to penetrate these protected markets but often witness depressed world prices as a result of oversupply.

These problems point to the importance and the benefits of diversification.

Remember

- The terms of trade of countries with significant concentration of primary exports are obviously affected: a decreasing long-term trend in non-fuel commodities leads to a deterioration of the long-term terms of trade of developing countries. It means that a developing country would have to export a greater and greater volume of, for example, coffee to import a machine (which is self-defeating because by increasing volumes of a good its price will be further depressed).

- This long-term deterioration of the terms of trade of developing countries is referred to as the Prebisch-Singer thesis.

This implies that the gains from trade are unequally distributed between developed and developing countries and that, if there is no change in the structure of world production, inequality will widen.

Remember

- A structural characteristic of many developing countries is that primary product food exports are a very high proportion of total exports. For these countries, short-term price swings as well as long-term downward trends can be devastating.

Remember

- The role of the World Trade Organization (WTO) is controversial with respect to 'the rules of the game' of international trade. Many claim that the rules are bent in favour of developed countries and that the interests of developing nations, especially the smaller and poorer ones, are not effectively promoted. These are some of the issues:

  - developed countries continue to maintain their subsidies on agriculture

  - they have been accused of making increased use of non-tariff barriers towards developing country exports

  - they insist on the protection of intellectual property rights

  - environmental and labour-related concerns are not a priority.

Remember

- Concerning regional integration between developing countries, the theoretical arguments are the same but empirically there seems to have been more trade diversion than trade creation.

- Bilateral agreements between the USA or the EU and a developing country have been accused of 'arm-twisting' as the bargaining power is not balanced.

- Resources on the regional agreements in the world can be found at the WTO site www.wto.org, click the 'Trade topics' drop-down menu; then 'Regional trade agreements'; then the 'RTA database'. In this database you can retrieve information by country and, on a world map, you can see for each country you choose its participation in regional trade agreements.

Remember

- Import substitution has been practised by almost all countries including the USA. It has also been a stepping stone to the successful export-oriented strategy of East Asian economies. It may be theoretically sound but its implementation carries significant risks.

Example 1

Explain why agricultural commodities exhibit wide short-term price volatility.

The main reason is that the short run supply of such products is affected by random factors, of which weather is the single most important. Given that these markets are competitive, any supply-side shock will automatically translate as a price change in the market.

These supply-induced price swings will be pretty big because of the low price elasticity of demand (PED) for such products. These commodities do not have close substitutes.

In addition, market conditions and so price may be affected by speculation as these products are traded in world commodity exchanges.

Example 2

Provide possible benefits of increased regional cooperation among developing countries as well as two reasons why such attempts have had limited success.

Possible benefits are:
- increased trade creation as a result of the resulting expanded market

- economies of scale that may lead to more exports outside the bloc

- greater political and bargaining power in negotiations with developed economies

- a decreased level of dependence on developing countries' markets.

The reasons for which many such attempts failed or resulted in limited success are:

- the structure of production and of trade in developing countries lacks a sufficient complementary nature and has resulted in more trade diversion than trade creation

- many developing countries have encountered significant organizational and administrative problems

- political rivalry both between and within countries has also been an issue.

Exercise 1

Go to the WTO site at www.wto.org to read its side of the story. Download the pdf publication *Understanding the WTO* from the WTO site, which has Chapter 6 dedicated to developing countries. Then use an Internet search engine to find sites where the role of the WTO is in doubt and critics voice their concerns. The BBC site is a good starting point: type the terms (BBC, WTO, profile) into an Internet search engine and you will find the relevant page. Write a short essay discussing the role of the WTO (GATT) with respect to both developed and developing countries. Remember that developing countries are not only China, India and Brazil.

Exercise 2

Research one of the following regional trade agreements:
- Mercosur (The Southern Common Market)
- Asia Pacific Economic Cooperation (APEC)
- COMESA
- SADC
- ASEAN
- EAC

Find out when it was set up; which countries are members; what type of agreement it is; and examples of issues of interest within it. For example, by entering the terms 'BBC, Mercosur, profile' into an Internet search engine, you will find relevant information on the BBC site. Alternatively, you can start researching COMESA or APEC in Wikipedia, which has useful information and further links.

Foreign direct investment and multinational corporations

Remember

- Multinational corporations may seek to establish production units in countries with cheap labour, but if a country has cheap labour it does not necessarily mean that it will attract foreign direct investment. It is the overall economic and political framework of a host country that matters to the decision.

- To find statistics on flows of foreign direct investment around the world visit www.unctad.org and click 'Statistics' at the top of the page.

Tip

In order to evaluate the role of multinational corporations, it may be convenient as a starting point to think of the 'filling the gaps versus widening the gaps' approach. Gaps include:

- actual versus desired levels of investment
- actual versus desired levels of foreign exchange
- actual versus desired levels of tax revenues
- actual versus desired levels of employment
- actual versus desired levels of skills
- actual versus desired levels of technology.

Exercise 1

Download the latest World Development Report from the World Bank site, locate Table 5 on trade, aid and finance, and find the data on 'Foreign direct investment net inflows ($ millions)'. Which **developing** countries attract the most foreign direct investment? Using your background knowledge and other information from the Internet, try to find which factors may be responsible for your findings.

Exercise 2

Multinational corporations are a source of controversy. There are many sites that are devoted to 'watching' the activities of multinational corporations. A quick Internet search will reveal many of these sites. An interesting exercise is to use such a site, find out about alleged reprehensible activities of some corporation (there are many that have been accused of wrongdoings) and then conduct a detailed research on the accusations. You should also go to the company's Internet site to find out about employment and other practices. For example, an oil trading company, operating in more than 40 countries and accused of dumping waste that allegedly caused injuries and health problems in the local population, claims that 90 % of its employees are local nationals.

Exercise 3

Evaluate the role of multinational corporations when establishing a presence in a developing country. What are the factors that one has to examine to make a judgment?

Exercise 4

Explain why each of the following is a reason for which MNC's invest directly into developing countries, or a reason that explains why some countries attract more foreign direct flows than others (or both).

- avoidance of tariffs
- low wages / labour costs / differences in labour costs
- high levels of human capital and labour productivity
- extent and power of labour unions
- proximity to markets
- stable macroeconomic environment
- clearly defined property rights and a secure legal framework

- public policy including tax treatment and profit repatriation
- environmental laws, regulations and their enforcement
- export-oriented economy
- high and/or growing levels of income
- stage of development
- cultural similarities
- stable political environment
- quality of physical and informational infrastructure
- membership in wider free trade areas/trading blocks
- natural resource endowments (and their geographical distribution) including climate.

Foreign aid

Remember

- The type of aid matters when assessing its potential effectiveness. Tied aid, when the funds must be spent to buy (import) goods and services from the donor country, is typically considered least effective as recipients are often asked to buy products that either they do not need or that could have been imported from elsewhere at lower prices.

- Much to the surprise of many, foreign aid includes so-called concessional loans and not just outright grants that don't need to be repaid. Lending is concessional if interest rates are lower than market interest rates and repayment periods longer.

  Motives for official assistance include:

  - the moral, humanitarian motive
  - the political motive
  - the economic motive.

  The above categorization is often sufficient in explaining the identity of the donor (whether it is a country, a multilateral institution or an non-governmental organization), the type of aid granted (whether it is tied, project or programme aid) as well as the size and size differentials of official assistance flows to developing countries.

- Much of the criticisms of aid are criticisms of its administration, both within the recipient countries and on the part of donors (for example criticisms of tied aid, conditional lending, spaghetti bowls of requirements imposed by different donors).

- The consensus on the aid versus trade issue is that it is a non-issue: both are necessary in a complementary fashion. The particulars of course, as with almost everything in development economics, vary across time and countries. Aid without an exporting presence (trade) in a globalized world is futureless, while trade without aid is not possible in many developing countries because of the binding constraints of poor infrastructure and/or institutions.

Tip

- Visit http://stats.oecd.org and click 'Development > Aid activities'. Click 'Creditor reporting system' and then you will find all the information you need to compare and contrast the extent, nature and sources of official development assistance to any two or more countries you want by selecting the country from the drop-down menu 'Recipient'. You will find information on the size and composition of aid arranged by donor country for bilateral aid as well as by different multilateral organizations for multilateral aid. Clicking a magnifying glass will uncover detailed information on the size of the flow, whether the flow is a grant or a loan, the purpose (whether it is education policy or basic health care) and the channel of delivery (whether it is through the public sector or non-governmental organizations, for example).

- Work in groups to collect all the necessary data for a few countries (not more than four). Organize the data in a meaningful way and then proceed to 'compare and contrast' in terms of the 'extent, nature and sources' you found. Present the data to your class (or to the world through "Prezi" or any other format).

Exercise 1

Visit a blog related to foreign aid, find an issue of interest, research it further and present your findings to your class or to the IB world. There are many interesting blogs such as:

- www.kristof.blogs.nytimes.com/tag/foreign-aid
- www.aidwatchers.com
- http://blogs.oxfam.org
- www.guardian.co.uk/global-development/poverty-matters
- www.aidinfo.org
- www.oxfamblogs.org/fp2p

Exercise 2

The policy advice of the International Monetary Fund (IMF) has often been described as 'anti-developmental'. Why is it, in your opinion, that this description is adopted by some academic circles? (See for example the Stiglitz critique). What are the major criticisms that the IMF has faced in the past 15 years? (Hint: capital account liberalization; market-based pricing; trade liberalization; privatization; research the term 'Washington consensus').

Or could it be that the IMF is often blamed for things it has no control over?

4.7 The role of international debt

Foreign debt

Remember

- The debt burden of a country can be measured through various indicators, which include:
  - the debt to exports ratio
  - the debt to national income ratio
  - the debt service to export earnings ratio (the proportion of export earnings needed to repay principal and interest on debt).
- The high costs on the development path of a highly indebted developing country are a result of:
  - diminished ability to import necessary capital goods

- the adverse effect on private (foreign and domestic) investment of the debt overhang as a result of the fear of higher taxes, profit repatriation constraints and periodic recessions
- the social costs of a diminished ability of governments to undertake social investments in health care, education and social infrastructure
- the risk of becoming entangled in a debt trap where debt servicing requires further accumulation of debt obligations.

Example 1

Explain why countries borrow from foreign creditors. Under what general conditions is external borrowing meaningful?

A country will need to borrow to finance a (or part of a) current account deficit that is not financed by foreign investment inflows, foreign aid inflows or a decrease in foreign exchange reserves. External borrowing to finance a short-term current account deficit is considered acceptable as it allows the country to avoid disruptions in production, consumption and employment because import purchases are not interrupted.

If the borrowing is to be a recurring long-term practice, it must be channelled into strengthening export industries (which will contribute to increased foreign exchange earnings) or import substituting industries (which will decrease future expenditures on imports). External borrowing, in other words, should aim at facilitating directly or indirectly (for example through infrastructure investments) production of tradables. Either generating or saving foreign exchange must be directly or indirectly achieved. The average annual rate of the resulting additional net foreign exchange earnings must exceed the average rate of interest paid on the external debt.

Example 2

Explain the meaning of the term 'debt rescheduling'.

Since the debt crisis of the 1980s there have been several debt rescheduling plans and initiatives, for example the abortive Baker plan, the Brady plan, the Trinidad and Toronto initiatives by the Paris Club (a group of creditor governments of OECD countries) and the World Bank – IMF, HIPC initiatives.

The goal of these plans was to make the debt service payments manageable by lengthening loan maturities, reducing interest rates on new borrowing, facilitating debt buy-backs (in which a debtor country buys back its own debt at a discount) or debt swaps. Debt swaps include:

- debt for equity swaps, where debt is exchanged for ownership stakes in a newly privatized, previously state-owned firm

- debt for nature swaps, where debt is exchanged for agreements by a debtor country to set aside land as protected reserves.

Debt relief initiatives aim to relieve very poor countries of their unsustainable debts and to promote credible reform policies for growth, poverty reduction and human development. To qualify, countries had to meet certain conditions. The conditions for the HIPC initiative require that: the country must be very poor; the country must 'face an unsustainable debt burden that cannot be addressed through traditional debt relief mechanisms'; and must have 'established a track record of reform and sound policies through IMF and World Bank supported programs'.

(www.imf.org/external/np/exr/facts/hipc.htm)

Strengths and weaknesses of market-oriented and interventionist policies

Remember

- In discussions about the role of markets and the role of the state in the process of development, keep these points in mind.
  - Markets provide signals through changing prices.
  - Prices transmit information and can coordinate behaviour.
  - The profit motive creates the incentive to use resources efficiently.
  - Competition leads to cost cutting, lower prices and the drive to innovate.
  - Markets permit choice.
- However, market failures exist and are pervasive in less-developed economies, as in the case of:
  - public goods such as national defence, law and order, price stability, basic infrastructure
  - positive externalities such as in the provision of education and health services
  - negative externalities such as in air, water and soil pollution, and problems related to the management of common-access resources
  - asymmetric information, adverse selection and moral hazard such as in credit markets and insurance markets.
- Markets do not protect the vulnerable or ensure that income is equitably distributed. The state is necessary not only to provide but also to enforce a conducive institutional framework within which markets can operate.
- Lastly, governments very often fail miserably as a result of corruption, rent seeking, excessive red tape, regulatory capture, limited information, misguided policies, short-term horizons, etc.

Exercise 1

Download the *World Development Report 1997 – The State in a Changing World* from the World Bank, http://www-wds.worldbank.org. Turn to Box 1.4 (p. 26), 'The economic rationale for state intervention and some definitions', which succinctly explains why government intervention is necessary. You will find ways in which the state can improve development outcomes as well as examples of how the state can inflict harm (p. 31). Read the paragraphs on the 'lawlessness syndrome' (p. 41) to comprehend the importance of effective property rights and the costs of corruption and red tape. Read examples of why public investments in health, education and infrastructure promote development objectives (p. 52). There are many other illuminating sections in this report but many are outside the scope of this course.

How to write an extended essay in economics

Writing an extended essay in economics is a popular choice in many schools.

If you like the subject and you do not mind spending time collecting data outside the library and by using the Internet then perhaps it is also a good choice for you.

What to do

First, try to think up a topic that is interesting to you and is definitely related to the theory you are learning.

Thinking of an interesting and appropriate economics topic is half your job. This is where many extended essays go wrong. Candidates often decide to research topics that are either only remotely related to some specific area of theory they can employ or are much too broad, making a meaningful investigation that will satisfy the very specific criteria an impossible task within the 4,000 word limit.

Invest a lot of time trying to come up with a topic that is not only interesting to you and worthwhile investigating but that also clearly lends itself to economic analysis proper.

Once you come up with a specific promising idea, sit down and draft a detailed research proposal (RP) which you should hand in to and discuss with your supervisor.

The research proposal (RP) you draft should include the following information.

Information on the research question (RQ)

- It should present an explicit formulation of the topic. Phrase it in the form of a question (i.e. with a question mark at the end).
- It should include an account of why the specific research question may be interesting and worth studying. Make sure that the answer is not completely obvious. Having phrased the topic as a question will help you determine whether it is trivial or not. Trivial questions are a bad idea. Also, make sure that the treatment will not be merely descriptive but also analytical.

- Consider these points.
    - Is the topic narrow enough?
    - Is it linked to your own local community or environment? It doesn't have to be, but if it is you know that most probably it is not too broad. The examiner also knows that you most likely have not only relied on secondary sources and the Internet.
    - Is it possible to limit the investigation to less than 4,000 words?

Information about the theoretical backbone you plan to employ

- Give a detailed account of the area (or areas) of economic theory that your topic will relate to. This is very important. The most common mistake is for candidates to choose a question that really belongs in business and management or some other discipline. Your account of the area of economic theory that you will employ should be as specific as possible. Writing, for example, that the topic relates to oligopoly issues is too broad. Try to specify the framework in greater detail. Is it issues of interdependence that you will examine? Is it issues of collusion? Is non-price competition

relevant? Will game theory be useful?
- Include a preliminary list of possible theoretical diagrams (adapted to your specific research question) and why each may be useful in your analysis. When drawing, for example, a diagram to illustrate interdependence, do not use 'firm A' and 'firm B' but the actual names of the firms you are focusing on.
- Write a list of all the economic terms you expect to use in your essay. If there are not that many terms in this list, then maybe it's time to search for another topic.

Information about the primary and secondary data you plan to use

- Describe the information that will be needed to answer your specific research question.
- For each piece of information listed, include a brief explanation of why it may be needed; why will each piece of information be collected?
- Consider: Where will the information be found? What are the sources?
- If you plan to collect data (prices charged, quantities bought or sold, rents paid, etc.) where will you collect the data from? What period will the data cover? How many data points do you expect to collect? Will the sample collected be representative? Will it be large enough? Can you foresee any data limitations?
- If you plan to use a survey, questionnaire or interview, decide what questions you will ask and explain why each one will be asked. What kind of answers do you expect to get? How would these answers help you answer the RQ? Too often candidates who design surveys or questionnaires or plan an interview include questions that are of absolutely no use in their work.

Analysis of the data

- How do you expect to analyse the data or results? Will you look at trends? Will you use averages? Will you present percentage changes? Will the analysis be qualitative only?
- How do you plan to present your data or results? Will you include tables, charts and/or pie charts? Whichever of these you decide to use, make sure that you do not just drop them into the essay. They need to be analysed, discussed and evaluated.
- Is it possible to combine the economic theory you consider relevant with your possible data or results?
- How will your analysis help you arrive at meaningful conclusions?

Bear in mind

Each extended essay is assessed against a set of criteria. The criteria are very detailed and include 11 different categories. Your supervisor will provide you with a copy of the criteria and they can be found in the official *IBO Extended Essay Guide*. You must realize that you are **not** asked to write a dissertation. The extended essay will **not** be your *magnum opus*. The end product must only satisfy the specific set of criteria that the IB has designed. The extended essay is a simple exercise designed to introduce candidates (who are still secondary school students) to the structure as well as the 'ingredients' of professional research papers. So, relax and enjoy the process. At the end, you should be proud of your work.

Advice on the economics internal assessment exercise

The internal assessment in economics requires candidates to produce a portfolio of three commentaries on published news article. They should be based on three of the four different sections of the syllabus from three different sources.

Advice point 1

Make sure you enjoy the work you do

Find articles on issues that are of interest to you and that manage to intrigue you. If you are not at all curious about what is written in the article it will become more difficult to produce good-quality work.

Advice point 2

Find an appropriate article

- This is probably the most important step in producing high-quality work. First, the article you choose should be the right length. Many candidates focus on long articles. This is a big mistake. Lengthy articles are 'very much discouraged' (*IB economics guide*, p. 91). Very short articles are also a bad choice. Usually, articles that are between ¾ of a page and one and a half pages long are the best. Anything less than half a page is too short and does not have enough information to work on. Anything longer than one and a half pages has too much information, making it difficult for you to remain focused.

- Avoid articles that have already done the job you are asked to do. The article should be of a reporting nature and not a commentary or an editorial. Many students consider *The Economist* magazine as the best possible source of articles, but most experienced IB teachers disagree because, as Dr. Manuel Fernandez, OCC adviser for IB economics, has commented, they 'tend to convey already a self-contained economic analysis and the student is left with nothing much that can be used for a meaningful comment'.

- Choose articles explicitly linked to an element of economic theory you have been exposed to. Start searching with something specific in mind.

For example, in microeconomics, articles related to developments in agricultural markets (or, more generally, commodities) can be analysed using demand and supply tools and investigating elasticities, taxes and subsidies, minimum prices, buffer stocks, etc; articles that report on pollution-related issues, or on health and education policies, may be analysed within the theoretical framework of externalities, merit and demerit goods, taxation, subsidies, etc; articles related to competition issues or to activities of large oligopolistic firms may be examined through the theory of market structures (for HL commentaries).

- In the opinion of many teachers, the best way to find an article is by skimming through hard copies of papers you find at school or at home. One big side benefit is that, by the time you find your article of choice, you will have read through quite a few other interesting articles on totally unrelated issues.

- If you do not have access to hard copies of papers then the Internet is there to help. Virtually all newspapers have an online version and most are searchable. Bookmark on your laptop papers of global and of local interest.

- Limit your search to articles written in the same language as your commentary. The *IB economics guide* explicitly states that 'the article should, where possible, be in the same language as the commentary', otherwise an accurate translation must be provided, which is extra and rather difficult work.

Advice point 3

Read the article very carefully, 'connect' with the theory and get down to work

- Underline the sentences or paragraphs that contain all the 'juicy' material.

- Writing a commentary is straightforward. Just think of reading an article and then visiting an optician to buy a pair of spectacles. Each pair of spectacles this specific optician has in stock is rather special: each is a particular economic theory, a concept or a diagram. Your task is to pick the appropriate pair or pairs and then write down what the article is about after putting on the specific 'econ' spectacles you chose. Think: aren't I 'reading' much more into this article now than I would have read into it six months before taking this course?

- Now divide a piece of paper or a word file into three separate sections: 'Terms', 'Diagrams, concepts and theory' and 'Evaluation and judgments'.

- Start off by writing down all the economic terms found in the article as well as any economic terms that you think may be included in your commentary. Next, write down which diagram or diagrams you think you could use in your commentary. If you cannot easily think of at least one diagram, throw away the article and start searching for a new one. Once you have your diagram or diagrams you pretty much have your theory organized. Write the essentials of the theory you are employing, making sure that your exposition is intertwined with the particulars of the article. For example, if you are to explain the

easy monetary policy that New Zealand is adopting, refer to the New Zealand Central Bank and to the New Zealand dollar which may depreciate. Do not explain theory in a vacuum. Remember that you must 'explain the linkages between the article and economic theory', not just the theory. In the 'Evaluation and judgments' section of your notes, write down your opinion about implications, limitations, alternative viewpoints, biases, etc. In order to satisfy criterion E, 'Evaluation' (worth 4 points), you are asked that 'judgments are made that are supported by effective and balanced reasoning'. This is your moment as a junior economist in a round table of professionals when they ask you for your valued assessment (of the policy, of the performance or of another issue).

- Now for the rest: start writing your commentary so that a friend who is intelligent but who is not taking economics understands what the issue is all about, ensuring that you also offer your judgment or evaluation of the issue.

The criteria

There are five criteria against which each of your commentaries will be graded:

Criterion A	Diagrams	3 points
Criterion B	Terminology	2 points
Criterion C	Application	2 points
Criterion D	Analysis	3 points
Criterion E	Evaluation	4 points
Total		14 points

and one internal assessment criterion for the whole portfolio:

| Criterion F | Rubric requirements | 3 points |

for a maximum of $3 \times 14 = 42 + 3 = 45$ points.

Below are the descriptors for achieving the maximum points for each criterion.

These are the five rubric requirements.

- Each commentary does not exceed 750 words.
- Each article is based on a different section of the syllabus.
- Each article is taken from a different and appropriate source.
- Each article was published no earlier than one year before the writing of the commentary.
- The summary portfolio cover sheet, three commentary cover sheets and the article for each commentary are included.

Needless to say, no points should be sacrificed from criteria A, B and F. Criteria C and D are also relatively easy to satisfy. Care and practice are required to satisfy criterion E. Remember that if you have selected an appropriate article, satisfying criterion E will also be possible.

Criterion	You earn	Descriptor
A	3 points if	relevant, accurate and correctly labelled diagrams are included, with a full explanation
B	2 points if	terminology relevant to the article is used appropriately throughout the commentary
C	2 points if	relevant economic concepts and/or theories are applied to the article appropriately throughout the commentary
D	3 points if	there is effective economic analysis relating to the article
E	4 points if	judgments are made that are supported by effective and balanced reasoning
F	3 points if	all five rubric requirements are met

Command terms and their use in the economics syllabus

The table below includes command terms **explicitly** mentioned in the learning outcomes of the economics syllabus and classified within AO1, AO2 and AO3. The meaning of each command term is given (quoted from the official syllabus glossary) as well as one example of each taken from the learning outcomes.

	Term	Student is asked to do the following	Example
1	Analyse (AO2)	Break down in order to bring out the essential elements or structure	...analyse the impact of indirect taxes on market outcomes
2	Apply (AO2)	Use an idea, equation or principle, theory or law in relation to a given problem or issue	(HL) ...apply the Marshall-Lerner condition to explain the effects of devaluation
3	Compare and contrast (AO3)	Give an account of similarities or differences between two (or more) items or situations referring to both (all) of them throughout	...compare and contrast two education indicators for economically more-developed countries and economically less-developed countries.
4	Define (AO1)	Give the precise meaning of a word, phrase, concept or physical quantity	...define the term unemployment
5	Describe (AO1)	Give a detailed account	...describe, using examples, common access resources
6	Discuss (AO3)	Offer a considered and balanced view that includes a range of arguments, factors or hypothesis. Opinions or conclusions should be presented clearly and supported by appropriate evidence	...discuss the possible advantages and disadvantages of a monetary union for its members
7	Distinguish (AO2)	Make clear the differences between two or more concepts or items	...distinguish between GDP and GNP/ GNI as measures of economic activity
8	Evaluate (AO3)	Make an appraisal by weighing up the strengths and limitations	...evaluate government policies to deal with the different types of unemployment
9	Examine (AO3)	Consider an argument or concept in a way that uncovers the assumptions and interrelationships of the issue	...examine the possible consequences of overvalued and undervalued currencies
10	Explain (AO2)	Give a detailed account including reasons or causes	...explain the two components of the capital account, specifically capital transfers and transaction in non-produced, non-financial assets
11	Outline (AO1)	Give a brief account or summary	...outline the current status of international development goals, including the Millennium Development Goals
12	State (AO1)	Give a specific name, value or other brief answer without explanation or calculation	...state that supply-side policies may be market-based or interventionist

Also:

(1) The following command terms are not explicitly mentioned in the learning outcomes but may still be used in lieu of other equivalent command terms: list (AO1); comment, suggest (AO2); justify, to what extent (AO3).

(2) 'Explain' (AO2) is the typical command term found in the Foundations section. Each of the following is encountered only once: outline (AO1), distinguish (AO2) and examine (AO1).

The AO3 command terms: synthesis and evaluation

AO3 command terms are reserved only for part (b) questions in HL and SL Paper 1, worth 15 of the 25 marks, as well as for part (d) questions in HL and SL Paper 2, worth 8 of the 20 marks.

There are six command terms in the economics syllabus from the AO3 'synthesis and evaluation' category.

The first four are:
- compare and contrast
- discuss
- evaluate
- examine.

Then there are these two which are not explicitly mentioned in the learning outcomes:

- justify (give valid reasons or evidence to support an answer or conclusion)
- to what extent (consider the merits or otherwise of an argument or concept – opinions and conclusions should be presented clearly and supported with appropriate evidence and sound argument).

Below you will find all learning outcomes included in the official syllabus where AO3 level command terms are explicitly mentioned. Next to each, in a parenthesis, is the section of the syllabus in which it is found. Of course, many draw on more than one section of the syllabus. Make sure that you are very well aware of how to deal with each and every one of them.

Compare and contrast

- **HL** Compare and contrast, using a diagram, the equilibrium positions of a profit maximizing monopoly firm and a revenue maximizing monopoly firm. (Micro)
- **HL** Compare and contrast, using a diagram, a monopoly market with a perfectly competitive market. (Micro)
- **HL** Compare and contrast, using diagrams, monopolistic competition with perfect competition, and monopolistic competition with monopoly. (Micro)
- Compare and contrast a fixed exchange rate system with a floating exchange rate system. (IE)
- Compare and contrast the different types of trading blocs. (IE)
- Compare and contrast the GDP per capita figures and the GNI per capita figures for economically more-developed countries and economically less-developed countries. (DVLP)
- Compare and contrast two health indicators for economically more-developed countries and economically less-developed countries. (DVLP)
- Compare and contrast two education indicators for economically more-developed countries and economically less-developed countries. (DVLP)
- Compare and contrast the HDI figures for economically more-developed countries and economically less-developed countries. (DVLP)
- Compare and contrast the extent, nature and sources of ODA to two economically less-developed countries. (DVLP)
- Compare and contrast the roles of aid and trade in economic development. (DVLP)

Discuss

- Discuss the consequences of imposing an indirect tax on the stakeholders in a market. (Micro)
- Discuss the consequences of providing a subsidy on the stakeholders in a market. (Micro)
- Discuss the consequences of imposing a price ceiling on the stakeholders in a market. (Micro)
- Discuss the consequences of imposing a price floor on the stakeholders in a market. (Micro)
- Discuss the implications of the direct provision of public goods by government. (Micro)
- **HL** Discuss possible government responses (to monopoly power). (Micro)
- Discuss why, in contrast to the monetarist or new classical model, the economy can remain stuck in a deflationary (recessionary) gap in the Keynesian model. (Macro)
- Discuss why, in contrast to the monetarist or new classical model, increases in aggregate demand in the Keynesian AD or AS model need not be inflationary, unless the economy is operating close to, or at, the level of full employment. (Macro)
- Discuss possible economic consequences of unemployment. (Macro)
- Discuss possible personal and social consequences of unemployment. (Macro)

- Discuss the possible consequences of a high inflation rate. (Macro)
- Discuss the possible consequences of deflation. (Macro)
- **HL** Discuss, using a short run Phillips curve diagram, the view that there is a possible trade-off between the unemployment rate and the inflation rate in the short run. (Macro)
- **HL** Discuss, using a diagram, the view that there is a long run Phillips curve that is vertical at the natural rate of unemployment and therefore there is no trade-off between the unemployment rate and the inflation rate in the long run. (Macro)
- Discuss the possible consequences of economic growth. (Macro)
- **HL** Discuss the real-world relevance and limitations of the theory of comparative advantage. (IE)
- Discuss the arguments in favour of trade protection. (IE)

- Discuss the arguments against trade protection. (IE)
- **HL** Discuss the implications of a persistent current account deficit. (IE)
- **HL** Discuss the possible consequences of a rising current account surplus. (IE)
- Discuss the possible advantages and disadvantages of a monetary union for its members. (IE)
- Discuss the positive outcomes on development of market-oriented policies. (DVLP)
- Discuss the negative outcomes on development of market-oriented strategies. (DVLP)
- Discuss the strengths of interventionist policies on development. (DVLP)
- Discuss the limitations of interventionist policies on development. (DVLP)
- Discuss the view that economic development may best be achieved through a complementary approach, involving a balance of market-oriented policies and government intervention. (DVLP)

Evaluate

- Evaluate, using diagrams, the use of policy responses to the problem of negative externalities of production and consumption. (Micro)
- Evaluate, using diagrams, the use of government responses to the problem of positive externalities. (Micro)
- Evaluate, using diagrams, possible government responses to threats to sustainability. (Micro)
- **HL** Evaluate possible government responses when asymmetric information is present. (Micro)
- **HL** Evaluate the role of legislation and regulation in reducing monopoly power. (Micro)
- Evaluate the use of national income statistics. (Micro)
- Evaluate government policies to deal with the different types of unemployment. (Macro)
- Evaluate government policies to deal with the different types of inflation. (Macro)
- Evaluate government policies to promote equity. (Macro)
- Evaluate the effectiveness of fiscal policy. (Macro)
- Evaluate the effectiveness of monetary policy. (Macro)

- Evaluate the effectiveness of supply-side policies. (Macro)
- Evaluate the effect of different types of trade protection. (IE)
- Evaluate the possible economic consequences of a change in the value of a currency. (IE)
- **HL** Evaluate the effectiveness of the policies to correct a persistent current account deficit. (IE)
- Evaluate, with reference to specific examples, each of the following as a means of achieving economic growth and economic development.
  - a Import substitution
  - b Export promotion
  - c Trade liberalization
  - d The role of the WTO
  - e Bilateral and regional preferential trade agreements
  - f Diversification. (DVLP)
- Evaluate the impact of foreign direct investment (FDI) for economically less-developed countries. (DVLP)
- Evaluate the effectiveness of foreign aid in contributing to economic development. (DVLP)

Examine

- Examine the assumption of rational economic decision-making. (Foundations section)
- Examine the role of price elasticity of demand (PED) for firms in making decisions regarding price changes and their effect on total revenue. (Micro)
- Examine the significance of PED for government in relation to indirect taxes. (Micro)
- Examine the implications of cross price elasticity of demand (XED) for businesses if prices of substitutes or complements change. (Micro)
- Examine the implications for producers and for the economy of a relatively low income elasticity of demand (YED) for primary products, a relatively higher YED for manufactured products and an even higher YED for services. (Micro)
- Examine the possible consequences of a price ceiling. (Micro)
- Examine the possible consequences of a price floor. (Micro)
- Examine the output approach, the income approach and the expenditure approach when measuring national income. (Macro)

- Examine, using diagrams, the impacts of changes in short run (macro) equilibrium. (Macro)
- Examine, using diagrams, the impacts of changes in the long run (macro) equilibrium. (Macro)
- Examine the possible consequences of overvalued and undervalued currencies. (IE)
- Examine how the current account and the financial account are interdependent. (IE)
- **HL** Examine the effects of changes in the terms of trade on a country's current account. (IE)
- Examine, with reference to a specific developing economy and using appropriate diagrams where relevant, how the following factors contribute to economic development:
  a education and health
  b the use of appropriate technology
  c access to credit and micro-credit
  d the empowerment of women
  e income distribution (DVLP)
- Examine the current roles of the IMF and the World Bank in promoting economic development. (DVLP)

The AO4 command terms

These include: Calculate, Construct, Derive, Determine, Draw, Identify, Label, Measure, Plot, Show, Show that, Sketch, Solve.

These command terms are predominantly used in higher level (HL) specific learning outcomes. The following are the instances of AO4 command terms **not** specific to HL outcomes.

Term	What you are expected to do
Calculate	Calculate PED, XED, YED and PES
Construct	Construct various diagrams
Draw	Draw various diagrams
Identify	Identify consumer and producer surplus on a diagram; identify the four factors of production
Show	Show that substitutes have a positive XED whereas complements have a negative XED; that normal goods have a positive YED whereas inferior goods have a negative YED